MY CREDIT SCORE
IS MY SUPERPOWER

FROM MORTGAGE FACILITATOR TO FAMILY
MONEY GURU — HOW I OUTSMARTED DEBT
AND BECAME THE BUDGET AVENGER

TUMEKA JINKS

Copyright © 2025 by Tumeka Jinks

All rights are reserved, and no part of this publication may be reproduced, distributed, or transmitted in any manner, whether through photocopying, recording, or any other electronic or mechanical methods, without the explicit prior written permission of the publisher. This restriction applies to any form or means of reproduction or distribution.

Exceptions to this rule include brief quotations that may be incorporated into critical reviews, as well as certain other noncommercial uses that are allowed by copyright law. Any such usage must adhere to the specified conditions and permissions outlined by the copyright holder.

Book Design by HMDPublishing.com

CONTENTS

1. The Foundation of Financial Freedom 4
2. Meet The Budget Avenger 15
3. My Superpower: Credit Scores Explained 26
4. From Debt To Dreams 36
5. The Family Financial Planning Strategy 47
6. The Power of a Strong Network 58
7. Budgeting Basics For Everyone 69
8. Saving Like A Superhero 79
9. Investing 101: Your Path To Wealth 89
10. Avoiding the Credit Pitfalls 100
11. Navigating the Mortgage Maze 110
12. Family Legacy and Financial Responsibility 121
13. Tax Strategies for the Everyday Hero 131
14. The Entrepreneurial Mindset 142
15. Raising Money-Savvy Kids 153
16. Financial Freedom Through Community 164
17. OVERCOMING FINANCIAL SETBACKS 175
18. Celebrating Your Financial Wins 186
19. A Day in the Life of a Budget Avenger 196
20. Your Journey Begins Now 206

CHAPTER 1
THE FOUNDATION OF FINANCIAL FREEDOM

Understanding Credit Basics

Welcome, dear reader, to the marvelous world of credit! It is a land where numbers dance, excitement brews, and financial jargon reigns supreme. Now, before you panic and feel that pang of dread curling in your stomach because finance has always been the gargoyle in your attic, let me assure you—it's all in good fun! In fact, understanding credit is a lot like trying to decipher your family's Thanksgiving dinner seating arrangement. It may seem complicated, but once you've got it figured out, you can actually enjoy the feast without worrying if Uncle Bob is going to discuss his conspiracy theories for the umpteenth time.

First, let's embrace the idea that credit is simply a reflection of how trustworthy you are with borrowed money. It's like your popularity score at the high school reunion—if you've paid your debts, rung the bell, and danced like nobody's watching, your score will go higher! When you go to borrow money for that shiny new car or fabulous vacation home, lenders will glance at your credit score, which ranges from 300 (you might as well be using Monopoly money) to 850 (the financial equivalent of "You do you, boo!"). The higher the score, the more confidence your lender will have in you. And we want our lenders to be as confident as possible! Nobody wants a lender that was unsure if they will show up like a bad date at a romantic dinner.

Now, imagine if I told you that credit isn't just a solitary adventure—no, my friend! Credit is more like a roller coaster ride at the state fair. It dips. It sways. Sometimes it might even make you want to scream! But don't worry, we'll get through it together. Credit has two main components—revolving credit and installment credit. Revolving credit (think credit cards) is like a never-ending buffet—just because you have it doesn't mean you should pile your plate high with designer shoes and gourmet snacks. On the other hand, installment credit, like a mortgage or a car loan, is kind of like a dance competition; you have to stick to an exact routine to impress the judges and fulfill your obligation.

Next up, let's discuss the credit report—that document that behaves more like a deep, dark secret than a financial tool. It's the Netflix documentary of your spending habits, detailing everything you've paid on time (the heartwarming coming-of-age story) and the missed payments (the drama-filled betrayal). Credit bureaus gather this information, and it's a tale worthy of an Oscar for best performance! The data in your credit report comprises your payment history, amounts owed, length of credit history, new credit inquiries, and types of credit used. Spoiler alert: if you miss a payment, it's like accidentally posting a bad hair day photo on social media; it sticks around and won't be forgotten easily.

But you aren't doomed! If managing credit were a video game, there would be cheat codes! You can boost your credit score and pave the way to financial freedom! Pay your bills on time (because our moms weren't kidding when they said time is money), keep credit card balances low (under 30% is like wearing a cute outfit that says "I've got my life together"), and avoid unnecessary credit inquiries (showing up to six places in one night wearing the same outfit is a definite no-no).

So, here's a fun twist! Credit is not only about the numbers; it's about your financial behavior, lifestyle choices, and yes, even your values. It determines whether you can afford to grab a fresh organic smoothie every morning or whether you're limited to the sad vending machine snacks of doom at work (trust me, we love vending machines, but not their choices). A good credit score gives you the freedom to live your best life, from splurging on that dream vacation to owning a home where you can disengage and hide from the world when family gatherings get too chaotic.

So, as we embark on this journey through credit, remember: it's not just numbers and reports; it's a learning curve, a series of chaotic adventures, and an opportunity to express our financial superhero spirit. As we take our first steps into the wild and exciting realm of personal finance, may we do so with laughter, lightness, and the distinct sound of our wallets ringing just a little bit happier! Cheers to mastering the art of credit, one quirky step at a time!

The Importance of a Good Credit Score

The coveted good credit score! It's like the golden ticket of the financial world, akin to finding an unexpected treasure map in your attic while sorting through last year's holiday decorations. A good credit score can take you places—literally and figuratively! You might be thinking, "Why do I need a good credit score? Isn't cash king?" Well, my friend, while cash certainly has its charms (like the ability to buy ice cream in the dead of winter—bless that creamy goodness), a good credit score is the crown jewel in the realm of financial success.

Let's start by discussing the role a good credit score plays in our everyday lives. If you've ever tried to rent an apartment, you probably noticed that landlords treat your credit score like the ticket price at a sold-out concert. A dazzling score opens doors to the coolest venues, whereas a lackluster score might find you showing up at the corner bar with the flimsy karaoke machine instead! Landlords may look at your score and judge whether you are trustworthy enough to let you into their rental paradise, or if you'd be the type to throw impromptu dance parties that annoy the neighbors. Spoiler alert: a good score says, "I promise to pay my rent on time and only do the Macarena at reasonable hours!"

But wait, there's more! What's the one thing we all dream about, pacing back and forth like a contestant on a cooking show? Homeownership! A solid credit score is your ticket to the delightful world of mortgages and the joy of lumbering around a house after that "Welcome Home" signing ceremony (complete with confetti combat). A good score can lower your interest rates, which, let's be honest, is like getting an extra scoop of that poolside pineapple sorbet when you only paid for one. Lower interest rates mean lower monthly payments, which translates to more margaritas and less sacrifice at the expense of your summer vacation dreams (a sound financial strategy indeed!).

Have I mentioned what a good credit score can do for your business endeavors? Ah, the entrepreneurial dream! As an entrepreneur myself, I can tell you that having a good credit score can turn you from a mere mortal into a financial gladiator ready to conquer business loans like a seasoned champion in the Colosseum of finance. It's almost like wearing a majestic cape that assures everyone you are equipped for success! Lenders will flock to your door, waving cheques, ready to back your exciting new plans—whether you want to launch an organic cat cafe or a holographic tuxedo rental service for pets. Availability, my friends, is the name of the game in the business world.

And yes, I need to mention that your credit score often becomes the gatekeeper guarding the lands of car insurance! In many scenarios, the better your credit score, the lower your insurance premiums will be. That means you can treat yourself to a new ride without cringing every time you see a bill! Imagine the thrill of driving around in your shiny new car while your friends question how you've managed to do it without going broke. The secret is simple: you have mastered the importance of a good credit score.

Now, let's not forget the social perks of having a good credit score! That's right, folks—there are actual social benefits! You can proudly roll up to gatherings as the "Wise Financial Wizard" in the family, bestowing your magical knowledge on your wide-eyed cousins. You'll become the person everyone consults for tips on escaping the clutches of credit card debt. Need a family to block out those unwise spending habits? A good credit score earns you that placement at the head of the table, where family gossip is seamlessly woven into money-management strategies!

But what about emergencies or the unexpected twists life throws at us when we least expect it? A good credit score can be the lifebuoy you throw to yourself when financial tides rise unexpectedly. A roof leak, a fender bender, or a surprise cake order for Aunt Flossie's retirement party can all be tackled without dismantling your personal finances because you can secure a loan to weather the storm.

So, my credit-contemplating comrades, it's clear: a robust credit score is more than just a number. It's your ticket to Wonderland, a passport to financial adventures, and quite frankly, the superhero cape you didn't know you were missing. Strap on your belt and get ready to jump into the exciting riptide of credit improvement—because a good credit score is where the magic truly begins! Cheers to debt-free adventures ahead and living life without the weight of financial dragons lurking around!

How Credit Affects Your Financial Journey

Credit—often perceived as the modern-day sorcerer that can weave spells of financial dreams or conjure nightmares with but a blink of an eye! Let's take a moment to examine how this enchanting potion, known as credit, truly affects the tapestry of our financial journeys. Buckle up, dear reader, and try not to spill your coffee as we embark on this thrilling and humorous quest through the labyrinth of credit-related decisions that shape our lives.

To kick things off, let's think of credit as that dramatic friend in your group who's always the center of attention—the one who gets invited everywhere, often oversharing easily and inciting a range of reactions! Credit can either be your bestie or the source of existential dread. Would you invite that friend on a vacation to Hawaii? Of course! But would you take them skydiving on a whim? Perhaps not! Similarly, when credit behaves—hello, excellent score and responsible borrowing!—you can go on delightful adventures such as buying your dream home, snagging that shiny new car, or simply enjoying brunch without worrying about becoming a debt-saturated crab.

But allow me to reveal the underlying truth: how you manage your credit can either supercharge your financial journey or send it tumbling down a rabbit hole of chaos resembling a scene from a cheesy horror movie. And we all know how much we love budget horror! One minute you're dining out at that fabulous new restaurant, blissfully unaware of the financial roller coaster awaiting you. The next moment, BAM!—your credit card bill arrives and reveals more zeroes than you'd like to confront. It's like discovering that the usual watering hole is now a dive bar with questionable karaoke.

Credit impacts your ability to secure funds, and here's where it gets juicy! When you need to borrow, lenders, much like a scrutinizing bouncer at an exclusive club, will check your creditworthiness before rolling out the red carpet. If they see a well-maintained credit score, they'll be happy to open the gates and whisper sweet nothings like "low-interest rates" and "flexible terms." But if your score is less than stellar, brace yourself—lenders will raise an eyebrow akin to your unamused mother and may sadly turn you away, leaving you standing outside in the pouring rain of financial despair.

Want to travel? Pack your bags, but don't forget your credit score! Airlines and hotels often peek at your credit profile like a nosy neighbor on an afternoon stroll. "Oh, did she just book a vacation without checking her credit score? How quaint!" Your credit affects your travel plans; wanting to book that last-minute trip to Fiji may become a wild chase akin to a modern-day treasure hunt, where instead of gold doubloons, you gather all the documents to secure financing, only to find out your credit isn't quite up to snuff.

Now, let's break into the magical world of entrepreneurship! If you've got a brilliant business idea brewing in your mind that might rival the next best-selling taco-flavored pizza, your credit score can be the wind beneath your wings! Lenders and investors will utilize your credit to gauge how responsible you are, ultimately deciding whether they want to back your entrepreneurial ambitions. So, if you harbor dreams of launching a tech empire, wearing crisp suits, or throwing extravagant pizza parties for your employees, investing time into your credit score is tantamount to laying a solid foundation for your empire.

On the flip side, your journey may lead to roadblocks due to your credit choices! Picture this: just when you think you're rolling along, a sudden, unexpected expense demands attention. If your credit is less than favorable, you may find yourself in a tizzy, aimed with desperation in your plea to secure funds. Understandably, this can feel like a financial emergency, compelling you to pull the chandelier to your throat like a melodramatic opera star—unless, of course, you've cultivated your credit wisely, and then it's simply another challenge to meet head-on.

Finally, let's not forget the emotional toll credit can take on your life! Much like a love affair fraught with ups and downs, your credit journey can cause heart palpitations when you receive the shocking news of a denial letter. Or it can elate you when you receive that gratifying mortgage approval, making you feel giddy as a schoolchild on the last day of school. Your credit score can create a dramatic narrative, and—just like the plot twists in your favorite movies—it can ultimately lead to transformative growth, teaching essential life lessons along the way.

So, my fellow financial journey warriors, understand this: your credit score isn't merely a number; it's an ever-evolving entity that will accompany you and narrate your adventures along the way. Whether you grow to embrace your credit or learn valuable lessons from it, remember, laughter is the best medicine, even in the sometimes hilariously uncomfortable world of personal finance! Keep that score on point, and let's make our financial journeys as fabulously memorable as a holiday family reunion, minus the awkward small talk. Cheers to credit—and may it always treat you kindly!

Common Myths About Credit

Myths about credit! They swirl around like tall tales at a family reunion, often more exaggerated than Uncle Joe's fish stories. You know the ones—usually steeped in misunderstanding, confusion, and the scent of biscuits fresh out of the oven. It's time we set the record straight on these tall tales, so grab your favorite snack and sit down, my friends, because we have some credit myth-busting to do!

First and foremost, let's talk about the ever-popular myth that carrying a balance on your credit card helps elevate your credit score. Oho! If I had a dollar for every time I encountered this gem of misinformation, I could afford a luxury vacation to Tahiti—without a credit card in sight! The truth is, carrying a balance only fuels a wildfire of high interest rates and potential debt. Picture your credit score as a child: it's happier and more well-adjusted when you teach it not to be greedy. Whenever possible, you should pay off your credit card in full each month, because a zero balance is like giving your credit score a gold star for excellent behavior! After all, wouldn't you rather take vacation selfies on the beach rather than thousands of selfies with your debt collector?

Another myth that raised its ugly head is the assumption that checking your own credit score will hurt it. Anyone who has ever tried to piece together a puzzle knows that you can't figure out how to make the final picture without peeking at the pieces! Checking your credit score is like getting a glimpse at your financial future—knowledge is power, my friends! Honestly, monitoring your own credit is more of a gentle caress than an all-out assault. Just beware of those third-party credit inquiries—those might look suspicious, like someone borrowing your favorite sweater and not returning it; those definitely can leave a mark on your score!

Next up, let's address the blockbuster myth that closing old credit accounts is a wise financial decision. My friends, it's more dangerous than mixing soda and milk for a midnight snack! Closing old accounts can actually shorten your credit history, and if there is one key component to your credit score, it's the length of your history. So, if you've got an ancient credit card collecting dust in the back of your wallet (it still has that nostalgic picture from back when you believed in low-interest rates and unicorns), keep it open! Use it occasionally, maybe treat it to a pizza night so it knows you still care, and watch your credit score soar like an eagle witnessing a sale on ramen noodles!

Let's not forget the myth that credit scores are a secret, only known among shadowy figures talking in hushed tones over a campfire. It isn't some mysterious elixir concocted by financial wizards. Your credit score is very much a public affair, and you have the right to know it! In fact, you can snag one free credit report each year from each of the three major credit bureaus. Think of it as a gift from the financial gods, a moment of self-reflection where you can reassess your financial choices from last fall's questionable impulse buys on novelty socks.

Ah, and here comes the classic belief that if you've declared bankruptcy, your financial life is forever doomed and rendered unworthy of love or credit. Sound familiar? It's akin to thinking that your high school mishap with the dance recital will follow you around like a ghost haunting your every step. Fear not! Declaring bankruptcy can be a start-over button in your financial game—sometimes life throws curveballs, and you've got to learn how to catch them, my friend. After a few years, you'll find your score climbing back to a respectable level, like a phoenix rising from the ashes—or a burned piece of toast you bravely attempted to salvage!

And lastly, let's address the myth that all credit scores are created equal—ah, this one is a whopper! Just like people, scores can be quirky, and each credit bureau has its style and flair. So, one bureau might think your financial choices make you a rockstar, while another is confused about the decision to order pizza twice a week without sufficient funds left for essential items. Monitor all your scores so that you know which version of yourself is being portrayed to the world.

So, let's toast to unraveling the misconceptions surrounding credit! Now that we know the truth behind these dreaded myths, we can spread the good word like it's a hot cake at a church picnic. Remember, sift through the chaos, listen to the experts, and please—let's make sure we don't let these myths define our financial journey! Keep your sense of humor intact, and we'll navigate the whimsical world of credit together! Cheers to clarity, comedy, and a credit score that would make even your skeptical Uncle Joe proud!

Getting Started on Your Credit Journey

Getting started on your credit journey! It's like embarking on a thrilling expedition to find the treasure of financial independence, complete with unexpected twists, occasional dangers, and perhaps a pirate or two—or at least a few family members who have no qualms about commenting on your spending habits. If you're ready to hoist the sails and steer the ship toward credit enlightenment, let's break out the map and delve deep into the treasures (and pitfalls) waiting ahead.

First things first, let's clear up the essential basics—understanding how credit works is like learning the intricacies of a good cup of coffee. You don't just throw water and beans together and pray for magic! No, you must heed the details: the grind, the temperature, the steeping time! Similarly, credit is made up of three significant components. There's your payment history, which accounts for 35% of your score. Imagine it like your attendance record in high school; if you were the class clown who never showed up, you'd flunk out fast! Next up, we have amounts owed, making up 30% of your score. It's like the cake portion—you want just the right slice without overindulging! Last but not least, we have the length of credit history, where patience is key. Lenders want to know you're a reliable friend, someone who pays them back without dodging their calls.

Once you've set your bearings and know the lay of the land, it's time to venture into the credit wilderness—navigating that treacherous terrain where good credit exists! The first step? Get yourself a credit card, friends! This is where some feel the tingling excitement of joining a special club that comes with the distinct privileges of "spending money you absolutely should not be spending." But remember, the key here is to use your card wisely, treating it like a musical instrument—not just for grand performances but also for daily practice. Start with small purchases, and pay off that balance promptly. You want to earn those sweet, sweet brownie points—or in this case, points that improve creditworthiness.

Now, let's acknowledge that getting started with credit can feel daunting—a bit like being the new kid in school trying to navigate the cafeteria seating chart. You've got the cool kids, the wise ones, and the ones who have no qualms about spending everything on the latest gadget. A credit limit is not a suggestion; it's a guideline! So stick to spending about 30% or less of what you've been allocated. This will show that you've got a handle on your finances and can hold your head high (much like a peacock flaunting its magnificent feathers).

Next up, let's pause here for a significant moment of enlightenment: paying your bills on time is absolutely crucial. I can't stress this enough! Picture the sense of dread watching your credit score plummet faster than a lead balloon if you miss a payment. Creditors report your payment busyness to the credit bureaus like they're live-tweeting your financial drama! And believe me, we want that drama to end up in a Netflix series, not a horror movie. Set calendar reminders, use apps, or even enlist family members. Harness the power of a well-timed notification!

As you move forward, continually monitor your credit regularly—this is like keeping your finger on the proverbial pulse of your finances. You wouldn't neglect your garden and expect roses to bloom, right? Credit monitoring allows you to track your score, catch any discrepancies, and address them before they spiral out of control. And let's face it, if you do find a mistake, it'll be more satisfying than finding a long-lost sock that actually matches! Plus, it helps you take responsibility for your credit health, and that's pretty badass.

Now, dear readers, don't forget about the power of a good support system! Surrounding yourself with fellow credit adventurers who understand the importance of good credit can feel like an essential ingredient in your proverbial recipe for success. Join online communities, forums, or even weekly coffee meetings with friends where you swap tips and tricks. Sharing your victories and failures creates an empowering environment, turning the whole process into a hilarious bonding experience. Warning: spare the cringeworthy finance jokes; I cannot be held responsible if your friends "groan" at your money puns!

Finally, know that credit is a journey filled with missteps, mishaps, and triumphs—aha, the thrill of both the struggle and the victory! Think of crediting as a Netflix series packed with plot twists and character development: one moment you're binge-watching with your popcorn, and the next, you're sidelined with suspense! With that in mind, remember that mistakes are part of the process; everyone stumbles at some point. The trick is to get up, dust yourself off, and refocus on the path forward.

So, gather your financial compass, shape your ambitions, and embrace the adventure that lies ahead! Together, we'll plow through the challenges of maintaining good credit, armed with positivity, humor, and perhaps even a few snacks. Let's set sail on this exhilarating credit journey with confidence and a gleam in our eyes—because if you're tackling finances with laughter, you'll surely emerge victorious, no golden eyebrows required! Cheers to your credit journey; it's time to get started!

CHAPTER 2
MEET THE BUDGET AVENGER

The Journey from Mortgage Facilitator to Financial Guru

When I first jumped into the world of finance, I thought my life journey would play out as a lovely sitcom. You know, like that episode of *"Friends"* where the pals miraculously find ways to avoid the doom of adulthood! Instead, my tale morphed into that of a quirky superhero who could defuse financial crises with nothing but sheer determination and a killer spreadsheet addiction. As a mortgage facilitator, I found myself on the front lines, explaining to countless bewildered clients how a mortgage is not something you just put on a credit card and hope for the best. Spoiler alert: it's way more complicated (and much worse for your credit score).

In those early days, my prospects were bright—or, shall I say, a shade of confusion? I often encountered clients who walked in with a look on their face as if they'd just been told that listening to the *"Macarena"* was a financial plan. I would sit them down, armed with a whiteboard and an enthusiastic grin, and outline the basics of credit, which is akin to explaining the concept of 'Secure the Bag' to someone who still thinks *"Fortnite"* is a video game about gardening. They were baffled, but I was fueled by the exhilaration of potentially being the money-saving Yoda they never knew they needed!

It wasn't long until my friends started calling me "Financial Guru" instead of just "Tumeka." I felt like a hipster barista who had suddenly discovered the art of latte making: one minute you're serving up hot water with sadness, and the next, you've turned it into the fanciest cappuccino money can't buy. Honestly, it's wild—one moment I was locking in interest rates and pushing paperwork in the beloved world of mortgages, and the next, I transformed into the Budget Avenger, slashing overly sweetened spending habits like a rogue ninja through the dark alleys of financial hell!

But here's the part that makes everything more interesting: I didn't just magically become a financial sorceress because I wore a cape and waved a wand. Nope! I had my own series of epic financial blunders, or what I like to call "character-building moments." There was a time I played fast and loose with my credit cards, racking up more debt than an overenthusiastic taxicab driver during New Year's Eve. You know the drill—dinner here, shoes over there, and all the random stops at those "one more latte" cafés that somehow cost more than my first car. Those blunders taught me some of the toughest lessons, but also gave me ample material for this satirical masterpiece!

Friends, let me tell you, the more I learned, the more I realized that I must transform this chaotic adventure into a source of inspiration for others. After numerous "light bulb moments" while sitting on my living room floor surrounded by stacks of receipts, I cracked the code. Yes, even in a world of credit scores and debt, humor and joy can blossom like a well-watered money tree! I hung up my superhero cape and decided to embrace everything uncomfortable that I once felt. Being vulnerable and sharing all my hilarious finance fails became my mission. Who knew that sharing my experience of comprehensively failing at adulting could lead to something as uplifting as financial empowerment?

Community became my secret weapon. I started organizing workshops, potlucks, and money-makeovers—turning my lessons into laughter. Let's face it, folks: who wouldn't want to attend a *"How to Budget Without Losing Your Mind"* event hosted by a quirky Black woman with a penchant for sequined capes? The more I engaged with my community, the more I realized that we could help lift each other up, one belly laugh at a time! And before I knew it, I was not only guiding people through the maze of mortgages, I was actively engaged in their financial growth, too.

And so the journey continued, evolving with every challenge and every laugh. From a simple mortgage facilitator to a full-fledged financial guru, I learned the art of blending serious lessons with laughter, thus creating a delightful recipe for financial success. Now, not only do I wake up smiling, but I also have a band of loyal followers who cheer on the Budget Avenger! As I lead the charge toward financial freedom with humor and heart, I encourage you all to grab your capes and join me on this hilarious ride because, let's face it, life's too short to treat finance like a boring tax seminar!

Recognizing My Passion for Financial Empowerment

Let me take you back to a time when my mornings were caffeinated with ambition and my evenings were marinated with doubt. I had recently transitioned from a mortgage facilitator into a full-time financial guru, and while I danced in the euphoric glow of newfound independence, a question loomed overhead like a sitcom rain cloud— "What do you really want to do with your life?" Sure, I could finagle loan parameters and explain interest rates like a passionate school teacher juggling pint-sized delinquents. Still, there was something more substantial, a calling hidden deep within my frugal heart. It was the "Aha!" moment that sparked my passion for financial empowerment.

Picture this: I'm sprawled out on my couch, surrounded by a sea of financial classification manuals, spreadsheets, and sticky notes that threaten to suffocate me with their neon hues. The TV flickers in the background, dishing out a mind-numbing infomercial about vacuum cleaners that promise to suck up everything but your dreams. Suddenly, a thought strikes me—what if I could help people who feel as lost as I once did, especially those caught in the unrelenting grip of financial struggle? My passion surges like a rollercoaster ride, spiraling me into an epiphany: financial empowerment isn't just about numbers; it's about helping people regain their money mojo!

It became apparent to me that money can often feel like that awkward third wheel in a relationship; we know it exists, but hey, we'd rather not discuss it. Yet, what if it weren't? What if we could break that stigma and transform financial discussions into open dialogues sprinkled with laughter? This was it! I realized I could blend my quirky sense of humor and relatable personal stories with practical financial advice – kind of like mixing a fun dance party with a business meeting. So there I was, a determined diva passionate about making money discussions as enticing as a slice of my mom's famous pecan pie.

Thus began my journey into the glorious realm of financial wellness workshops. I embarked on a mission to reach those who experienced budgetary FOMO—fear of missing out on financial literacy. Every time I stepped onto that stage to present, I felt as if Tony Stark himself was scheduling a meeting for a superhero reveal: "Ladies and gentlemen, welcome the Budget Avenger!" The rush I felt was electric; my passion was blossoming, and the thrill of empowering others ignited my inner joy.

But trust me, taking the plunge felt like jumping into a kiddie pool full of sharks. The hesitations crept in like bad romance movie plot twists. "What if I make an absolute fool of myself?" I'd think. Isn't that the nightmare we all dread? To spill the entire pot of beans while armed with half-baked knowledge and a PowerPoint that even my cat would find boring? Yet, as I looked into the eager eyes of the audience, the sweet, tremulous energy reminded me this was bigger than me. This was about providing them with the tips and tools to take back control of their financial lives—teenage dreams upgrade!

Every chuckle, every "light bulb" moment from someone in the crowd who was just beginning to grasp the complexities of budgeting, only solidified my resolve. I got to share my penchant for gaffes and mistakes elegantly packaged as snacks of wisdom! "So, you too thought 'buy now, pay later' was a superpower? Welcome to the club! You won't be the last to learn that the real superheroes use credit like they use veggies in a smoothie—carefully and sparingly!"

As I continued to weave my passion for financial empowerment into my workshops, I felt an exhilarating rush; this could positively impact people's lives! I saw the transformative potential; like a mad scientist concocting a potion for world peace, my version, of course, involves personal checks and savings accounts! It hit me like a ton of bricks: financial literacy could change the course of families, lifting them out of cycles of debt and confusion, providing them with a map to money-mountain tops and opening doors to opportunity.

In the end, recognizing my passion for financial empowerment was like unearthing a fabulous pair of dancing heels buried under stacks of bills. What began as a question turned into my mission—spreading the wealth of knowledge, one skillful joke at a time! Now, armed with my cape, humor, and a stuffed piggy bank full of dreams, I march forward, ready to revolutionize the way we view money. My journey is ongoing, but boy, it's an exhilarating ride, complete with absurd escapades—who wouldn't want to join in on that hilarious madness of finance? Because at the end of the day, it's not just about making sense of money, but teaching everyone we can dance through life and still keep our wallets in check.

Turning My Personal Struggles into Lessons

Personal struggles—those delightful little nuggets of wisdom that can transform us into stronger, smarter, and slightly crazier versions of ourselves. If there were ever a trophy ceremony for life's toughest lessons, my name would be etched right there on the golden plaque under the title "Most Likely To Trip Over Her Own Financial Feet." Trust me, my journey through the vast forest of debt and financial confusion was practically the equivalent of trying to skateboard on a tightrope strung between two skyscrapers—unsteady and full of plunging uncertainties!

A significant struggle I faced involved my encounter with credit cards. It was love at first swipe; the thrill of buying now and paying later felt as intoxicating as guzzling down a cheeseburger after a particularly rigorous juice cleanse. As a burgeoning mortgage facilitator, I convinced myself that I could handle the allure of credit. "I'm responsible; I can totally rock the world of credit cards," I thought, puffing up my chest like a peacock trying hard to impress another peacock with its feathery glory. Spoiler alert: I fell into the trap of debt faster than my kids can say "it's time for dinner."

Suddenly, I was grappling with a tidal wave of statements, inches thick, showcasing my bad decisions. I learned that the phrase "minimum payment" does not mean that paying the minimum qualifies you for a "cool kids" club—it merely prolongs your financial heartbreak! After months of the very adult habit of ignoring those pesky bills, I finally had to sit down and really face the symphony of my poor choices. I can still remember that moment when I dramatically threw myself on the couch, sobbing into my pile of overdue notices. "Why must the universe punish me so?" I whined, deeply contemplating whether I should start a support group for fellow credit card victims who were nursing hangovers from their reckless spending episodes.

As I grappled with my missteps, I recognized the power of my stories. I took those all-too-fresh memories and transformed them into the teachings I hoped to share with others. After all, wisdom is best served with a side of humor, and who doesn't appreciate a hearty laugh about their missteps? The key realization was that my mistakes didn't just define my downfall; they also laid the foundation for my credibility as a financial guru. After all, those struggles equipped me with the experience to understand people's genuine fears of money. I knew all too well how daunting it is when financial statements read like cryptic messages from an ancient civilization: "What on Earth does this even mean, and why do I owe so much?"

Empowered by my new outlook, I decided to craft relatable anecdotes perfect for my workshops. "Now gather 'round, my confused financial friends! Let me regale you with the charming tale of the time I mistook glitter and impulse buys for retirement savings—a true tale of fabulous folly!" With tales of my own financial faux pas, I painted the picture that it is okay to fumble, fall, and rise again, budget in hand, as long as you don't let those blunders define who you are. Plus, I'll take any excuse to turn my cringeworthy moments into comedic gold!

The great part of turning struggles into lessons was not just about writing them off with a comedic twist. I nurtured empathy for those who struggled, drawing from a wellspring of experiences that gave me a greater understanding of the emotional weight tied to money. Losing sleep over bills—been there! Stressing over how to give your kids a good life while slogging through paycheck-to-paycheck limbo—done that! Letting money define your self-worth—oh, honey, please! It's time to shatter those chains.

Over the years, my personal struggles became a roadmap for my audience, guiding them through the confusing labyrinth of financial emotions. So much wisdom can be mined from life's absurdities; it's practically a goldmine! My journey transformed every stumbling block into stepping stones, ensuring others could learn and grow while having a good chuckle at my ventures. Weaving those experiences into humor became a superpower of its own; suddenly, I wasn't just some uptight financial advisor in a wool sweater spouting facts—I became their relatable Budget Avenger, armed with sweet laughs and life lessons galore!

To sum it all up, turning my personal struggles into lessons became the turning point of my life and career. I realized the power of my mistakes—to enlighten, uplift, and inspire others to stop the cycle of self-criticism and just start laughing at the chaos life throws our way. After all, if we can't share our blunders and make sense of our financial messes together, then we're missing out on the very best part of growth: finding joy amidst the struggles. Grab your popcorn, folks—it's all part of the hilarious financial show!

Building a Brand: The Rise of the Budget Avenger

The birth of a brand! It's a miraculous transformation that begins with a flicker of inspiration, leaping into a firework explosion of identity. Picture me, clad in thrift-store find leggings and a hand-stitched cape (that may or may not have been a bedspread at one point), as I set off on a journey to market my brand: the Budget Avenger! My husband, Sims, joked that I was on a quest to save everyone from financial doom, which was oddly correct. But little did I know that building this brand would be as chaotic and magical as a toddler holding a glitter explosion during craft time.

At first, my vision was as clear as a foggy day in London. Sure, I wanted to empower folks with financial wisdom, but what did that truly mean? Was I going to wear glasses and have tea parties with stuffed animals while discussing balance sheets? Or should I create something more cheeky, like financial tutorials delivered through a YouTube channel where I wear outrageous costumes? The possibilities were endless! Spurred by enthusiasm and armed with a notepad, I started brainstorming. I even slapped together a mission statement that read something like, "Transforming Dreams into Dollars" while snickering at how ridiculous it would sound if plastered on a billboard.

As I rolled up my sleeves, I quickly learned that building a brand requires more than simply being fun and quirky (though trust me, I had that locked down!). I realized I needed to craft a compelling story, something that engaged people with my journey while being relatable and humorous. That's when I embraced my transformation from the somber mortgage facilitator to the Budget Avenger! I began telling my tale; one of ups and downs, debts and sneaky budgets, while keeping a light heart and whimsical approach. It sounded good in theory, but man, I had moments where I felt like a clown instead of the superhero I envisioned, like the time I showed up to an event in matching outfits with my own inflatable money bag sidekick. Honestly, that was just a little too much.

Then came my revelation: I had to use social media to amplify my message. I mean, let's face it—everyone is glued to their phones like they're delivering the hottest gossip about the latest reality star. I tapped into platforms like Instagram and Facebook, where I encapsulated financial nuggets of wisdom into relatable memes, all while peppering in personal anecdotes. I'd pair photos of my kids' antics with captions that read something like, "Remember, when saving your pennies, use your 'inside voice'—because no one wants to hear you struggling at the checkout line!" My mission? To normalize discussions about money while creating an atmosphere where others could learn, engage, and let out a good guffaw!

With my trusty sidekick—who, in reality, was simply my laptop—I designed colorful graphics, organized online workshops, and hosted "Money Madness Fridays," where I donned ridiculous costumes (because why not?). I found that my animated approach resonated with people! They laughed, learned, and, dare I say, even shared my content with friends and family. Little by little, the Budget Avenger brand began to take shape like a clay figure sculpted by an overzealous artist. My notoriety grew, and I started to feel like I was on the cusp of something truly special—nobody else had championed the fusion of humor and financial literacy quite like me!

Before I knew it, folks began reaching out, asking how they could work with me, and I thought, "This is it! I am the Financial Fun Guy!" Workshops turned into consulting gigs, and my reputation as a relatable, funny financial guru expanded like my collection of oven mittens (which you'll learn about later). I couldn't have been more thrilled to witness people become excited about budgeting and money management, all thanks to a blend of laughs and real advice.

But, my friends, no true rise to greatness comes without its pitfalls. There were moments when I questioned my brand presence. Was it too silly? Too chaotic? Should I tone down my quirkiness and embrace a more serious demeanor? Yet, in staying true to myself and my mission, I learned that authenticity was paramount. I wasn't just here to sell financial advice; I was here to build a community of fellow warriors fighting against the struggles of the budgeting battlefield.

In the end, the rise of the Budget Avenger became more than a mere branding exercise—it morphed into a movement, encouraging laughter and empowerment, allowing me to connect with folks on their financial journeys. I realized that finance wasn't just about numbers; it was about people connecting, engaging, and, most importantly, having fun while they chase after their dreams. Armed with my cape, a delightful sense of humor, and my ever-growing brand, I forged ahead into the financial fray, ready to empower even more lives, one budget at a time! Who knew laughter could be such a powerful tool? Cheers to all my fellow budget avengers out there!

The Role of Humor in Financial Education

Humor is the magical ingredient that can turn even the dullest topics into a joyous fiesta! When it comes to financial education, the role of humor is like that of an inflatable bouncer at a kid's party: it keeps the mood light, makes everything more inviting, and allows us to jump higher than ever before! Let's face it, most people cringe at the idea of discussing finances. It often brings to mind images of dusty calculators and spreadsheets so boring that they could make a grown adult weep quietly into their coffee. But by injecting some humor into those dreary discussions, I found we could transform trepidation into celebration, and that's when the magic really happens!

First and foremost, humor serves as an incredible icebreaker! Picture yourself in a workshop filled with eager—but somewhat tense—faces, all staring back at you like deer caught in headlights as they think, "Oh no, please don't make me calculate my budget." Enter yours truly, ready to hit them with the punchline: "Ladies and gentlemen, welcome today, where we learn to spend wisely and cry less! Just kidding, we'll still cry—but it'll be tears of joy!" The laughter cascades around the room, and suddenly, my audience is engaged, open, and ready to tackle the trickiest financial topics without fear of judgment. Who knew that a lighthearted quip could break down the barriers of financial drudgery?

But humor isn't just for eliciting laughs; it also aids retention! When I weave a funny story about budgeting mishaps, listeners relate on a personal level. Sure, they might remember the lesson, but who wouldn't remember that time I dramatically revealed my credit card statement, pretending it was a treasure map leading to "the land of bad decisions"? Laughter enhances our cognitive abilities, so when people chuckle, they release endorphins, making it easier to learn and remember. Humor plants those nuggets of wisdom in their brains so they can recall them in moments of spending temptation, like facing down a glittery aisle of shoes during a post-holiday sale.

It's science—if laughter can help people remember to save instead of splurge, I'm all in!

Let's not ignore the fact that humor builds camaraderie and fosters community. While financial discussions can often feel isolating and intimidating, cracking a few jokes creates a shared experience and encourages collective laughter. When we come together to laugh about our budgeting woes or compare financial faux pas, it forms a bond that builds trust and encourages vulnerability. Think about it: how many times have you shared an awkward moment related to spending, only to have someone chime in with a similar story? That sense of connection brings people together, making it easier to open up about their own struggles with finances. Now that's a recipe for a whole new world of support and understanding!

Moreover, humor provides the perfect vehicle for dissecting serious topics. We can discuss meticulous budgeting and the harsh realities of debt without boring our audiences to tears. "Let's talk about the horror of living paycheck to paycheck—sounds fun, doesn't it? Splendid little life lessons that show you just how close you were to that latte, which turned into a mortgage payment!" With that playful jab, I maintain my audience's attention while inspiring them to engage with the material. Every laugh is a step toward gradual acceptance, turning overwhelming topics into digestible, approachable nuggets of understanding.

Finally, let's not overlook the reality check humor provides. It reminds us that finance isn't just about numbers and calculations. It's about real people with real feelings navigating a complicated world of money. When I share my own financial foibles under the guise of humor—my regret over impulse buys or how my money tree apparently only produced leaves—it validates the struggles so many face. It's not foolproof, and we shouldn't be ashamed of it. By embracing humor, it reinforces the notion that budgeting and finances are human experiences, filled with quirks and quirks—after all, we're all just here trying to figure out how to afford a taco truck and pay rent on time!

In summary, humor plays a starring role in financial education by breaking down barriers, aiding retention, fostering community, facilitating difficult conversations, and emphasizing our shared experience. It transforms mundane topics into magical discussions filled with heart, laughter, camaraderie, and a healthy dose of realness.

As I dance through this wonderful world of financial empowerment, I invite you to embrace humor as your trusty sidekick. Together, let's boldly navigate the often chaotic and hilarious maze of personal finance, all while laughing heartily at the absurdity of it all. Because if we can tackle our financial futures with a smile and a lighthearted attitude, then frankly, we can take on anything, like negotiating that last cupcake at the office party!

CHAPTER 3
MY SUPERPOWER: CREDIT SCORES EXPLAINED

What is a Credit Score?

Let's kick things off with the burning question most people have when they first step into the world of credit: "What the heck is a credit score?" If you've ever wondered whether it's related to your performance in dodgeball back in school (it isn't, but wouldn't that be fun?), or maybe if it dictates how many avocado toasts you can have in a month (I wish—then I could truly control my brunch game), relax! A credit score is a three-digit number that measures your creditworthiness: a blend of your financial past and present that essentially decides whether you get the green light for that loan, mortgage, or even the coveted credit card with... (drumroll, please) a fabulous rewards program!

Imagine your credit score as a report card for adults, except unlike that one time in fifth grade when you didn't quite grasp long division, this report card could dictate where you live and drive—yep, no pressure!

Scores typically range from 300 to 850, where 300 is basically the financial equivalent of wearing socks with flip-flops, and 850 is akin to being able to leap tall buildings in a single bound. A score above 700 is generally seen as "good"—not to brag, but I often hover around there, and it opens quite a few doors, including those to the "reasonable interest rate" club. Trust me, you want to be associated with the cool kids in that realm!

Now, your credit score isn't just plucked out of thin air by some evil financial overlords. Oh no, it's calculated based on your financial behavior over time—like a nosy neighbor who keeps track of everything you do. The major scoring models consider five key components: payment history, credit utilization, length of credit history, new credit, and types of credit in use. You can think of it like a recipe—too much of one thing (late payments!) and not enough of another (having various credit accounts) could spell disaster. It's like trying to bake a cake with mostly flour and no sugar. What's a cake without sugar? Just a sad gluten pile.

Let's break each of those down a bit, shall we? Your payment history accounts for a whopping 35% of your score! Basically, if you want to keep your score looking more like "Hallelujah!" than "Oh no!", you better pay those bills on time—no one wants to be haunted by the ghost of missed payments past! Then, there's payment utilization, which sounds fancy but is basically your credit card balance in relation to your credit limit. If you've maxed out that shiny, new credit card, you're waving a big red flag—think of it as trying to squeeze into jeans that were cute in high school (we've all been there, right?).

Length of credit history is another slice of that pie, because those relationships you've nurtured with credit accounts can give you a more favorable score. The more seasoned your accounts, the better! It's like being the wise sage in a financial fairy tale—no one trusts the newbie who just jumped in last week. New credit inquiries may seem harmless, but they can sting your score if you're applying to a dozen places like you're shopping for a new outfit. Stagger those applications, people! Don't treat your credit like a clearance sale.

Finally, the variety of credit accounts adds some zing to your score. Lenders prefer folks who can juggle multiple types of accounts, like credit cards and loans. Imagine trying to party while only listening to the same monotone song—yawn! Mix it up and show them you can groove with different tunes.

So, there you have it—a credit score is not some secret coded language or a new TikTok dance move; it's a vital number influencing your financial journey! By understanding what it is and how it works, you're putting on your financial superhero cape and ready to conquer the credit world. The more you know, the better you can manage your finances, and who doesn't want to sleep a little easier at night knowing their credit score is on point? Here's to living your best financial life, one credit score at a time!

The Factors That Impact Your Credit Score

Alright, folks, let's dive into the juicy world of credit score factors. If a credit score were a meal, the factors impacting it would be the ingredients—the cilantro lurking in your guacamole or that questionable mystery meat in your burrito. Just like you wouldn't want anything off-putting to ruin your culinary experience, you certainly don't want clashing elements messing with your credit score, which, let's be real, is basically the lifeblood of "adulting."

First up on our ingredient list is the hefty 35% payment history—an absolute diva that demands top billing! This factor is all about your record of making payments on time. You know that feeling when you order a pizza and repeatedly track the delivery on that suspicious little app? Your payment history is akin to that; it's watching every move you make. If you pay your bills late or—gasp—skip them altogether, it's like receiving a terrible review on your favorite takeout. "Would not recommend." Thanks, but no thanks! Good ol' FICO doesn't take late payments lightly; consider it a written warning—eventually, it will show up as a scowl on your beautiful credit profile!

Next, we have the infamous credit utilization ratio, which accounts for around 30% of your score. Picture this: you have a credit card with a limit of $10,000, and you decide to throw caution to the wind while shopping, so you blissfully max it out. Congratulations! You've just declared war on your credit utilization! You can think of it like those "All you can eat" buffets; the key isn't just how much you can pile on your plate, but how much you can manage without facing a catastrophic food coma. Keeping your utilization under 30% is the sweet spot—like enjoying dessert but still being able to fit into your favorite pants.

Length of credit history comes in at a respectable 15% of your score, like the wise elder in a village who quietly observes before delivering profound advice. This factor considers how long your credit accounts have been open, so the earlier you start building credit—responsibly, of course—the stronger your financial reputation will be. Imagine this: the older your credit account, the more stories it can tell. "Back in my day, we had to walk uphill both ways to get a credit card!" Yes, we're talking grandpa vibes. So start early and nurture those accounts like they're your little seedlings—water them well and they can grow into sturdy oak trees.

Then we have new credit, which makes up 10% of your score. Eager to bring new friends into your circle of credit? Chill out! Every time you apply for a new credit card or loan, it's like a credit card application ghost popping up and saying, "Boo!" Too many inquiries can raise eyebrows and make lenders question whether you've suddenly fallen into some financial mishap. Think of it as your socialite friend who tries to befriend everyone at a party—not everyone is cool with that! So pace yourself, and remember: quality over quantity!

Lastly, rounding out our list is the type of credit accounts you have—this factor contributes a solid 10% to your score. It's not just about how many credit cards you have; lenders want to see that you can handle different types of credit—car loans, mortgages, credit cards, you name it! Think of it as being a well-rounded adult; no one wants to be the person who can only do one dance move at a party. By showing you can juggle different types of credit, you're essentially saying, "Hey, I've got macaroons, and I can cover your fries, too!" Be a credit buffet!

So, there you have it—the factors impacting your credit score are like the ingredients in a successful dish. Combine your payment history, a low credit utilization ratio, a long credit history, a sprinkle of new credit, and a variety of credit types, and you'll have a recipe that will make your credit profile deliciously appealing. Embrace these factors, handle them wisely, and you'll be on your way to being the ultimate "Credit Crème Brûlée" that lenders can't help but adore! Here's to cooking up a score that shines brighter than Aunt Edna's sequinned pants at a family reunion!

How to Check Your Credit Score

Alright, buckle up, my financially savvy friends! Let's dive into the thrilling world of checking your credit score. It's not quite the same adrenaline rush as bungee jumping or trying that outrageous new hot sauce at your favorite diner, but trust me, it can still get your heart racing, particularly if you haven't checked in a while. First things first: knowledge is power! Do you really want to be left in the dark, wondering if your credit score is as fabulous as your Aunt Edna claims her lypo was? That's just too risky, folks!

Now, checking your credit score isn't akin to cracking a secret code or deciphering ancient hieroglyphics; it's easier than finding your Netflix password after your fifth glass of Merlot. We live in a technological age where every minute detail of our lives is exposed (thanks, social media!), so it's only fitting that accessing your credit score should be relatively painless. You can get your score from various places, but proceed with caution—avoid websites that promise a "free" score but really just want to sneakily sign you up for a subscription service without your knowledge. You're looking for clarity here, not another monthly charge clouding your financial future!

The best way to kick things off is to head to reputable websites that are specifically designed for this purpose. Places like AnnualCreditReport.com let you access your credit report for free once a year, which is like the holy grail of credit checking, my friends! Think of it as being granted a magic wish to scream at your credit report once a year—"What have you been doing?!" You're entitled to get your hands on three reports, one from each of the major credit bureaus (Experian, TransUnion, and Equifax). This gives you a chance to compare and see if any of them are harboring dark secrets or shady judgments against you.

And let's face it, folks, checking your credit score doesn't have to be drudgery. Grab your favorite snack, kick back, and make it an event! Talking about credit scores actually can be entertaining! Set the mood with your best playlist, perhaps some classic tunes or even some '80s hair bands, while you sip on that herbal chamomile tea that's supposed to be miraculous for your stress levels. I like to call it "Zen-onomics." You'll feel more relaxed as your fingers hover over the keyboard, awaiting the magical number that could grant you access to a shiny new house or car.

Keep in mind, however, that there are several ways to ease this process. If you're the cautious type (and who isn't these days?), consider monitoring services that will give you periodic updates on your score so you don't feel like you're living under a rock for most of the year. These services can send alerts to your phone. Imagine that moment of realization when you see those words flash across your screen: "Your credit score has changed!" Cue the dramatic music!

This keeps you proactive rather than reactive during exceptional financial storms.

Just a heads-up—emotionally, it's perfectly acceptable to experience an array of feelings upon seeing your score. Most people do! You might experience excitement, dread, or a sudden urge to purchase a full-wheeled cart of kale and revert to a health craze while staring at the number that feels closer to a GPS pin dropped in the middle of nowhere to be found (or not found!). Remember, though: a credit score isn't the end-all, be-all of your financial worth. It's more like a snapshot of your financial journey. But trust me, it's a powerful snapshot that needs to be framed properly—at least until you improve it!

Once you've checked your score, it's essential not to just stare at it like it's a Picasso painting hanging in a museum. Make sure to review your credit report for any discrepancies or errors. Think of it like an unsecured diary—you never know what wild nonsense might have made its way in if you weren't paying attention. If you find an error, dispute it like your unofficial title is "Credit Score Vigilante."

In summary, checking your credit score is way easier than trying to put together IKEA furniture without the instructions. You have options galore at your disposal, and the world of credit checking is at your fingertips. Whether you go for the yearly free report or decide to monitor it throughout the year, just do it! Checking your score empowers you to know where you stand and take charge. Who doesn't love feeling like they're in control of their financial fate? So roll up your sleeves, grab that metaphorical magnifying glass (not literally, please), and get to your score-checking journey. The adventure awaits, and it's better than binge-watching anything on Netflix!

Debunking Credit Score Myths

Gather 'round, my curious financial warriors! It's time to tackle some of the most ridiculous myths surrounding credit scores. Do you know those stories floating around like a ghost at a Halloween party that just won't go away? They lurk in the corners of conversations, looming larger than the last slice of Grandma's pumpkin pie. Let me assure you, it's time to grab your flashlight and expose these credit score monsters!

First up, let's take on the monster that claims you must carry a credit card balance to build your score. Oh boy, I can't even begin to tell you how many times I've had a client look at me with wide eyes and explain, "But I thought I had to owe money to look creditworthy!" No, my dear friend, no! You don't actually have to owe anyone anything to make your score sparkle like a diamond at a high-end jewelry store. In fact, this myth is tantamount to saying you need to wear the same pair of dirty socks all week to prove you're a good person. The truth is, paying your balance in full each month demonstrates financial responsibility and is applauded by FICO's elite. So let me be crystal clear: carrying a balance can actually hurt your score!

Next, let's chat about the creeping suspicion that checking your own credit score will send it plunging faster than a contestant on a reality TV dating show. This myth is as ludicrous as claiming eating pizza on a Sunday makes you unworthy of love! What you want to do here is learn how to differentiate between "hard" and "soft" inquiries. When you check your own credit—also known as a soft inquiry—it's like giving yourself a high five; it's all good! However, when a lender checks your score to approve your loan or credit card application, that's a hard inquiry. The best practice? Checking your credit often, on your own, so you can monitor it for inaccuracies and get a leg up on your financial goals, is a surefire way to feel like the confident superhero you truly are!

You may have also heard that having multiple credit cards is a surefire recipe for disaster and will catapult you into debt faster than you can say "buy one, get one free." Well, let me tell you this: just because you have several credit cards doesn't mean you need to max them out like they're on life's clearance rack. Why? Because a diverse mix of credit types can actually benefit your score! Think of your credit cards as flavor-enhancing sprinkles on your financial cupcake. The key, of course, is moderation! Like that friend at the party who loves to jump into every conversation. If you can't manage your cards effectively, it may be time to take a breather.

And who could forget the ancient belief that closing old accounts will magically boost your score like it's being given a shot of espresso? If only! Only in the great land of myth is that true. Closing old accounts can actually damage your credit history, which is a key component of your score. When you close an account, you shorten your history and potentially increase your credit utilization ratio. Picture this: you've been running a marathon for years (like a tortoise, if you will), and suddenly one day, you decide to sit down on the running path and give up. The finish line feels farther away than ever! Keep those old accounts open—let them quietly bask in the glory of being aged and smart.

Now, let's discuss the notion that credit scores are set in stone. Nope, they're more fickle than a cat at bath time! Your credit score can fluctuate based on a variety of factors, so it's essential to keep the lines of communication open with your credit accounts. Likewise, many people believe that credit repair services will wave a magic wand and make all their credit woes disappear. Unfortunately, no magic is involved—just proactivity and your own good sense!

Lastly, let's debunk the myth that only wealthy people can maintain good credit scores. Cue the dramatic music! This belief is simply false. Good credit scores are attainable for anyone who follows solid financial practices, regardless of income. It's about making smart decisions, budgeting, and staying responsible in managing your debts. Anyone can claim the title of "Credit Score Royalty" with the right attitude and habits—even that cousin of yours who swears by their life hacks for thrifting!

Folks, there you have it! We've shed some light on those pesky credit score myths that are far too prevalent in our financial folklore. Remember that knowledge is your ultimate weapon in this credit journey—so armor yourselves with the truth, laugh off the absurdities, and strut confidently through the world, brandishing your financial wisdom like a gleaming sword! You are now well-equipped to tackle the credit landscape and achieve your goals, one myth at a time.

The Importance of Credit Scores in Financial Decisions

Gather 'round once more, my financial warriors! It's time to explore why credit scores are like the GPS of your financial journey—without them, you could wind up lost in the wilderness of financial despair. Imagine driving cross-country with no map, no GPS, and only a crinkled old road atlas from 1997 that your uncle gave you. You might end up somewhere you never wanted to be—like that one intersection with four different Starbucks and no way to choose just one! Credit scores serve as your guideposts in the financial world, steering you toward better opportunities and away from the terrible traps that can drag you down. So, let's dive in, shall we?

First off, let's talk about the direct impacts on borrowing costs. Think of this as the magical number that determines whether you pay the nice, pleasant interest rates or the rip-off "I can't believe you're charging this". Rates. When lenders look at your credit score, they're trying to gauge how trustworthy you are with money—basically playing a little game called "Will I get my money back?" A higher score generally means lower interest rates, and we all know that when you save on interest, you can spend that extra cash on more fun things, like, I don't know—delicious snacks or fancy lattes! Lenders see you as less of a risk, which is exactly what you want.

Now, let's not forget how your credit score can affect your chances of getting approved for that dreamy mortgage or car loan you've been fantasizing about. Imagine you've found your ideal home, complete with a backyard that leads to a secret garden (or maybe just a place to host family barbecues). If your credit score is looking more like a speedy rollercoaster downwards—yikes!—then good luck getting approved for a mortgage! Lenders will want to be sure you can repay them, and your credit score is a reliable sneak peek into your financial habits. Think of it as the first date before the commitment; if they see red flags in your score, you might get stuck in "single" land while someone else snags their dream home!

But the fun doesn't end there—credit scores also play a significant role in securing rental agreements. Yes, my friends, these numbers affect more than just mortgages and car loans! Have you ever tried renting an apartment or securing a leasing agreement, only to be met with a predatory credit check? It's like a backstage pass to what you hope is the cool concert, only to find out you can't even get in because your score is low. Property managers want to ensure they're renting to responsible tenants, and your score is a big part of that equation. So, if you envision a vibrant apartment with eclectic décor and brunch-themed community picnics, you'll need to shine with that credit score.

Let's shift gears! Credit scores also serve as your ticket into the exclusive club of premium credit cards. Do you know those with fancy travel rewards and cash back points? Those rewards can feel like confetti in your wallet, but only if you've shown you can handle financial responsibilities. When you apply for these cards, lenders use your score to see if you're party-worthy. Suppose your score is up to snuff, congrats! You get to enjoy the perks of being "Cardholder Extraordinaire." Go ahead, let that frugal party hat fly off while you rack up those sweet rewards!

And let's not forget about insurance policies—yeah, they peek at your credit scores too! Insurers might use your score to determine your premium on various policies, such as auto or homeowners insurance. It's like setting up for a game you have no control over until the dice rolls. A higher credit score can lead to lower insurance premiums, giving you even more reason to love your score! Anytime your credit score can save you more dollars, it's a reason to do a happy dance!

Finally, don't overlook the psychological impact credit scores have. Having a good score can boost your confidence levels, helping you feel empowered as you strut through life like you own the place. It's not just about the numbers; it's a representation of your hard work and responsibility. When you know you have a solid credit score, you can tackle financial decisions confidently, much like striding into a room wearing your favorite outfit—the one that makes you feel like a million bucks!

So, there you have it! Your credit score holds a remarkable degree of importance in nearly every financial decision you make. From borrowing costs, housing opportunities, and credit card fun to insurance savings and boosted confidence, your score is a powerful tool that can lead you to success or, conversely, a world of confusion. Keep your credit score shining brightly, and you'll be well on your way to navigating the financial landscape like a pro—a superhero with a killer credit score, ready to seize every opportunity that comes your way! Now go out there and shine!

CHAPTER 4
FROM DEBT TO DREAMS

The Wake-Up Call: Recognizing the Impact of Debt

Debt! The very word is enough to make most folks break out in a cold sweat, much like that time I decided to cook Thanksgiving dinner for my family. Picture this: me, armed with a cookbook, a turkey the size of a small car, and my mother hovering in the background, ready to swoop in like a hawk at any sign of danger. Now, imagine that panicked feeling as you realize you've forgotten the pumpkin pie, and your beloved grandma is about to disown you. That's the essence of the panic one feels when they finally confront their debt!

But here's the plot twist: understanding the impact of debt doesn't have to feel like a family roast gone horribly wrong. My wake-up call came on a Tuesday—because, naturally, life always gets you when you least expect it, right? I had been blissfully ignoring my credit card statements piled up like laundry on the bedroom floor (you know the kind). It was one of those magical moments where I decided that I might as well open a few bills while binge-watching my favorite reality show, *"Dancing with My Debt."* The glittery numbers danced across the paper, taunting me like my children when I tell them they can't have dessert before dinner.

My eyes widened as I treated those numbers like they were a plot twist straight out of a soap opera. I felt like an amateur detective uncovering a complex conspiracy theory. "Is that really my debt?" I muttered, wondering if maybe the universe had played a trick on me. It was as if my finances had staged a coup, and let me tell you, I wasn't ready for this unexpected plot twist. The reality hit me: debt had not just crept into my life; it had taken up residence, started redecorating, and even left its dirty dishes in the sink. When I realized I was Miss Scarlet in the living room with a credit card, I knew I had to step away from the chaos.

Suddenly, it dawned on me that debt was much more than just a number—it was a monster lurking under my financial bed. You know the kind: the one that gets silly around Halloween but is deadly serious when it comes to gobbling up your resources faster than you can say "budgeting." I went through the stages of grief faster than a toddler can throw a tantrum: shock, denial, anger, and then, finally, acceptance. My mood swings resembled my poor attempts at home workouts—one moment, I'm pumped up, feeling unstoppable, and the next moment, I'd rather just sit on the couch and eat potato chips in my pajamas.

The impact of debt isn't just financial; it's a strain on relationships. Picture me trying to have a romantic dinner with my husband, Sims, while simultaneously worrying about our credit card bills. "Hey, honey, these mashed potatoes are delightful! Did you know that last month's minimum payment was late? Gosh, I love a good meal with a side of anxiety!" Not exactly what I envisioned for our date nights! There were days I couldn't even enjoy a cup of coffee without that ever-present feeling of guilt hovering over me, like an annoying relative who won't stop asking when you're going to settle down and have kids (sorry, Auntie Pat!).

Recognizing the impact of debt opened my eyes to how much it had invaded my space. Not the good kind of invasion either, like an exciting surprise party. This was the kind of invasion that made me want to shove all my bills in a box, bury them in the backyard, and hope the neighbors wouldn't notice. It's all fun and games until you realize that the receipts that look like confetti are actually signals that your finances are spiraling out of control. I'm talking about the kind of mess that requires more than just a cleaning lady—like an intervention from the entire family!

Ultimately, my wake-up call became the catalyst I needed to shift my perspective. At this moment, recognizing the impact of debt transformed me from a clueless ostrich (head stuck in the sand) to a resourceful Budget Avenger on a mission. Armed with knowledge, I decided I wouldn't let debt dictate my life anymore. No longer would I be the punchline to a bad financial joke! It was time for a revolution, my friends. If there's one thing I've learned in this rollercoaster ride, it's that acknowledging the monster under the bed is the first step to reclaiming your space, one dollar at a time. So let's raise our glasses (of water—because, remember, we're saving money now!) to recognizing the impact of debt and banishing it once and for all from our lives.

Transforming My Mindset: From Fear to Action

Transformation—a word that often conjures up images of butterflies breaking free from their cocoons, or a superhero putting on a cape. But let me tell you, transforming my mindset from fear to action was more like a raccoon caught in a trash can; lots of flailing about, some questionable decisions, and plenty of moments to laugh at in hindsight. It all began when I realized that living in fear of my debt was as productive as teaching a cat to fetch. Frankly, it was time to stop wallowing in worry and start wielding my financial sword like a true Budget Avenger!

Now, let's take a trip down memory lane to the dark days when my financial fears were as prevalent as Netflix shows. I would wake up in the middle of the night, heart racing, thinking about my credit card bills like they were chasing me with pitchforks. Whenever I heard the word "savings," I felt like someone had just slapped me with a wet noodle. I was paralyzed, a deer caught in the headlights of my financial woes. But one fateful day, with a cup of coffee that was ten times stronger than the usual brew, I decided that enough was enough. Just like that, I got the courage to kick my fears to the curb and embrace a new swagger—the "I Own My Finances" attitude.

The first step in this transformation was recognizing that fear is a terrible financial advisor. If I took financial advice based on my anxiety, I might as well be calling up my cousin who swears he has a foolproof scheme for skinning cats (don't ask!). I started telling myself that fear was just my mind's way of trying to protect me, like an overly cautious mother when her kid decides it's a good day to rollerblade down a steep hill. Sweet of it, but let's be honest: I was an adult now, and it was time to take control.

I distinctly remember a moment where I had an overwhelming urge to binge-watch yet another reality show and drown my stress in snacks. But instead, I decided to channel my inner superhero and tackle my debt head-on. I crafted a strategic plan—the type of plan that would make even Tony Stark jealous. My mission? To flip the script on my financial story. Instead of ruminating about my budget's tightness, I began to see challenges as opportunities. I asked myself, "What would happen if I viewed my financial struggles as a game?" With that idea, I laced up my imaginary superhero boots and marched into the battlefield of budgeting.

You see, embracing action meant I had to make some serious changes. I dove into learning everything about my financial situation. I channeled my inner nerd and became a credit score whisperer. I read blogs like they were hot-off-the-press romances. I watched videos on budgeting strategies, taking notes like I was studying for a final. I mean, if knowledge is power, I was ready to Hulk out on my debt! Little by little, my mindset shifted from being shackled by fear to being fueled by determination. At this point, my husband, Sims, thought I was putting a little too much excitement into spreadsheets, declaring, "Is that a rave I hear, or just you balancing the budget?"

With each small win, I felt my confidence swell like my favorite pair of stretchy pants after a family dinner. I paid off a credit card and celebrated instead of simply checking it off my list. Gleefully dancing around my living room, I channeled my inner Beyoncé, belting out, "I'm a Survivor!" to an audience of one—my confused cat, who barely noticed. It was those little celebrations that cemented this newfound perspective; I began to relish the process instead of viewing it as drudgery. Fear dissipated as if it had been kicked out by a bossy grandma enforcing house rules—one stern look at a time!

Before long, I realized that transformation isn't just about taking the right steps but about nurturing a mindset of resilience and openness. Fear will always whisper unkind things in my ear—it's almost as predictable as my mother's questions about when I'll give her more grandkids. However, I've learned that choosing action over inaction isn't just liberating; it's downright empowering! From then on, whenever I felt that familiar sense of dread creep back in, I'd shout back, "Not today, fear! I'm too busy being fabulous and financially savvy!"

Although I'm still a work in progress (let's face it, who isn't?), I know that the journey from fear to action is one filled with laughs, awkward triumphs, and perhaps a few cabbage patch dances in the kitchen. Life may throw challenges my way, but I've transformed that initial fear into fuel for action. And you know what? If I can do it, so can you! So, raise your glass (of maybe sparkling water) and let's celebrate our victories, knowing that we have the power to change our financial narratives, one fabulous step at a time!

Developing a Plan: Setting Financial Goals

Setting financial goals—a process that should ideally be as empowering as a fabulous makeover montage, but often feels more like preparing for a root canal! But let me tell you, developing a plan was perhaps the best commitment I've ever made (right up there with the one to marry Sims—sorry, honey!). It started with a moment of clarity, as all the best ideas do, when I decided that my financial dreams weren't just pipe dreams; they were plans waiting to happen!

I remember sitting down one day with an oversized cup of coffee—seriously oversized, like they're trying to compete with my ambitions—facing my computer screen as if it were the final boss in a video game. My first task: wrapping my mind around the concept that setting goals was essentially like deciding on a destination for a road trip. And honestly, if you don't have a destination, you're stuck driving in circles, wasting gas, and probably consuming too many snacks—never a good thing. So, with that metaphor freshly brewed in my mind, I grabbed a notepad and put my best financial foot forward.

The first thing I learned about setting financial goals was that specificity is key! I mean, let's be real: if you say you want to "get rich," that's a vague wish better suited for a genie than a realistic goal. So, inspired by my favorite DIY show (who doesn't love a good transformation?), I started crafting specific, measurable, achievable, relevant, and time-bound (yes, I just invoked the mighty SMART acronym—thank you, high school economics class!). My first target was to pay off my credit card debt, my arch-nemesis, within two years. I'm here visualizing that moment when I'd figuratively toss my credit card statement into the air like confetti, yelling, "Freedom!"

Next came the budgeting. They say a budget is like a diet for your finances. Just like I can't live off potato chips (as glorious as they are), I couldn't expect my financial health to thrive on reckless spending. I mapped out my monthly cash flow like an enthusiastic middle-schooler detailing their plans for world domination. I mean, who needs to find their way to financial stability when you can have a plan that looks like it came straight from a strategic mastermind? I listed my income sources and meticulously tracked my expenses, leaning on spreadsheets as if they were my best friends. Yes, my family might have rivaled my spreadsheets for affection, but nothing sparkled like that colorful chart of mine did!

With my goals outlined and my expenses tracked, it was time for a little budgeting magic. I had days filled with possibilities; no more fear of the dreaded "where did my money go?" question that had haunted me for far too long. My plan was all about prioritization. Do I really need those fancy coffee shop lattes every morning? How many times can I convince myself that yoga pants are "business casual"? Spoiler alert: more than I'd like to admit. So, I decided to allocate funds toward my debt paydown while also establishing a fun fund—because no one wants to live like a monk when they don't have to. Life is for living, not just budgeting, right?

As I moved forward, my goals started morphing into action items. I'd give myself simple "missions" each month: whether it was a determined no-spend week or hunting for the elusive coupon goddess. Let me tell you, nothing felt as rewarding as winning a battle at the grocery store when I bought two pounds of cheese for the price of one! Did I feel like a financial warrior? Absolutely! Each little success acted like a milestone that lit up my path, like road signs leading me towards my ultimate destination of financial freedom.

And yes, I had my ups and downs along the way. There were times I splurged on something that turned out to be an impulse, like that inflatable unicorn I thought would change my life. Spoilers: it didn't. But instead of wallowing in regret, I dubbed myself a "Financial Artist," painting my life with colorful mistakes and lessons learned. It's important to remember that no evolution is without a few missteps; it's just part of the process! Besides, those misadventures made the journey far more entertaining.

Looking back now, setting financial goals was like crafting my own superhero storyline. I started as an ordinary citizen of Budgetsville, facing the daunting villains called "debt" and "spending temptations." But with each goal I set, every plan I executed, I transformed into the Budget Avenger, fighting my financial battles with flair and determination! It may not have been a fairy tale, but it certainly made for a uniquely hilarious and empowering journey. So, here's to setting those financial goals, transforming dreams into plans, and striding forward with all the gusto of a bargain-hunting superhero! Because let's face it, we're going to need a little laughter every step of the way!

The Power of Persistence: Overcoming Obstacles

Persistence: it's like that stubborn stain on your favorite shirt that refuses to budge no matter how many times you scrub it. You know the one—no matter what technique you try, it's always there, mocking you, reminding you of your laundry mishaps. But when it comes to overcoming obstacles in my financial journey, I've learned that persistence is the secret ingredient that turns a mediocre soup into a gourmet dish. And trust me, my financial soup was a thick, murky broth of debt, disappointment, and more than a sprinkle of self-doubt.

Let me take you back to the moment when I first realized that I needed to harness my inner persistent warrior. Picture this: I'd just created my budget, goals neatly laid out, and I was feeling invincible—like I could conquer Mount Everest with a single leap. Fast forward a few months later, and life decided it was time for a plot twist, starring my bank account. My car broke down like an aging diva on stage, and the repair cost was enough to make me consider public transportation for the rest of my life. I mean, can we agree that "unexpected expenses" should come with a warning label, preferably in neon lights?

So there I was, faced with the reality of a shattered budget and an even more shattered spirit. My initial instinct was to yank the nearest blanket over my head and declare myself a hermit until the financial apocalypse passed. But then I thought about all the progress I had made (and that beautiful spreadsheet full of vibrant colors). The old me would've wallowed in despair and sulked over a tub of ice cream—don't get me wrong, I love a good emotional eating session—but the new me, the Budget Avenger, refused to let one little setback throw me off course.

This is where the magic of persistence came into play. Instead of allowing the repair bill to render me powerless, I decided to roll up my sleeves and get down to work. I knew I had to create a plan B, C, and maybe even D! That's right—this was my moment to embrace the chaos and methodically address the obstacles that life had thrown in my way. I cut back on non-essentials (goodbye to my daily overpriced teas) and found creative side gigs that turned me into a financial ninja! I did odd jobs, opened a pop-up bake sale, and even offered my services as a "budget guru" for friends. If there was a way to hustle, I was there, and my persistence paid off, literally!

Through it all, I realized something profound: Persistence is more than just plowing through challenges; it's about adapting. Like a chameleon at a color party, you've got to be ready to adjust on the fly. During my quest to overcome obstacles, I learned to switch my perspective when I encountered bumps in the road. Instead of feeling defeated, I began to see hurdles as opportunities for creativity. How can I make this work? What else can I do? Suddenly, I wasn't just surviving—I was thriving, even with all the changes!

Let's not forget the emotional roller coaster that comes with persistence. Some days, I'd feel like a financial rockstar, dancing around my kitchen like it was my concert stage, while on others, I'd be grumbling at the grocery store over rising prices, ready to do a poke dance in frustration. The key was to keep moving forward, even when the wilting plants in my house seemed to laugh smugly at my financial aspirations. Every time I celebrated a small victory—be it saving a few bucks or hitting a milestone—I was fueled by the reminder that persistence was my greatest ally in achieving financial freedom.

And speaking of small victories, let's talk about the power of community! During my roller-coaster ride, I sought motivation from friends, family, and online forums. I learned that sharing my setbacks and triumphs with others made obstacles feel lighter, like a well-shared burden. I even joined a local budgeting group where we gave each other high-fives over small wins while rolling our eyes at unexpected expenses. It's amazing how discussing the woes of debt with a good laugh can lift your spirits! The feedback and camaraderie I found in my support network reignited my zest for overcoming obstacles.

In the end, persistence doesn't just lead to overcoming obstacles—it shapes you into the hero of your life story. I went from a reluctant participant in my financial journey to becoming the mighty Budget Avenger! Armed with perseverance, I learned how to dance with challenges, persistence lighting my path like a disco ball. So next time life throws you a financial curveball, remember that even the stickiest of stains can be scrubbed out with the right dose of persistence and the willingness to adapt. Keep dancing, my friends; the world is watching, and your financial freedom is just one persistent step away!

Celebrating Milestones: Every Step Counts

Celebrating milestones—oh, where do I even begin? It's the part of my financial journey where I put on my party hat, do a little jig, and pop the confetti, sometimes all while still in my pajamas! For someone who spent years feeling like every month was an uphill battle against looming credit statements, learning to acknowledge my progress felt like discovering the secret stash of chocolate hidden in the back of the pantry. You know, the kind of joy that makes you want to shout from the rooftops—or at least skedaddle around your living room in merry abandon.

Now, amid my financial transformation, I quickly realized that celebrating milestones was as important as the effort I put into budgeting and saving. Imagine treating every small victory like a mini-celebration, like a surprise birthday party—only instead of balloons and cake, we had budget spreadsheets and challenges galore. And let me tell you, it radically shifted my mindset! I used to think, "I'll celebrate once I'm free from debt," but then I realized there's something smart about celebrating our small wins along the way. After all, if I waited for that grand moment to throw a parade, I might end up too old to have any fun!

My first official milestone celebration was after I successfully paid off my first credit card. Picture me, fists raised in victory, strutting around my house like I had just won a gold medal at the Olympics! I cranked up the volume on my favorite playlist (hint: it was very disco) and danced like nobody was watching. **Spoiler:** My cat was absolutely watching, judging my every move; it was like performing a one-cat show. I indulged in some humble treats (hello, half-price cupcakes from the bakery!) and even took a selfie to commemorate the occasion. There's something ridiculously satisfying about having a visual memento of your triumph—not only to remind you of your journey but also to show the world (or just your social media followers) that you are getting things done over here!

I also began hosting milestone parties with my financial tribe. With triumph in the air, we made it a point to celebrate not just my victories but everyone's. We held "mini-commencement" ceremonies whenever someone tackled a challenging expense or achieved a specific goal. There we were, decked out in our favorite "I Love Budgeting" shirts while clinking our glasses of sparkling water (because champagne isn't in the budget!). As we toasted to our hard work, each bursting laugh and joyous cheer felt like an affirmation that every little effort mattered. It felt like we were throwing an extravagant gala, albeit one with slightly less glamour and far more spreadsheets!

And talk about a delicious reason to gather—food is always a great motivation, am I right? Whoever succeeded in their monthly savings challenge had the honor of picking the theme for our feast! From "Flavors of Thrift" where we concocted mouthwatering dishes from pantry staples to "Discount Dessert Devilry" focused on using markdowns, my friends and I cleverly incorporated every level of saving into festive meal planning. Let me tell you, a humble pot of beans has never tasted so good when you drum up enthusiasm about it with a handful of friends and a dash of creativity!

Beyond the cheeky gatherings and dance parties, I prioritized keeping track of my progress through milestones on a visual board. I decorated it all flashy-like—a sparkly reminder that I was conquering my financial goals! Each payment was denoted with bright sticky notes and stars, adding a touch of fiesta to my otherwise routine-centered life. Whenever I dealt with setbacks or unexpected expenses (like the time my daughter's school "forgot" to mention there was a field trip fee), I glanced at my board to reflect on how far I'd come. It was like having my very own cheerleader encouraging me to keep pushing forward.

The emotional payoff of celebrating milestones started to transcend across all areas of my life. I was no longer just counting my steps on my path to financial freedom; I was dancing through them! They became moments of joy that linked us together with laughter and abundance, not just reflections of hard work. Remember, it's about building a life of fulfillment rather than just numbers, with a little glitter and sincerity sprinkled on top.

In conclusion, every step of progress counts, my friends! Having fun while simultaneously inching towards your financial goals is the ultimate best practice. So let's collectively slip on those party shoes, acknowledge each little victory, and throw confetti with glee, because we, *yes, we!*, are rocking this financial journey together. So, whether your milestone is as big as paying off debt or as simple as sticking to your budget for a week, do yourself a favor and celebrate it with the joy it deserves. Here's to your successes, my fellow warriors—cheers to the adventure yet to come!

CHAPTER 5
THE FAMILY FINANCIAL PLANNING STRATEGY

The Importance of Family Involvement in Financial Planning

When I decided to embark on my journey to financial freedom, I quickly learned that flying solo felt a bit like trying to swim with a ton of bricks tied to my ankles. You see, financial planning isn't just a task to check off your list or a lonely journey through complex spreadsheets filled with numbers that look like they were pulled from an alien spacecraft. Nope! That would be way too easy! Instead, I found that including my family in the financial mix turned this nerve-racking endeavor into a riotously enlightening circus. Yes, folks, welcome to the Big Top of budgeting, where the clowns trip over their own expenses and the tightrope walkers dance precariously on the line between wants and needs.

The first thing to consider is that family involvement in financial planning brings about a certain level of accountability. Just like Mom always said, "It takes a village to raise a child." Well, in my ever-expanding household, it takes a family to keep the credit score in check! Imagine this: Tiler, my towering teenager who could easily double as my bouncer, is tasked with tracking our family expenses. The kid has a laser focus on every dollar that floats in and out like a yo-yo in a toddler's hands. Little did he know, he would take this job seriously. Suddenly, Tiler becomes Mr. Moneybags, and I have to watch my back when it's snack time because he's ready to negotiate terms more strictly than a Wall Street banker!

Then we have Bristiney, my ultra-organized daughter, who treats every financial goal like a class project worthy of an A+. When she discovered that saving for a family vacation was on the table, she whipped out a PowerPoint presentation that was more impressive than my tax office pitch! She rallied the troops with catchy slogans like "Save Enough to Surf!" and created a family vision board that made my last entrepreneurial plan look like a kindergarten project. By rallying the family in such a vested way, I realized that involving loved ones is more than just sharing financial burdens; it also fosters teamwork! Who else needs a soccer team when you've got a family united by the singular goal of achieving financial success?

Let's not forget about the hilariously maverick moves my husband, Sims, brings to the team. He's been around the entrepreneurial block enough times to know that there's often more than one way to skin a cat. You have to appreciate the man for trying to see how "Start Fresh Today" principles could help us turn our next family dinner into an expense-tracking casserole party. Picture this scene: half-baked budget charts on the dining table, and Sims proudly proclaiming our dinner is now a "financial planning bonanza." Family involvements can lighten the mood and infuse your budget discussions with creativity and flair, although I still draw the line at turning family meetings into themed costume parties. Who needs superheroes when you can save like one?

By involving family members, we also unravel the stigma about money that exists in so many households. Weirdly enough, talking about finances should be as normal as discussing dinner menus or what Aunt Patricia did on her last cruise. The more we talk about our financial goals, the more we normalize budgeting, saving, and even splurging (within reason, y'all!). Remember, if we can chat about who left the refrigerator door open, why can't we discuss creating a solid budget? By demystifying the topic of finance, we pave the road for everyone to share their opinions, regardless of their financial prowess—or lack thereof. Finally, no one feels like they're being forced to take the money talk so seriously that they feel like they're trying to solve a Rubik's Cube!

Financial planning as a family is like putting together a comedy routine. One person may tell a joke, leading to a roguish riff that spirals into laughs and unexpected insights. Having everyone play a part in making financial decisions not only strengthens our family bonds but also brings humor and perspective into our lives. When we make mistakes—and trust me, we make them—there's no shame in the game because laughter creates a bridge over our financial faux pas. Think of it as our version of group therapy: "Hi, my name is Tumeka, and I may or may not have impulse-shopped during the one-day flash sale!"

In the end, family involvement in financial planning doesn't just keep our family on track; it creates a unique, nurturing environment where money worries take a back seat to laughter, creativity, and accountability. And on this financial crusade, it's nice to know that when you're budgeting, failure may be an option—but so is success, one hilariously awkward family meeting at a time. After all, who wouldn't want to be part of the greatest budgeting show on earth?

Setting Collective Financial Goals

When it comes to setting financial goals as a family, we need to face the reality that it's a bit like herding cats—furry, sassy cats. Each family member has their own ideas about where they want to channel their hard-earned cash. For instance, while my daughter Bristiney is content saving every penny to take our family to a tropical escape where sun-soaked bliss meets coconut drinks with tiny umbrellas, Tiler is firmly convinced that all financial advances should be redirected toward his basketball shoe collection. So, you can imagine the family discussions resemble more of a catfight rather than an organized summit on wealth creation! But therein lies the beauty: chaos is the spice of financial life!

Initially, I realized that the most contentious matter was getting everyone to agree on what collective financial goals truly mean. To tackle this, we decided to host a "Financial Family Summit"—fancy, right? Picture us gathered around the living room table, complete with oversized glasses of lemonade, and a massive whiteboard that would salivate any corporate exec. Except instead of serious jargon, I had colorful markers and our wishes written in glitter. Yeah, real professional. But guess what? This lighthearted take was a genius move because it set the stage for brainstorming and unleashed our inner teenagers, who suddenly assumed they were at summer camp.

So, we began the summit by throwing out random ideas like confetti—winning a family vacation, saving for a new car, or just having enough money left over to avoid ramen noodles for the rest of the week (which, let's be honest, nobody could bear). Once we had a diverse assortment of ideas plastered across the board, we began reeling it in. One thing I learned quickly is that you might have to fight for your dreams, and fighting over where money should go is no exception. Yet, collaborating as a family not only provided various perspectives but also opened up communication lines that made family members feel valued.

Then, we focused on refining those grand aspirations into measurable, achievable targets—because, let's face it, no one wants an unfinished family goal hanging over their heads like a piñata ready to shower disappointment. If we wanted to vacation in the Bahamas, we needed realistic timelines and budgets attached to it. After kicking around some numbers, I had my husband, Sims, pitching possible venues for our future beach getaway while simultaneously reminding everyone that "swimwear does not come cheap, kids!" The man has a one-track mind; you've got to love it.

And while we were at it, the kids caught on to something ingenious: if we split our goals into short-term, mid-term, and long-term categories—like a financial treasure map!—we'd have a much clearer path to success. If we could manage to save enough for ice-cream dates on Fridays (short-term answers), followed by a family camping trip to the nearby state park (mid-term), before ultimately grinding for our Caribbean Beach Adventure (long-term goals), our capitulation would be sweet! This is the family ambition set on sugar diets!

Of course, we had to accept that a family is an ever-evolving unit, so we reserved the right to revisit our goals regularly—kind of like a reality TV show where we anxiously binge-watch our own financial journey featuring twisted plot twists, disappearing cash, and surprise expenses that throw a wrench in our perfectly laid plans. For example, suddenly we found ourselves faced with unanticipated costs like dentist bills, and wouldn't you know it: the dream of adding Dad's prized fishing boat to our family portfolio got unceremoniously tossed into the "later" pile.

Through all of it, I learned that transparency is key. The more everyone knows about our current financial standing, the more involved we all become in decision-making. And, of course, facing our finances together creates a united front, muting the voices that squawk "No, we can't have that! We're saving for the Bahamas!" We might have different dreams, but the method of arriving at them is tied to a teamwork campaign where laughter is a requirement.

In conclusion, setting collective financial goals isn't just about surviving—it's about thriving, all while having the family dynamic of a sitcom episode! Embracing the chaos, turning the financial stress into laughter, and aligning our aspirations into a beautiful mosaic of jointly crafted dreams has become our newest family adventure. So here's to financial goal-setting—a thrilling escapade that may cause minor chaos but ultimately leads us toward financial freedom and, hopefully, a fabulous family vacation, too! Cheers to that, with our lemonade in hand, of course!

Creating a Family Budget Together

Creating a family budget together is like hosting a potluck dinner where nobody knows what anyone else is bringing, and everyone's hopeful but suspicious about what actually ends up on the table. Trust me, I've been there! I gathered my family with the enthusiasm of a marching band in a parade, ready to tackle our finances like the budget warriors we aspire to be. However, a hint of trepidation loomed in the air, like the smell of burnt popcorn about to waft through our living room. The kids were skeptical, and honestly, I couldn't blame them. After all, they were about to witness their mother attempt to navigate the budgeting waters as a collective—something akin to trying to herd the aforementioned rebellious cats.

First and foremost, I pulled out my trusty whiteboard, which I swear had been through more budget meetings than any corporate employee. I boldly declared, "Today, we create an all-inclusive budget, silly expenses and all!" Yes, ladies and gents, I included Tiler's aspirations of allocating "snack funds" for his daily dose of chips and soda. I mean, what's life without some humor amidst the numbers? As I laid out our monthly income and expenses, it suddenly felt like I was writing the script for a never-ending sitcom episode—complete with the dramatic tension of what we actually had coming in versus the ever-growing list of wants and needs that seemed to sprout like weeds in a neglected garden.

The first task? Identifying our fixed monthly expenses because apparently, bills are a thing, and they don't disappear, no matter how much you wish upon a star! We methodically penciled in our mortgage, utilities, groceries, and those "unexpected" expenses that really want to come crashing in like an uninvited guest. Whoa, wait a minute! Did someone just say "unexpected"? That term felt as slippery as a water snake! Everyone was armed with a calculating expression because, in no time, we realized that even with the best budgeting intentions, those pesky "surprise" expenses lurked like ninjas, ready to sneak up on us as soon as we turned our backs.

And here comes the best part: after we itemized our non-negotiables, it was finally time to flesh out the fun stuff—the variable expenses. Cue excited wiggles and uncontrollable whoops from Tiler, who fought valiantly for his snack budget that felt more like a stock market pitch! "Perhaps we can save on utilities this month and allocate it to more junk food!" he suggested. I couldn't resist a cackle since the sight of my 15-year-old negotiating a financial strategy like a Wall Street consultant made for hysterical entertainment. Watching the kids pitch their cases for individual wants was like a live-action game show where everyone competed for the title of "Best Persuader."

As we collectively squeezed all of our wants into the budget, I could feel family dynamics at play—Sims raising his eyebrow every time new requests got thrown into the mix. At the same time, Bristiney tugged at her heartstrings by citing future family trips and experiences. We faced the harsh reality that luxury and daily life often collide like cats and dogs in a sitcom where no one wins. So I introduced a fun twist: we designated a "Family Fun Fund," a line item that could be tapped into for spontaneous weekend adventures. Thankfully, a half-hearted debate followed about whether it should include trips to the arcade or if the latest video game purchase would qualify as "fun." Note to self: never include the words "family" and "fun" in the same sentence when dealing with teenagers—bad recipe.

Allow me to emphasize: compromise became the name of the game! That's right; we became low-key budget negotiators, convincing each other that a night out for pizza was more financially responsible than buying another pair of high-top sneakers. And, of course, we all engaged in the Wal-Mart-style "buy more, save more" mentality because we needed every last discount! But through these discussions, we traded high stakes for laughs—someone would always be tweaking a word or two to make their pitches more irresistible, turning what could've been a mundane budgeting session into a hilariously entertaining meeting that yielded both laughs and actual progress.

Let's not forget that tracking our budget wasn't a one-and-done deal; it required regular check-ins! To keep it lighthearted, we dub our catch-up meetings "Family Money Mondays"—the most hyped and the least anticipated day of the week. We traded judgment for giggles, colluding like members of a heist crew who'd just returned from a not-so-successful robbery. "So, uh, who ate the budgeted pizza night last month?" was an actual line spoken before we all burst into uncontrollable laughter, which is, of course, the whole point!

In conclusion, creating a family budget together has proven to be more than just numbers on a board; it's an experience filled with jests, playful negotiations, wild aspirations, and the delightful concession of realizing everyone's financial dreams are intermingled with a mountain of laughter. So let's tip our hats to the craziness because, at the end of the day, if we can budget while chuckling and finding joy in our financial journey, we're already winning! Plus, I think we've all learned that the best things in life may not always be free, but they sure can be darn entertaining, and that's priceless. Cheers to budgeting, y'all!

Communicating About Money as a Family

Communicating about money as a family can sometimes feel like trying to get cats to play fetch—disorganized, skeptical, and, quite frankly, mayhem incarnate. Somehow, however, I found myself at the center of this very circus. Sitting down to discuss finances with my husband, kids, and the occasional peeking pet can be an exhilarating experience, though not necessarily in the zen-like clarity I initially envisioned. Instead of peaceful discussions, I often encounter a whirlwind of "I need this!" versus "What do you mean we can't afford that?!" with the ferocity of a dramatic soap opera! Still, I genuinely believe these loud squabbles lead to richer conversations about money, and, wouldn't you know it? They keep me from going completely bonkers.

The first step in our family communication strategy involves creating a safe space. At least I thought it was safe until Bristimey decided that "safe" meant launching her latest crusade for tickets to that trendy concert we absolutely couldn't afford. I mean, I was picturing a cozy, pillow-filled living room setting where the kids shared their financial woes openly, akin to a heartfelt therapy session. What I got instead was a full-on negotiation, complete with dramatic gestures and Tiler bursting through the living room doors like a sports announcer on deadline. Our "safe space" quickly became a WWE wrestling ring for financial arguments, and you could almost hear the announcer's voice: "And in this corner, Tiler 'Money Muncher' Bailey, champion of snack funds!"

Then, just when I thought I had entered a fever dream of financial brawls, I introduced the concept of "Family Finance Night!" This is essentially where we all agree to throw our financial concerns—and hopes—onto the table for discussion, complete with snacks as reinforcements. Because honey, nothing breeds cooperation like crunchy snacks! Whether it's popcorn, chips, or leftover pizza, as soon as the munchables hit the table, the atmosphere shifts from combat to camaraderie faster than you can say "budget cuts." Letting everyone indulge in snacks during our chit-chats adds a delicious touch, effectively transforming our budget talks into mini-parties—because what's better than a money discussion fueled by nacho cheese and guacamole?

We made it a rule that everyone gets a chance to talk without anyone interrupting; thus, we became professional listeners. Well, most of us…because Tiler still manages to interject with questions like "Can we cash out our future for a gaming console?" in the middle of Sims expressing the need to save for a new mower. Trust me; this leads to some very amusing conversations where we gently remind our youngest that cashing in on future dreams requires more than convincing a bunch of adults to fork over their finances. It's a democracy here, buddy, and your voting rights do not extend to purchasing the latest superhero action figure!

However, communicating about money isn't all fun and games. Life inevitably rears its head with harsh financial truths that are so unbelievable, they belong in a bad sitcom. Honestly, I sometimes feel like a financial referee breaking up squabbles over whose financial needs come first—Tiler's never-ending pizza craving or Bristiney's desire to become the next Beyoncé (also not a cheap venture). This is when the rubber hits the road, and I find myself explaining why some dreams take priority over others instead of just shrugging my shoulders and declaring, "It's a tough world out there!" Because let's be real, the last thing I want is for my children to walk away with a worldview that money is merely a shiny object they chase without realizing the strategy behind it!

In these intense discussions, I often weave lessons on financial responsibility—the necessary evil of this budgetary bonding experience. I like to think that teaching my kids about budgeting, investing, and saving inspires a legacy of financial literacy that will honor my late-night rantings and financial prowess! But here's where it gets funny—no matter how serious I get with my advice, my kids inevitably bring in the "but Mom!" argument that derails my expressive preachings. At this point, I've come to embrace a slightly loony approach: if they can make me laugh while discussing money, I count it as a win, however dysfunctional it may seem.

So, communicating about money as a family is profoundly rewarding. It is messy, laughter-infused, and creates bonds that thread our family closer together—like a heartfelt quilt stitched with hopes, dreams, and those inevitable moments of indulgence (let's face it; snacking is essential!). And the more I encourage open discussions about financial priorities, the stronger we all become as a family, even if it's often punctuated by Tiler's unsolicited rap about "getting that cash." So, there's a method to the madness! Here's to embracing our collective financial fiascos, because behind every head-scratcher of a family money talk is an opportunity for growth, understanding, and bundles of laughter. Who knew budgeting could be such a riot? Cheers to our money-bound misadventures, my friends!

Celebrating Financial Milestones Together

Celebrating financial milestones together is like throwing a party for a pet rock; you must convince everyone it's worthy of the occasion while secretly knowing it's the funniest celebration you've ever planned. You see, as the self-proclaimed Budget Avenger in my household, I've learned that recognizing every tiny victory—be it achieving a savings goal or paying off a credit card—can transform our financial journeys into joyous adventures rather than solemn obligations. Why celebrate when achieving financial stability can be all fun and games? So, the stage became set for a series of delightful, offbeat celebrations that brought our family together without breaking the bank—or our sanity!

Let's be honest: I had little idea what to expect the first time we celebrated a financial win. I conjured a cute "Savings Success Celebration," eager to turn a modest achievement, like paying off our dishwasher, into an event every bit as extravagant as you'd find for a wedding. We gathered the kids in the living room, adorned in thrift-store party hats, and launched into a confetti shower that rivaled

New Year's Eve in Times Square! "You've saved $500 on a dishwasher we didn't know could break!" I announced. Tiler, ever the literalist, asked, "Do we get cake now, or is this just a budget meeting dressed up like a party?" Lesson learned: attaching cake to the celebration makes everything a whole lot sweeter, even if it came from a well-timed 'day-old' clearance sale!

Our next monumental moment arrived when we tackled our mountain of student loans! Oh, what a glorious day that was! We finally made the last payment, and I announced the news with the enthusiasm of a game show contestant winning a brand new fridge! To mark this epic conclusion, we decided to host a "Loan Liberation Celebration." I whipped up a batch of brownies and brought out some seltzers, and just like that, we had a full-bore celebration, complete with joyous cheers and a "welcome back to financial freedom" toast. However, I learned three days later that someone still needed to remind Tiler that money didn't magically reappear just because we'd celebrated—because he attempted to "borrow" my emergency fund for a brand-new video game release!

Then came the milestone of finally achieving a fully funded emergency fund (thank you, coupon clipping!). This was where the stakes cranked up a notch! I held a particularly animated family meeting: "Ladies and gentlemen, I present to you our brand-new *Emergency Goat Fund!*" Yep, I did that! I adorned the dining room table with a ridiculously large, inflatable goat as the centerpiece, dubbed "Billy the Budget Buddy!" The kids were instantly intrigued, like they had stumbled upon a treasure map! As I recounted the wild adventures we had encountered saving that fund, every unexpected hiccup became a badge of honor. The hilarity peaked when Tiler announced, "I propose we use the goat to 'butt' heads with future emergencies!"

Once we created a habit of celebrating financial milestones, it became a family tradition. For every holiday season, we would choose a particular finance-related theme. You'd be amazed to know that "Christmas Credit Card Payoff" ended up being quite a hit! Picture a holiday-themed scavenger hunt with cleverly rhymed clues, all leading to an important lesson promoting debt-free living; it's a blast! The catch was, every clue would guide us on a budget-friendly quest to find miniature presents along the way. Kids would engage and cheer every time we found a special treat—who knew financial literacy could be disguised as a joyous holiday quest?

Now, don't get started on our annual "Budgeting Olympics!" Imagine our family dressed like athletes, our faces painted with excitement (and a pinch of skepticism). With various events, such as "Fastest Grocery List Completion" and "Creative Coupon Clipping," we brought a sporty spin to the tedious task of budgeting. Each little victory took on a life of its own, and as a team, we celebrated our progress together, cheering each other on like we were at the Super Bowl (minus the million-dollar ads—and yes, we did sneak in wings on the budget!).

Sims became my partner-in-crime, turning my ridiculous ideas into an epic saga of wittiness and enthusiasm. "Can we just have a 'Money Motivator' award?" he suggested with a twinkle in his eye each time we achieved a goal. And suddenly my dream was no longer just about reaching the milestone—we were creating a family legacy packed with hilarious memories, ridiculous costumes, and experiences that would stick in our minds longer than any bank account statement ever could.

In conclusion, celebrating financial milestones together has reshaped our family's outlook on managing money. We've learned to embrace laughter, creativity, and absurdity, successfully turning what could have been solemn occasions into wild celebrations. And so, cheers to the inflatable goats, the scavenger hunts, the themed Olympics, and everything in between! As we gear up for each new milestone, we'll do so knowing that while money may come and go, the joy of celebrating it as a family, amid laughter and absurdity, is something we'll treasure forever. So, who's ready for some budgeting festivities? Here comes the confetti cannons!

CHAPTER 6
THE POWER OF A STRONG NETWORK

Building Your Financial Power Team

Gather 'round, future budget avengers! Today, we're diving headfirst into the exhilarating world of financial power teams. No, I'm not talking about the kind that wears spandex and flies around saving the universe from alien invaders (though that would be cool). I'm talking about assembling your very own squad of smart, savvy, finance-minded people who will help you navigate the chaotic battlefield of money management and help you conquer your financial goals like the superhero you truly are.

You see, assembling a financial power team is like building the Avengers, but instead of battling Loki and his army of Chitauri, you're up against debt, poor credit, and questionable investments. Each member of your team should have a specific area of expertise. You wouldn't want Black Widow trying to pilot Iron Man's suit, right? Similarly, you wouldn't want to recruit your Auntie Shirley, who still thinks "digital currency" is just a fancy word for the allowance she doles out to her cats. The point is, surround yourself with people who know their stuff! When I made that leap from mortgage facilitator to family money guru, I quickly realized the value of having experts at my side.

Start with a financial planner—your very own Tony Stark. They'll map out your financial destiny and help you plan for your future. After all, why wing it when you can have a roadmap? When I first spoke to my financial planner, I felt like I was in one of those heist movies. You know, the ones where a crew assembles to pull off an elaborate caper that only they—well, let's be real—only the financial planner understands. We crafted a plan tighter than a drum, ensuring that I was doing all the right things with my money instead of trying to pay for my kids' college tuition with Monopoly money.

Next on your list is a tax advisor—your very own Hulk, smashing through the chaos of tax laws! Sure, many of us love to play the "guess what I can deduct on my taxes" game (hello, any reasoning behind that last-minute online shopping spree?). Still, the truth is, you want a certified professional who can navigate the tax labyrinth for you. When I implemented my tax strategies, I felt like I had unleashed a hidden weapon—taxes suddenly seemed less like a horror show and more like a tailored suit that I could wear with pride!

Now, let's not forget about a mortgage broker. Sometimes, you need a Thor—a mighty force that can get you shelter without causing a financial storm! A good mortgage broker understands the ins and outs of home loans like Thor understands how to swing his mighty hammer around (and we know he does it with STYLE!). When I found my mortgage broker, it was like discovering a secret level in a video game where I could score perks I didn't even know existed. Talk about leveling up my financial game!

Then comes the insurance agent—think of them as your personal Captain America, shielded from disaster. They'll ensure you have the protection you need when life throws its curveballs, or in my case, when my son decides to "experiment" with firecrackers in the living room. (Spoiler alert: it ended with an unexpected trip to the fire department.) Having someone who speaks the language of policies and coverage is essential because those are the folks who'll help you ensure you're not left stranded without a parachute when something goes wrong.

Finally, assemble your tribe of finance-savvy friends! Remember, while superheroes are great, there's power in camaraderie and collaboration. These are the folks who will buoy you when you're feeling low about your budget or give you pep talks when you consider buying the latest, automatically folding laundry machine that you probably don't need but desperately want. You create accountability when you share your financial goals, lend support, and perhaps criticize each other's spending habits in light-hearted banter. Your squad will help you navigate the money world while keeping the laughter rolling—trust me, money talks can get dull if there isn't a punchline involved!

So, my fellow Budget Avengers, your journey to financial freedom doesn't have to be walked alone! Assemble your financial power team and make those superhero-style connections. With the right squad by your side, you'll not only conquer your financial mountains but also have a few laughs along the way. After all, who says money management can't be a barrel of laughs? Your financial superhero story awaits, and the best part is you're the one wielding the mighty calculator!

Networking for Success: Where to Meet the Right People

Networking—the sacred art of squeezing your way into social circles and magically discovering the hidden goldmine of fabulous financial geniuses. Trust me, I know what you're thinking: "Tumeka, isn't networking just an elaborate game of 'Who can schmooze better at the next overpriced banquet?'" Well, my dear financial adventurer, allow me to disabuse you of that notion. Networking can be as rewarding and delightful as a slice of double chocolate cake—especially when you approach it with sincerity, humor, and a sprinkle of congenial charm!

First and foremost, let's talk about the good old-fashioned networking events. You know the ones: a room full of people sipping overpriced wine while trying not to spill it all over their crisp white shirts. You walk in, and suddenly, it feels like a high school reunion where you desperately seek out the person from math class who never let anyone copy their homework. But fear not! As daunting as those rooms sometimes can be, remember that everyone is there for a purpose, just like you! When I waltzed into my first networking event, let's just say I was more nervous than a cat at a dog show. But after a few sips of sparkling grape juice (because I genuinely believe in responsible networking), I started striking up conversations about credit scores, financial planning, and why using a credit card for avocado toast can be a slippery slope.

The next place to meet the right people? Community events! Yes, darling, unleash your inner social butterfly and embrace those community gatherings—the farmers' market, the small business fair, or even your neighborhood's annual block party with that questionable potluck. You'd be surprised how many financial wizards hang out in your local parks, trying to sell you artisanal granola bars or the world's finest kale salad. Talking to someone while munching on homemade cookies may seem casual, but you never know if that cookie enthusiast is secretly a tax advisor on the side! My husband, Sims, and I have stumbled upon brilliant connections while grabbing a plate of "what does this even taste like," finger foods at these events. Don't underestimate the power of a good cookie; it could lead you to the wisdom of a financial guru serving kale!

Now, if you're not feeling particularly adventurous when it comes to social events, do like I did and join local clubs or meet-up groups. You can participate in everything from a book club that focuses on finance books (you'd be surprised how many exist, and shout-out to the fabulous authors making that happen!) to local entrepreneurs' gatherings that leave you with more ideas than an infomercial at 2 AM. Meeting folks who resonate with your financial dreams is the ultimate goal, and it's often at these meet-ups that the real magic begins. I once connected with a brilliant woman named Lisa at a "Financial Freedom for Fabulous Women" meet-up. We ended up exchanging ideas as if we were two kids in a candy store, and boom! I found my go-to gal for everything related to investing!

Let's not forget the beauty of online networking! While bartering homemade cookies at a local event has its charm, the internet has opened up an entirely new universe. Platforms like LinkedIn, Facebook groups, and even Twitter are teeming with individuals eager to swap advice on budgeting, credit, and wealth-building, without the awkward small talk about the weather. I remember the first time I joined an online group dedicated to financial literacy. It felt a bit like being handed the keys to a treasure chest. There were experts from all walks of life sharing their golden nuggets of wisdom. I even made "virtual" friends who understood the struggles of managing a budget while raising three kids. We now periodically hold Zoom chats to share our collective brilliance, and they've proven to be as supportive as an overstuffed couch after a long day.

And let's not overlook industry conferences and workshops! Think of them as the ultimate playground for grown-ups who are serious about improving their financial acumen. When I attended my first finance conference, I felt like I'd stumbled into a secret garden filled with knowledgeable professionals. Between the workshops, panels, and networking luncheons, I spent more time connecting with people than I did learning, though it's good to engage your brain too!

But the best part? You find mentors ready to shower you with wisdom, tips, and sometimes even referrals that will make your financial dreams come true. Talk about a win-win!

So, my fabulous financial friends, whether you venture into local events, join clubs, mix it up online, or participate in conferences, remember that networking is the lifeblood of success. Each person you meet could be a superhero waiting to help you conquer the world of finance! The secret? Approach each interaction with an open heart and a dash of humor, sprinkle in some sincerity, and don't be afraid to share a laugh (or a cookie) along the way. With the right connections, you'll be well on your way to not just achieving your financial goals but also enjoying every step of the journey! So, let's lace up those shoes and make those connections—your financial future is waiting, and it's going to be one epic ride!

The Importance of Mentorship in Personal Finance

Mentorship is the superhero blend of guidance, support, and occasional awkward moment when you realize your mentor is just as unsure about whether to invest in avocado toast futures as you are. But let me tell you, dear financial enthusiasts, mentorship in personal finance can make all the difference between a budget that runs smoother than a greased pig and a financial plan that resembles a tangled mess of unused holiday lights. So, grab your capes and let's venture into the importance of having a financial mentor by your side!

Let's start by painting a picture. When I first embarked on my journey toward savvy money management, I felt like a lost puppy in a pet shop filled with complex investment opportunities and credit score evaluations. It was overwhelming! During a community workshop on improving credit scores, I stumbled upon this financial guru named Gary (yes, even superheroes attend workshops). Gary had the kind of charisma that made you believe he could coax the sun into shining on a rainy Tuesday. He was a wealth of knowledge, and the minute he started dropping terms like "diversification" and "compound interest," I knew I had found my guiding light—or at least my financial Yoda.

And here's the kicker—mentorship is all about learning from someone who has been in the trenches! Picture yourself trying to assemble IKEA furniture without the instruction manual: you'll end up with a bookshelf that resembles a modern art sculpture rather than a place to store your novels. A mentor helps you decipher that instruction manual! They've been through the jungle of financial decisions, faced the ferocious beast known as "unexpected bills," and successfully emerged on the other side clutching a financial plan, rather than a pile of crumpled receipts. With a mentor's wisdom, you can avoid those pitfalls and navigate the complex world of finance with all the grace of a gazelle in a tutu—just a little wobbly, but still fabulous!

One of the best parts about mentorship is the accountability factor. You see, when you share your financial dreams and goals with a mentor, you've essentially made a deal that's tougher than any contract you'll ever sign. Suddenly, you're not just a free-floating fish in the vast ocean of budgeting; you have someone watching over you, urging you on, and holding your feet to the fire (figuratively speaking, of course—don't worry, no need to add pyro to our financial plans). When I had weekly check-ins with Gary, I knew I couldn't come unprepared, spouting my absurd justifications for impulse purchases of kitchen gadgets with names I could barely pronounce.

Now, let's chat about the emotional support that a mentor brings to the table. It's like having a cheerleader who also knows how to extinguish your financial fires with a simple "Let's talk about how you can make smarter decisions." As I navigated through the often terrifying waters of investments and debt management, I admitted to Gary that I was terrified of making a poor investment. Instead of scoffing or rolling his eyes, he gave me practical advice and shared stories about his own blunders in the financial realm—the kind that made me feel like I was in good company! Understanding that even the pros make mistakes provided me the comfort I needed to embrace the chaotic learning curve.

Perhaps the most critical aspect of mentorship in personal finance is the connections that come with it. When Gary told me about opportunities to attend industry conferences, it was like handing me a ticket to the VIP section of the finance world. Not only did I gain valuable insights about managing money, but I suddenly found myself immersed in a network bursting with other inspiring mentors and potential collaborations. Your mentor is essentially a giant spider, spinning a web of connections, and you want to be attached to that web!

In the wild ride of personal finance, mentorship ultimately gives you the confidence and skills to tackle your financial goals head-on. It's like having a trusty sidekick (who isn't underappreciated and stuck in the friend zone) by your side, ready to tackle life's financial challenges together. Without mentorship, budgeting can feel like a series of blindfolded darts, hoping to hit the target from across the room. With mentorship, it's more like taking targeted shots with laser precision—ninja-style!

So there you have it, my fabulous friends! Mentorship is the gold star on your personal finance journey. Whether your mentor is a longtime friend, a financial professional, or even that wise guy at the coffee shop who always makes astute comments about stock prices, finding a mentor who aligns with your financial aspirations is essential. After all, every superhero needs their sidekick—and in this saga of financial freedom, it's time to suit up, engage, and embrace the power of mentorship! Trust me; your future self will thank you, preferably in cash. Now, let's go find our mentors—you never know, your financial Yoda might just be hanging out at a workshop waiting to guide you through the galaxy of financial wisdom!

Creating Win-Win Relationships in Your Network

The elusive art of creating win-win relationships in your network! If networking is the grand dance of the business world, win-win relationships are the ballroom where everyone leaves the party feeling like they're carrying a plate of success, a few laughs, and maybe even some leftover cake. Who doesn't love cake? Imagine walking into a gathering, shaking hands left and right, and feeling that delightful spark of connection with people who genuinely want to lift each other up. Sounds dreamy, right? Well, my astute financial warriors, let's dive into how you can whip up those deliciously reciprocal relationships that transform your network from dull to positively scrumptious!

First and foremost, let's talk about the vital ingredient—you! That's right, walking into a networking event thinking you're going to charm everyone while hanging out your metaphorical "I'm here to take" sign won't work. You need to enter those interactions with a mindset geared towards sharing and supporting. Usually, I like to paraphrase a famous saying that goes something like this: "What's mine is yours, but please don't take my last piece of chocolate," because that's where I draw the line. But you get the idea! If you're genuinely listening, offering your insights, and making an effort to help someone else out, you'll create an invisible bond that's much stronger than the Wi-Fi connection in a crowded coffee shop.

Next up, share your knowledge and resources. Imagine you're at a party, and someone mentions that they need help with budgeting. Instead of fidgeting with your phone while secretly googling "how to awkwardly exit a conversation," lean in and share what you know! Offer your own personal experiences with budgeting tools or recommend an app that has saved your financial hide more times than you'd like to admit. Suddenly, you're not just a face in the crowd; you're the hero of the hour, sporting a shiny cape made of goodwill and generosity. People love to connect with those who genuinely want to help, and your generosity will spark an immediate sense of camaraderie. That's how you create those tasty win-win relationships!

Now, let's spice things up by focusing on reciprocity, which, believe me, is like the seasoning that brings your financial dinner party to life. Remember, these connections should flow like a well-oiled dance! It might start with you offering insights or resources, but don't miss the chance to lean back and allow others to do the same for you. You see, it's not just about tossing out helpful tidbits like confetti; it's about building a community where both parties feel valued and appreciated. When someone shares their knowledge or experience in return, you've officially entered the realm of mutual support! High-five, virtual style!

Think also about strategic alliances—similar to those buddy cop movies where the mismatched duo fights crime but ends up as the best of friends. For instance, if you know someone in real estate and have a kickass credit score guru secret weapon (wink, wink, that's you!), work together! Thank your connections for what they bring to the table and offer your expertise in exchange. You might end up collaborating on projects that could produce results more glorious than a double rainbow! It's all about creating opportunities that benefit each other, creating serious synergy worthy of a standing ovation at your financial soirée.

But here's the kicker: be authentic. Seriously—no one wants a 50% discount on a used car that's trying to pull off a magician's vanish act! People can smell insincerity from miles away, and it's as pleasant as eating a whole jar of pickles in one sitting. When you're genuine in your interactions, a beautiful element—the warmth of trust- unfolds. Trust turns those winning connections into lasting friendships and fruitful collaborations that can withstand everything from budget cuts to economic meltdowns.

Let's not forget the power of follow-ups! After establishing a connection, don't simply drop off the map like a fledgling magician whose card trick fails miserably. Reach out, send a quick email, or connect on social media. Share an article you found interesting or offer thoughts on a recent project they've disclosed. Follow-ups are the best way to show that you value the connection and are interested in seeing it grow, because let's be real, we all need a little extra love in our networks.

So, my fellow budget avengers, it's time to roll up your sleeves and cook up some winning relationships! Approach networking events with an open heart and the intention to share, listen actively, cultivate reciprocity, and build authentic connections. Each of these elements adds flavor to your company potluck, creating a banquet of mutual support and camaraderie. Trust me; there's nothing quite as gratifying as returning home at the end of a networking event with new friends, exciting opportunities, and a slice of cake (wishful thinking, but who's judging?). So, let's get out there and create some incredible win-win relationships that will fuel our financial triumphs, one connection at a time!

Supporting Your Community While Building Wealth

Supporting your community while building wealth—a noble cause that just might make you feel like a superhero without the spandex! It's a beautiful dance, really: on one side, you're out there chasing your financial dreams, and on the other, you're flipping the script by lifting others up along the way. It may sound bizarre, but trust me, there's a method to the madness, and your journey toward wealth doesn't have to mean stepping over others like you're playing a game of "the floor is lava." So, let's lace up our philanthropic shoes and venture into this engaging quest together!

First, let's address the elephant in the room: how do you support your community while growing your wealth without feeling like you're draining your wallet faster than a four-year-old can unwrap a candy bar? It starts with a mindset shift! Building wealth should not solely be about stacking cash in your bank account (although, don't get me wrong; that part is fantastic). It should also encompass a desire to create positive ripples in your community that can lead to growth for everyone. After all, when you contribute to the well-being of others, you're essentially planting seeds—hopefully not the kind that sprout into bad financial decisions! More like the seeds that flourish into support networks, local businesses thriving, and empowered individuals.

Now, here comes the fun part: find ways to showcase your skills for the greater good! If you're a financial whiz who knows how to whip up a mean budget, consider offering free workshops in your community! Imagine hosting a "Budgeting like a Boss" event at your local community center. I mean, who wouldn't want to attend? You can have snacks, free child care (if only to distract the kiddos with glittery art supplies), and engage participants in lively discussions about saving, investing, and avoiding that infamous impulse buy—the "I-need-it-now!" mentality. You'll be amazed at how giving back can actually reinforce your own financial knowledge while bolstering the skills of your neighbors!

Another exciting way to support your community is to invest in local businesses. Instead of heading to that big-box store like it was the holy grail, opt to shop at local vendors and small shops. Nothing feels better than drinking your fine artisanal coffee from a local café while simultaneously supporting the dreams of someone chasing their passion. And let's be real: who can resist sharing a story about discovering that one-of-a-kind, hand-knitted scarf made by a delightful older lady who remembers what it's like to fight a pair of knitting needles? When you support these businesses, you're not just contributing to your economy but building a community rich with unique offerings and color. Plus, you get the added joy of spotting that hand-knitted scarf on someone else and doing a secret little fist pump for the local artisans!

Then comes the power of collaboration. Let's say you're an entrepreneur growing your business while living in the neighborhood—this is where you roll up your sleeves and partner up! Join forces with local non-profits, school programs, or community initiatives whose aims align with your values. One of my proudest moments was collaborating with a local non-profit to host a financial literacy seminar for high school students. We tackled everything from budgeting to planning for their futures, which—spoiler alert—also encouraged them to become engaged citizens. Those teens exploded with questions, especially when they discovered investing could be as thrilling as a rollercoaster ride (minus the nausea). Engaging collaboratively means you earn some good karma points while making a real impact!

And we must talk about volunteering, folks! No, it's not as grim as doing laundry while watching paint dry; it can actually be exciting! Being present in your community shows that you care and are ready to roll up your sleeves to help others. Whether it's serving meals at a shelter, tutoring kids, or contributing your time to a financial literacy initiative, your involvement demonstrates that wealth is not just about money—it's about creating a supportive environment. The stories you'll hear, the connections you'll make, and the gratitude you'll receive will fill your heart (and maybe even slim down your wallet a bit) in ways you couldn't imagine.

There's also a psychological boost that stems from giving back. Studies have shown that those supporting their community feel happier and more fulfilled. Imagine the difference you'll feel when you transform from a mere accumulator of wealth into an active participant in enriching the lives of others! You'll be that glowing, cheerful person who enters the room like confetti at a party, and trust me, that kind of energy is contagious! People will want to surround themselves with you, linking their growth with your own. Think of yourself as the sun, radiating warmth and light, and you're nourishing both your financial ambitions and the ambitions of others.

In essence, supporting your community while building wealth is good for your heart and bottom line! The more we lift each other up, the more we uplift ourselves, creating a cycle of growth and prosperity that just keeps giving. It's like planting a community garden that flourishes with diverse plants and characters, fostering a beautiful ecosystem of nurturing and achievement, all while you're still chasing your dreams. So, my fellow financial adventurers, step out, spread those wings, and together, let's create thriving communities full of wealth, both financial and powerful connections, because nothing is quite as rewarding as building wealth in ways that elevate us all!

CHAPTER 7
BUDGETING BASICS FOR EVERYONE

Understanding Your Income

Understanding your income is like trying to understand your teenager's obsession with TikTok dances—momentarily confusing, occasionally hilarious, but ultimately essential for your sanity. Your income is the lifeblood of your financial plan, and just like a sitcom family trying to navigate through a chaotic dinner, you want to keep it balanced, predictable, and not at all awkward. As an entrepreneur and a self-proclaimed Budget Avenger, I can assure you that nothing is more important than knowing exactly how much dough you're bringing in, where it's coming from, and making sure it doesn't mysteriously vanish into the ether after a weekend of impulse buys at the local farmers' market.

First things first, let's break down what income actually is. Income isn't just a fancy word thrown around during tax season or a random figure on your paycheck. It's the money you're obviously receiving in exchange for your hard work, genius ideas, and the countless hours spent pretending to enjoy meetings. This includes wages, salaries, bonuses, freelance gigs, and any side hustles you've decided to embark upon (because apparently, one job just doesn't scream "overwhelmed" enough). So go ahead, pat yourself on the back—we're dealing with multiple income streams, like a financial river running through your life. If you're not careful, you might end up with income that looks more like the wild rapids of an adventure park than a peaceful stream.

Next, we have to account for the "other" income. You know, the kind of income that makes you feel slightly guilty, like when you eat the last slice of cake but don't admit it to anyone. This could include rental income, capital gains, or even that sweet surprise from a tax refund that you didn't see coming. If something lands in your pocket and you didn't have to break a sweat for it, you should feel a thrill of excitement, not unlike finding an old twenty-dollar bill hidden in your winter coat. Take a moment to celebrate that win! Just remember, with that delightful surprise comes the responsibility to manage it wisely; don't rush to blow it all on that trendy fidget spinner you've been eyeing.

Now, let's discuss the concept of net income versus gross income—the financial equivalent of apples and oranges. Your gross income is all the money you make before the government swoops in like a hawk on a fresh squirrel. It's the grand total, the big picture, the siren song that pulls you into daydreams of extravagant vacations and luxury cars. On the other hand, your net income is where the fun ends, because this is the amount you take home after taxes, deductions, and all those pesky withholdings. The cruel twist here is that gross income looks so exciting, yet by the time it hits your bank account, it feels deflated, almost like your favorite balloon when a child accidentally lets it go—it's just sad!

Once we've mapped out the territory of income types, it's equally important to assess the stability of your income. Are you a fan of the paycheck-paying kind of income, or do you venture bravely into the world of commission-based earnings with a heart full of dreams and a dash of anxiety? Consider it a financial rollercoaster—it's thrilling, but if you have a weak stomach (or a crippling fear of heights), strap in tight and hold on! The more consistent your income, the better you can budget and strategically plan; yet when you have an income that resembles a game of Musical Chairs—sometimes there is a chair waiting for you, and other times you're left standing—your budgeting strategy requires some serious flexibility. You might have to embrace an elastic approach to your finances or be ready to dance like the world's best cha-cha dancer to make ends meet.

In the end, what matters is that you take stock of your income's nature. Pin down your monthly income with the prowess of a hawk capturing its prey, and keep your finger on the pulse of any changes that might occur. Remember, understanding isn't just about knowing; it's about taking action! With this knowledge, you'll be equipped to plot your financial course like a true Budget Avenger, ready to triumph over obstacles like unexpected expenses and uninvited guests during family dinners. So, let's embrace this journey, laugh a little at the craziness, and sail confidently into the budgeting waters of life, armed with the knowledge of our income—and hey, if we have to poke fun along the way, all the better!

Identifying Fixed and Variable Expenses

Identifying fixed and variable expenses is like sorting the contents of a teenage room—it's a messy affair. Still, once you get through the chaos, it can be surprisingly enlightening, if not a little horrifying. Fixed expenses are those boring but necessary costs that stay the same, like a stubborn cat refusing to move from your lap. You know the ones I'm talking about: rent or mortgage payments, insurance premiums, and the endless subscriptions to things you can't quite remember signing up for, like that last season of that crime drama you can't even finish. On the other hand, variable expenses are the unpredictable wild cards in your budget, bursting with spontaneity like a conversion van at a music festival—fuel costs, groceries, entertainment, and the impulsive "I'll just grab a coffee" moments that sneak up on you when you swore you were being good.

Let's start with fixed expenses and address the elephant in the room: WHY do we have to pay these? The answer, my friend, is because the world can be a cruel place, and apparently, people believe everyone should live under a roof and not on the streets. I mean, who made those strange rules? But in reality, fixed expenses make us feel semi-stable, like a seesaw that somehow balances itself. These are the costs we can predict, and most importantly, we can count on them to suck the joy out of our bank account every single month. Ever notice how your mortgage is there, just eagerly waiting like a child on Christmas morning to gobble up any extra cash you thought you were saving? Yes, those fixed expenses love to remind us that adulting is for the brave and the financially alert.

Now, let's transition to the wild and unruly world of variable expenses. These expenses are the circus performers of your budget: they come and go, swoop in unexpectedly, and can be quite entertaining until they've drained away your funds. You think you're being responsible, living your best financially prudent life, and boom! You're suddenly deep into the world of impulse buys, fancy dinners with friends, or those cute little 'limited-time' sales that make you feel as though you have to buy something before it disappears forever. Variable expenses are like that friend who convinces you to stay out for one extra drink—you think it's innocent enough. Still, suddenly you wake up with regret, a headache, and no money left in your pocket while staring at your debit card, proclaiming, "How did I get here?"

I recommend gathering all your bank statements, receipts, and possibly a magnifying glass to identify these expenses because you'll need to dissect every little purchase like an alien autopsy. Fixed expenses will stick out like sore thumbs—same amount, same time, every month. Variable expenses, however, will require a detective's hat and possibly a few snacks to keep you going. You'll want to identify patterns in your spending: how often do you grab takeout? Spoiler alert: If the delivery driver greets you by name, it might be time for a little self-control.

One crucial step in this entire undertaking is creating categories for your expenses. Picture it: you have "Fixed Fan Club" and their devoted members (you know, rent, insurance, maybe even your Netflix subscription that you only use to watch reruns of shows you already binged). On the flip side, you have the "Variable Virtuosos," which can evolve into an epic story about your shopping, hobby supplies, or the surprise treat purchases that seem harmless until they trigger a chocolate avalanche in your pantry.

So why bother making this distinction between fixed and variable expenses? Well, my fellow financial warriors, knowing the difference allows you to wrestle your budgeting like a tag-team wrestler in the ring. With fixed expenses, you can plan accordingly—knowing how much you absolutely must pay allows you to have that moment of peace. With variable expenses, however, you can flex your budgeting muscle and control the chaos that seems so ready to overthrow your financial structure.

Remember, everything takes practice. It's like learning to ride a bike—at first, you wobble, and your expenses spill out like an exploded piñata, but with time, you'll get the hang of it. By meticulously separating these expenses, you'll be empowered to create a budget that aligns with your lifestyle and your values. So grab that detective hat, unleash your inner Sherlock, and get to sorting. You'll feel like a financial rock star before you know it, flinging fixed expenses to the side like last year's fashion trends while strategically managing those pesky variable expenses like the budget boss you are. Just keep your eyes on the prize: financial freedom, sanity, and maybe a little less regret over those impulsive snack runs!

Creating Your Budgeting Framework

Creating your budgeting framework is like constructing a house of cards—one wrong move, and it all comes crashing down faster than my hopes of maintaining a strict diet with a family full of foodies. But fear not! With a solid framework, you won't just be balancing the cards; you'll be building a fortress against your financial fears, complete with a moat and maybe even an inflatable unicorn for some added flair. Whether you want to break free from the shackles of debt, save for that dreamy vacation, or finally impress your in-laws with your financial acumen, building a proper budgeting framework will be the bedrock of your financial success.

First up, let's establish some goals because what's a budget without a destination? Think of it as the guiding star in your financial night sky. Your goals can be short-term (like saving for that fancy coffee machine that you swear will turn you into a caffeine connoisseur) or long-term (like saving for your kid's college fund, which is basically a mini lottery—you buy in, and hope it yields a return). Write these goals down! You'd be surprised how putting pen to paper can help cement your intentions into reality. Visualize it like writing a letter to Santa Claus, except this time, you'll actually be getting what you ask for if you play your cards right.

Next, you'll want to determine your income again, but this time, you'll look at it in the context of your spending. It's like a detective puzzle; you'll need to piece together clues to understand what amounts of money you actually have available to work with and how that correlates to your goals. List all your income sources again, and if you're feeling daring, consider incorporating a wild card for the occasional side hustle (because who can resist earning some mad cash by pet-sitting for the neighbor's three cats?). Knowing your total income helps frame your budgeting structure, and also helps illuminate those cold, hard truths about how much you're really dealing with.

Now that you have your goals and income settled, it's time to map out your expenses. Remember our earlier chat about fixed and variable expenses? This is where they come into play. You'll want to calculate your total fixed expenses (the rent, the bills, the horrifying yet necessary insurance) and then predict your variable expenses based on past patterns. You might want to not only make categories but implement an 'emergency' category, just in case the fridge decides it wants to start spewing out food like a spoilage carnival gone awry.

Once you have your total estimated expenses, it's time for the magic to happen—creating your actual budget. On good old-fashioned paper or a funky app that pings you every time you spend a little too much on avocado toast, set aside amounts from your income to cover those expenses. This is where math becomes your best friend, like that one buddy who bakes cookies for you when you're sad (and who can say no to cookies?). You'll want to allocate funds towards needs first, then your wants, and finally, sprinkle in some fun savings.

But don't forget one vital rule: building space for some flexibility is as essential as knowing when to drop that last slice of pizza at a social gathering. Things won't always go according to plan—unexpected expenses will strike like a ninja! You'll want your framework to allow for adjustments. If you overspend one month, for heaven's sake, don't give yourself a wide berth of grief! Instead, modify your spending for the next month as needed and remind yourself that budgeting is a journey, not a sprint.

Finally, monitoring and revisiting this framework is where the real magic lies. It's like keeping an eye on that new plant you bought—ignore it, and you'll face wilted leaves and a whole lot of regret. Report back to your budget regularly to ensure you're on track and adjust it if necessary. Just be sure to celebrate any accomplishments along the way! Did you meet your monthly savings goal? Treat yourself to a mini-celebration, even if it's just a dance party in your living room with the cats.

Creating a budgeting framework isn't a daunting task; it's a pathway to financial clarity. By laying out your expenses, income, and goals with a touch of humor and a sprinkle of determination, you'll construct a budget that's not just functional but also liberating. Building this financial safety net will empower you to face the uncertainties of life head-on, equipped with the knowledge that you are, indeed, the Budget Avenger you set out to become! So grab that budgeting hat and measure twice—because once you build this framework, you won't just be playing house; you'll be creating a financial legacy that would make even your grandmother proud.

Incorporating Savings into Your Budget

Incorporating savings into your budget is like trying to convince your taste buds that kale is actually delicious—it's a tough sell, but once you get the hang of it, the benefits are totally worth it. Think of savings as that 'secret sauce' that elevates your financial meal from bland to gourmet. Without it, you're just chewing on expenses and debts like overcooked broccoli (nobody wants that). But once you master the art of saving, you'll find yourself comfortably sipping a smoothie made with real fruit—now there's a tasty visual!

To kick off this endeavor, we must first confront the psychological warfare that savings can sometimes wage in our minds. Let's face it: saving money feels an awful lot like telling your friends you're on a diet when the dessert menu arrives. One moment, you're feeling proud of your commitment to a healthier lifestyle, and the next, you're eyeing that chocolate lava cake like it's old high-school drama you just can't escape. The truth is, saving money can invoke feelings of deprivation. Still, it's our duty as modern financial warriors to pivot that mindset and treat savings like a big, fluffy marshmallow on top of our hot chocolate, making our financial lives sweeter and more enjoyable.

So let's position savings as one of your main expenses right from the get-go. Budget your savings the way you would your rent—funds ought to be allocated in your budget right alongside your fixed expenses. It's called "paying yourself first," and it transforms the concept of saving from an afterthought into a proactive strategy that puts your financial well-being front and center! You budget your essentials and fun splurges, so why not treat savings with the same level of importance? You wouldn't forget to pay your utility bill, would you? Well, your future self deserves attention too!

Now that you've accepted savings as a "must pay," we can jazz things up a notch and introduce different savings categories! I like to think of savings as a joyous celebration, not a chore, akin to throwing a party where every penny plays a part. You might have an 'Emergency Fund' category, for those "Where's the nearest repair shop?" moments, or even a 'Vacation Fund' for when the allure of sandy beaches and umbrella drinks calls your name like a siren. Want to buy the flashy new gadget that just dropped? Create a 'Fun Fund'—watch those savings swell as you squirrel away cash for those whims!

As you incorporate these savings categories, remember, the goal is to make it manageable and achievable. Don't set yourself up for disappointment by aiming to save 90% of your income immediately; that's not just unrealistic, it's a financial recipe for burnout. Start small by setting aside a percentage of your income, maybe 10% to start? As you grow comfortable with saving, feel free to increase that percentage. Celebrate those milestones! Lost a few pounds off your credit card debt? Treat yourself to a coffee! Just remember to keep it budget-friendly—unless your savings allowance allows for that $7 pumpkin spice latte each week.

Utilizing technology is another way to enhance your savings game. Automatic transfers can be as thrilling as winning a game of bingo! Set up your bank account to automatically shift funds into your savings account right after payday. This way, you won't even be tempted to "borrow" that cash back for that late-night pizza run. Besides, who can resist the relaxing sensation of seeing that savings account rise like the temperature on a hot summer day!?

Finally, your journey to incorporating savings into your budget wouldn't be complete without evaluating and reevaluating! As you settle down to review your budget each month, take a close look at your savings. Have you hit your targets? If so, fabulous! If not, don't beat yourself up. Financial progress is just that—progress, not perfection. Take a moment to analyze what's working for you and what could use some tweaking, and adjust accordingly. Life changes, and so should your habits!

Incorporating savings into your budget means paving the way toward financial freedom and empowering yourself for the future. Instead of seeing savings as a dull chore, see it as an adventure filled with possibilities—an investment in that dazzling birthday trip you've longed for or simply the peace of mind that comes from knowing you're ready for the unexpected. Just remember to don your financial superhero cape and treat those savings like the VIP they truly are. With these strategies in place, you'll be saving up like a pro, making your future self do an exuberant happy dance! Now, who doesn't want that?

Tracking and Reviewing Your Budget Regularly

Tracking and reviewing your budget regularly is like going to the dentist—you know you should do it, but there's always something more appealing on Netflix or a chocolate cake just begging to be devoured instead. Yet, just as regular dental check-ups ensure your pearly whites stay intact (and avoid that dreadful whole mouth of cavities), keeping tabs on your budget will help you maintain a solid financial foundation and prevent nasty surprises from creeping up like outdated fashion trends. Let's be real: nobody wants to discover they're suddenly funding a burgeoning shoe collection they never intended to start!

Now, the first order of business is to determine how you'll keep track of your budget. This is where the fun starts! Some people prefer the classic pen-and-paper method, where they can doodle smiles next to their savings. Others lean into the modern age with budgeting apps that make you feel like you're managing a high-stakes operation, complete with pie charts and colorful graphs that would make any accountant weep for joy. Whichever route you pick, commit to it! Think of it as choosing your financial alias: are you more "Excel Wizard" or "Budget Notebook Enthusiast"? Either way, you'll want a system that works for your lifestyle and allows you to seriously engage with your finances, without dropping your phone in the toilet while attempting to enter your latest trip to the coffee shop.

Tracking your budget requires commitment—a quality I like to think of as "financial discipline," which sounds fancier than just saying you're stubborn. Set a regular time—preferably weekly or biweekly—where you can review your spending. This is your moment to shine, your "money date," if you will. Pour yourself a cup of something nice (maybe even indulge in that fancy coffee you've been saving for) and sit down to review the previous week's accounts. Remember, this isn't a revelation-based experience; you want to track your spending with a focus on awareness, not anxiety. So go ahead—grab those receipts, and get cozy with your numbers like you're about to binge-watch your favorite show.

Once you've gathered your data, it's time for the annual episode of "What Happened This Month?" Spoiler alert: it's usually a combination of good intentions and impulsive decisions. Did you stay within your budget, or did your grocery expenses balloon like a kid's face at a birthday party? This is where the magic happens—truthful self-reflection will be your new best entertaining. Embrace it as a necessary part of your financial journey—one that will get more exciting as you develop a greater understanding of your spending habits, goals, and accomplishments. So grab your favorite drink, dig into the depths of your budget, and start unveiling the mysteries of your financial life! With this knowledge and dedication, you'll find yourself marching toward financial freedom while enjoying every moment, avoiding unplanned detours, and perhaps making a joyful noise about your triumphs as you go! Cheers to that!

CHAPTER 8
SAVING LIKE A SUPERHERO

The Importance of an Emergency Fund

Let's talk about emergency funds, those magical little treasures we keep hidden away for the unfortunate days, when life decides to throw us a curveball or two. Now, I don't mean the kind of emergencies where you can just wave a wand and make it all go away, like stepping in gum on a nice pair of shoes or burning dinner for the third time this week. I'm talking about real emergencies—like your washing machine deciding to show you who's boss and flooding your laundry room. Or maybe your beloved car develops a personality of its own and starts making noises only dogs can hear, leading you to an expensive repair that you somehow didn't budget for. Oh, the joys of adulthood!

So why is having an emergency fund so vital? Well, my friends, imagine waking up one day, and instead of your usual routine of coffee, emails, and dodging your husband's "what's for dinner?" questions, you discover that the universe conspired against you. Suddenly, you have medical bills bigger than a mortgage payment, and you're forced to sell your favorite plant to afford them. Now, I love plants—Betsy the Snake Plant has been with me since my days of financial struggle. I refuse to let Betsy down or be subjected to the emotional torment of selling her to cover unexpected expenses!

An emergency fund acts as your financial superhero. It's the cape that swoops in to save the day when life decides to drop an anvil on your financial plans. Financial experts recommend saving somewhere around three to six months' worth of living expenses. Some may think that's excessive, while others might feel that sounds way too comforting, like a cozy blanket you pull over your head when life's troubles get too real. But the truth is, when that unexpected expense hits, you want to be prepared, not left scrambling through your couch cushions searching for spare change.

Now, let's dig a bit deeper. Building this precious fund can feel daunting, like deciding to exercise for the first time in a decade—you know you need to do it, but your couch is calling your name. The key is to start small. You don't have to stash away $6,000 overnight (though if you can, then heck, you should let Betsy know you're in the big leagues now). Instead, start by aiming to save just $500. Think of it like setting a goal to binge-watch just two episodes of your favorite series instead of the entire season. Small wins keep you motivated and make it feel less like climbing Mount Everest armed only with a soda can.

One tip is to use a separate savings account for your emergency fund. You can call this account "Betsy's Backup" so you always remember what it's there for. This way, when temptation arrives in the form of a dreamy online sale beckoning you to splurge on that inflatable unicorn you didn't know you absolutely needed, you won't be swayed. You can remind yourself that Betsy needs a backup plan and that inflatable unicorns can wait until after you've successfully defended your financial future.

In my own experience building my emergency fund, things had to get crafty. I set aside a little cash from every paycheck, like a secret stash of snacks you're not supposed to share with family. I tried to avoid touching it, even when my husband, Sims, sweet-talked me into joining him on a spontaneous weekend trip (what can I say? The man has a way with words!). Every time I added to the fund, it felt like I was powering up in a video game, ready to face off against whatever financial villain dared to approach.

In the end, life will always throw its curveballs, and while we can't control everything, we can prepare ourselves to handle what it dishes out. An emergency fund provides peace of mind. Instead of hyperventilating about an unexpected bill, you'll be calm and collected, showing the universe that you're ready for whatever comes your way. So, put on your savings cape and start building your fund today, because every superhero needs a safety net—even if that superhero is just you trying to navigate the wild world of adulting. Plus, trust me, Betsy the Snake Plant will thank you for it!

Setting Savings Goals That Inspire

Setting savings goals is like trying to plan a family vacation to the ultimate theme park. Everyone has different ideas about what fun looks like, and somehow, Uncle Dave always thinks he can talk us into a road trip in his ancient minivan. But the secret to teasing out those unaffordable desires, like a scorching sunburn at the beach, is finding inspiration that fuels your financial fire. After all, if I'm going to attempt to save for the extraordinary rather than that towering stack of bills that often resembles my 10-year-old's more ambitious LEGO projects, I need to dream big and set goals that leave me feeling motivated instead of defeated.

Picture this: it's 8 a.m., and instead of the usual fight for the last cup of coffee with Sims, I'm daydreaming about a lavish vacation on an island where the towels are somehow always fluffy, the breeze is just right, and my only responsibilities are to sip fruity drinks and avoid sunscreen trauma. I mean, who wouldn't choose that over budgeting for new tires or the electric bill going through the roof? Dreaming about paradise can ignite a spark when it comes to setting savings goals. The first step? You have to figure out what inspires you most. Maybe it's a getaway to the Amalfi Coast or finally renovating that outdated kitchen that's beginning to feel like a time capsule from the 90s. Whatever it is, write it down and let it serve as motivation on those days when do-it-yourself pizza night appears more appealing than setting aside cash.

Now, it's important to ensure that those goals are not just pie-in-the-sky fantasies painted in rainbow colors. Let's face it; if I set my sights on saving $10,000 for a yacht when my current financial status only permits that inflatable pool shark I named "Captain Bubble," I'm probably setting myself up for disappointment. Think SMART: Specific, Measurable, Achievable, Relevant, and Time-bound. (Okay, okay, I know it sounds like I'm an accountant trying to drop some jargon on you, but trust me, it's like the holy grail of savings goals.) Set a target that you can actually accomplish, like saving $2,000 for a re-enactment of that beach vacation. Then break it down into smaller tasks, like saving just $166 a month for the next year. It's a mindset shift that won't imply you have to forsake that well-deserved third cup of coffee as yet another sacrifice on your Savings altar.

Next, let's talk about creating a vision board. You might think this is just something for Pinterest-loving youths with colorful feathers and glitter, but it's a real game-changer! Grab a poster board (yes, I said poster board—my mom had a stack of them when I was a kid for less than glamorous school projects), magazines, and scissors. Cut out images that represent what you want; if it's that island vacation, find a picture of palm trees that looks like it's begging for your Instagram presence. Create a visual representation that makes you so inspired that every time you walk by it, you're compelled to save a little extra. Putting it in a spot where you will constantly lay your eyeballs on it will make those savings goals pop like confetti at a kid's birthday party!

Rewarding yourself along the journey is also a critical factor in maintaining that motivation. So maybe this means treating yourself to an extra slice of pizza after hitting your monthly savings target, but not the gourmet kind that costs an arm and a leg. I'm talking about the local pizzeria where they know your name (and probably where it's only an arm). Little rewards keep you on track and remind you that you're not missing out on the fun while chasing your dreams. It's a delicate balance, much like figuring out if I can keep my daughter from stealing my expensive skincare products while also setting aside those necessary funds.

Remember, life has a funny way of tossing unpredictable plot twists into our plans. That means you may need to reassess your goals from time to time. A sudden car issue, an unexpected medical bill—these life detours can be annoying. But instead of letting those roadblocks crush your spirit, make adjustments as necessary. Keeping the focus on your ultimate inspiration will ensure your goals feel refreshing instead of suffocating.

In closing, motivation is key to staying on track with savings. Setting inspiring goals can ignite a passion for budgeting that your 10-year-old should not notice! Write down those dreams, create your vision board, reward small wins along the way, and remember, it's all part of the ride. I mean, if we can survive family gatherings and Uncle Dave's travel suggestions, we can definitely tackle savings goals with a smile—and maybe a little laughter along the way!

Creative Ways to Cut Expenses

Cutting expenses. It's like trying to convince a teen to let you see their text messages. You know it needs to happen, but the pushback can be fierce. As someone who has navigated the colorful world of budgeting, I can tell you that cutting expenses doesn't have to feel like applying for a loan to buy toothpaste—you just need to get a little creative! So sit tight, grab your unicorn mug filled with coffee, and let's explore how I've done more with less, while still keeping that sparkle in my eye.

First, let's discuss dining out. Who doesn't love the joy of bypassing soggy leftovers in exchange for a decadent plate of something you can't pronounce at your favorite restaurant? Spoiler alert: I, too, appreciate the miracle of a perfectly crafted guacamole. But let's be real, those little morsels of joy add up faster than you can say "how many more days until payday?" So here's my radical idea: find a local food truck or dine-in spot that serves deliciousness without the "do you want to trade your left kidney for a special this week?" pricing. You can eat well at half the price! Even better, make it a fun challenge—pick a night where your family has "takeout" while you whip up gourmet replicas at home. Trust me, your kids will love creating their very own "Kitchen Wars" as they try to outdo each other's culinary creations. You might even accidentally discover that Tiler can whip up a taco better than the fancy restaurant down the street!

Next, let's tackle your grocery bill. You'll find that grocery shopping can be as tricky as a high-stakes poker game: you never know who's bluffing. Pro tip: Meal planning is where the real savings magic happens. That means sitting down with your favorite snacks and browsing Pinterest for recipes that can easily feed a family of four for under twenty dollars. There's something delightful about plotting out meals while snacking on chips, thinking, "Today, I'm a budget genius!" Combine that with making and sticking to a shopping list, like an unstoppable financial force. And if your family gives you any lip about eating veggie stir-fry for the third time this week, just remind them that if they want to consistently chow down on gourmet cheese puffs, they'll have to contribute to the grocery fund!

Another sneaky trick is to embrace generic and store-brand products. I know, I know—there's a stigma attached that shopping "off-brand" means less quality, like wearing last year's trends. But think of it this way: when did your favorite snack last make you feel like you were at a red-carpet event? Spoiler alert: never! So grab that off-brand cereal—it's just as crunchy, trust me. You'll be amazed at how those little changes in the grocery aisle can chip away at your expenses without sacrificing the flavor of your breakfast. Plus, when Uncle Dave comes over for Sunday dinner, you can proudly tell him your "gourmet" budget-friendly meal was brought to you by the generic wonders!

Now let's talk about subscriptions. You may not realize it, but your monthly bills may be secretly plotting to drown your wallet in a tsunami of streaming services, music apps, and meal kit subscriptions. So, before you mindlessly pay these fees, take a moment to assess what you truly use. Does that one obscure streaming platform really give you enough joy to keep on board? Or is it just a vault for old sitcom reruns you swore you'd revisit? If you can't remember the last time you caught up on that series, it's time to say goodbye. Channel your inner Marie Kondo and let those budget-sucking subscriptions go!

Also, don't neglect to check out local resources. Many communities have programs that offer free activities, events, and even food! Yes, you heard me correctly. Some of those lovely patches of green we call parks host free outdoor movie nights, concerts, and all sorts of family-friendly shenanigans that won't cost you a dime. So grab your chairs, blanket, and snacks (bonus points if they're from those carefully planned grocery lists), and enjoy a night that celebrates all the delightful entertainment life has to offer.

Cutting expenses requires a bit of creativity, humility, and a pinch of whimsy. Embrace the idea that cutting costs doesn't mean you have to give up life's pleasures—just imagine the stories you'll tell about that night Tiler attempted to recreate Gordon Ramsay's finest, all while keeping your decorative but very functional unicorn mug close by! Financial freedom requires a playful twist on serious commitments, with laughter mixed in. So get to it, and start saving so you can travel the world guilt-free and leave Uncle Dave scrambling to figure out his own expenses!

Automating Your Savings

Oh, the glorious world of automation! It's like having a personal assistant who doesn't steal your lunch or judge you for binge-watching reality shows instead of folding laundry. Automating your savings can feel like a fairy tale; you set it all up once, and like magic, money appears in your savings account as if the financial fairy dusted it there while you sleep. Allow me to paint a picture of how this fantastical saving adventure can transform your money game, so buckle up, buttercup—this is going to be wild!

Let's start with the hard truth: saving can sometimes feel like dragging a boulder uphill while deciding between a kale salad and pizza. You know it's the right move, but the motivation can wane faster than your enthusiasm for a housecleaning day. Enter automation: it swoops in like your own personal superhero, saving you from mental exhaustion by making the entire process effortless! Imagine this—the moment that paycheck hits your bank account, like clockwork, a percentage effortlessly glides into your savings. No stressing about whether you've spent too much on artisanal plant-based snacks this month. No more ensuring that the last croissant didn't tip your finances over the edge. You simply set it and forget it; poof! Savings increase like the plot of a good sitcom.

But how, you ask? First, I recommend taking a good, hard look at your paycheck. What percentage can you comfortably siphon off before the threat of cash starvation looms? Maybe start small—5% will do just fine to commence your journey into the automated world. Seriously, it's less than the last trip you made to that fancy coffee shop that symbolizes adulthood responsibility. You'll feel like a financial guru in mere moments—filled with your favorite coffee or tea!

Next, set up a direct deposit feature with your bank. Many companies allow for multiple accounts, so when your paycheck arrives, it distributes funds to where they need to go, like delegating chores among family members. The trick is to set it up so a pre-determined percentage of your paycheck automatically flies into your savings account without you lifting a finger or even thinking about it. "Oh look!" you'll say, "There's money in my savings account! How very responsible of me!" It's almost a dopamine rush, and the best part: nobody gets burned out by the hassle!

Of course, there are always exceptions to the magical workings of life. Just when you think you have it all under control, life reminds you it has a knack for throwing pesky curveballs, like car troubles or unexpected school expenses. The beauty of automation is that it helps create a strong safety net to catch you when these difficulties arise—think of it as your very own financial trampoline! Those savings can be a lifesaver, and it's comforting to know that your future self will thank you as they continue to glide through life, a cool breeze blowing against their post-laundry hairdo.

Now, I know some of you may be thinking, "But Tumeka, what if I want to touch that money?" Ah, dear reader, great question! This is where the fun begins. Automating your savings doesn't mean you can't access your hard-earned funds; it merely means that you must make a conscious effort to withdraw them. Most banks nowadays have convenient apps. So, when the urge to spend arises, you can slow down for a second and ask yourself: "Do I want that random takeout meal, or do I want to continue my journey to financial freedom?" Sure, it's only pizza today, but before you know it, you could find yourself on a magic carpet ride around the world—dining on pizza in picturesque pizza places instead of settling for "double cheese" every week at your neighborhood joint.

While automating your savings can be slightly boring and may initially feel a tad counterproductive, it's a critical element to building wealth without sweating bullets over the little things. Automating savings allows for consistent growth, and that's where the real magic lies.

To reiterate, this whole process is like training your brain to become a savings ninja. Automating allows you to create a bridge over troubled financial waters without even breaking a sweat. You'll quickly realize how your money can work for you while you sip on margaritas, imagining future plans instead of feeling guilty and drained about every dollar spent. So, raise your glasses, my friends. Cheers to savings automation! Here's to watching our money grow while we continue living like the budget-savvy superheroes we were always meant to be!

Celebrating Small Savings Wins

Oh, the exhilaration of small savings wins! They may seem so unassuming, like little ants marching in a line, but trust me—if you look closely, they pack a powerful punch. Much like those tiny snacks you forget are at the bottom of your purse until you desperately need a hit of sugar, small savings victories revive your budgeting spirit. You see, financial freedom is not just about giant leaps; it's also about those adorable little hops that can make the journey feel like a fantastic trampoline experience!

So what exactly constitutes a "small savings win"? Let me paint you a vivid picture. Perhaps you found a coupon for your favorite face cream; or maybe you managed to dodge buying that overpriced latte and opted for the homemade blend instead. Maybe you even cooked dinner four nights in a row instead of bending to the pressures of takeout! Each of these moments is a reason to pop a mini bottle of sparkling water and celebrate like you just won a mini lottery. Why? Because every dollar saved adds up, and those little victories are crucial in cultivating the mindset needed to flourish financially.

Furthermore, celebrating those wins keeps you motivated. Let's face it, saving money is like scraping gum off the bottom of your shoe—sometimes painful and tedious, and you wonder why you even bothered in the first place. Recognizing small victories has the power to turn that frown upside down. So here's my first tip: create a "savings jar" designated for your small wins! You can add a quarter, a dollar, or whatever tickles your fancy every time you achieve one of those mini-desk victories. Watching that jar fill up will feel like unearthing jewels of personal finance. Once it's full, treat yourself to something fun that you've been eyeing—a new plant for your collection, a cozy pair of socks, or even a small outing with the family. The psychological boost you gain from seeing your savings grow will motivate you even more!

Now, let's combine savings with creativity, shall we? How about staging a "savings party" with the family? Because if we're going to cut expenses, we might as well make it an enjoyable experience! Gather everyone for a fun family meeting, complete with snacks (thanks to your successful attempts in the kitchen). Share the juicy details of the small victories you've achieved. Did your daughter Bristinney score a great deal on school supplies? Hearty high-fives all around! Tiler might have figured out how to plan a week of lunches for only ten bucks—give him the superhero award! Emphasizing accomplishments, regardless of size, fosters a sense of triumph and community. Plus, who doesn't enjoy basking in the warmth of each other's savings efforts?

The supportive atmosphere you create when celebrating small wins can also remind you to keep striving for more. When you reflect on all of your accomplishments, don't overlook the importance of those little battles won—like gently saying "no" when someone offers to split a round of fancy coffees. Recognize that you're building a stronger, more robust financial foundation while turning down the temptation to splurge superficially.

Each time you resist the urge to overspend, you're getting one step closer to your financial goals—and that's a celebratory moment worth embracing!

Now for my favorite part: create a motivation wall! Grab a board (I promise they're still cool), pretty artwork, photos of places you dream of visiting, and quotes that get you jazzed up about money. Every small win adds to the wall, growing with each passing month. It transforms into a visual tapestry of your journey toward financial freedom. You'll remember the small victories that pushed you forward whenever you pass by it. Not to mention, it provides casual family entertainment; your kids will love reminding you how fancy that "dream home" they might never live in looks!

Finally, let's talk social media! If you're brave enough, share your small victories online and invite your friends to do the same. It's a delightful way to connect with others while keeping yourself accountable. Imagine posting about saving $20 on groceries or repurposing an outfit for a school event! You'll see likes and virtual cheers flooding in, and it's a definite mood booster. The more you share, the more accountability you create; it might even inspire your friends to adopt similar habits—and that's a win for everyone!

In the end, never underestimate the power of celebrating small savings wins. They may seem inconsequential compared to grand gestures, but those mini-triumphs pave the way for a fulfilling financial journey. Every dollar saved, every coupon redeemed, every skipped latte adds up to your ultimate freedom fund. So dance around your living room, reward yourself, assemble the family for snack time celebrations, and give yourself a big ol' pat on the back! Because my friend, saving money should be as joyful as hanging a piñata filled with treats, and you deserve to enjoy every sweet moment along the way!

CHAPTER 9
INVESTING 101: YOUR PATH TO WEALTH

Understanding the Basics of Investing

Investing. Ah, the very word sends shivers down the spine of many a responsible adult. I mean, why invest when you can simply shove everything under your mattress where it's safe, right? Or better yet, why not just donate your cash to a sitcom laugh track and be done with it? But listen up, my friends! Investing is like dipping your toes into a pool of dollar bills, and trust me, you don't want to stay on the sidelines just watching others make a splash. In fact, investing can be surprisingly thrilling—the kind of thrill you get when you find an extra fry at the bottom of the bag, or on a more serious note, when your money actually grows and multiplies like rabbits on a very fertile farm.

Let's start with the most basic idea of investing: putting your money to work so that it can earn more money. It's like a little family of dollars—you know, Papa Dollar is off getting a divorce and wants a fresh start, so he goes to find Mama Dollar to start a bigger family, and suddenly you're sitting on a wealthier little nest egg. Investing can be likened to planting a garden of greenbacks. You take some money, plant it in a few financial pots, and hope something fruitful pops up. But unlike my Aunt Beverly's attempts at gardening (rip, poor, wilting succulents), if you give your investments proper care and attention, you'll yield a harvest that can outshine any casserole your family gathers around on Thanksgiving.

Now, let's address the elephant in the room—risk. I'm not talking about that high-stakes game of Jenga you play at family gatherings, where Uncle Bob makes everyone nervous with his questionable moves. No, I'm referring to the risk factors involved in investing because let's face it, investing isn't a warm-and-fuzzy cuddle session. It's more of a roller coaster ride that occasionally goes off the rails. Some investments are riskier than others (look out for seeds labeled "pumpkin"—trust me on that), but risk and return generally go hand in hand. If you fancy a riskier investment (like stocks in my cousin Martinez's smoothie shop), the potential returns can be enormous, but watch out! The downfalls are equally dramatic. Think of your funds as actors in a Broadway show—if they don't get the reviews they're hoping for, they could be heading straight to the unemployment line.

So, how do you navigate this thrilling yet terrifying adventure into the land of investments? Oh boy, here comes the fun part! Knowing what to invest in isn't something you learn overnight. It requires research—yes, I know, that nasty word—what will the internet provide you with this time? From tracking companies' performance as if you're investigating a ten-part limited Netflix series to analyzing market trends to make your own predictions like a fortune teller with a crystal ball. But don't panic; I won't send you down a rabbit hole so deep that you get lost like Alice. It's all about finding reliable resources. Read some investment books and follow financial podcasts. Heck, subscribe to "Budget Avenger: The Musical!"—okay, I just made that up. But it sounds catchy, right?

And while we're venturing into the icy waters of investing, let's also chat about your mindset. This isn't the cash grab that'll set you up with a penthouse in Manhattan overnight. No, investing is more like a long-distance run, not the 50-meter dash you took during gym class.

Patience is key, and there will be bumps in the road, twists in the maze, and surprise pizza deliveries that could be signs of a market correction (okay, maybe not the last one, but pizza is always welcome, isn't it?). Like romancing, investing takes time, heart, and the occasional cringe when you realize you've gone entirely off course in your financial adventure.

As I wrap this up, I want to leave you with this thought: investing is not just for Wall Street wolves. It's for everyday heroes like you and me. It's about taking control of your financial future, where you don't have to rely on Uncle Bob's "wisdom" about investing in the next big thing (his last choice was Beanie Babies, and we all know how that turned out). Educate yourself, start small, and build your knowledge and confidence over time. The more you engage with your finances, the more empowered you feel. In the end, you just might find that investing can turn from a confusing puzzle into a marvelously entertaining board game—complete with witty banter, snack breaks, and maybe even a little undeserved win here and there. So, strap in and let's kick-start this journey together! You're well on your way to becoming the next Budget Avenger!

Types of Investments: Stocks, Bonds, and More

Alright, folks! Buckle up because we're diving into the wild and wacky world of investments, and trust me, you're going to see more colors than a pile of crayons owned by a particularly enthusiastic toddler. When it comes to investing, the choices may seem overwhelming, like picking the right flavor at an ice cream parlor after a bad breakup. Don't worry, I'm here to help you sift through stocks, bonds, and all the delightful financial toppings that come with it!

First on our investment menu: stocks. Ah, stocks—the shiny stars of the investment universe. When you buy a stock, you're essentially purchasing a tiny piece of a company. It's like saying, "Well, I'm no Spielberg, but I'd like a sliver of his next blockbuster!" (And let's be honest, if my twelve-year-old nephew can pull off a TikTok dance video, we're not far from finding overnight sensations, right?) Of course, with stocks, you want to pick the winners, not the losers. That means keeping an eye out for companies that show promise, growth potential, and, most importantly, a good sense of humor! Who knew the stock market could have more drama than reality TV?

Next up, we have bonds—not the super-spy kind like James Bond, although, wouldn't that be fun? In the investment realm, bonds are a bit more sober. Basically, when you purchase a bond, you are lending money to a corporation or the government, and they promise to pay you back with interest. It's like being the parent who spots their kid a few bucks for that latest video game, but instead of playing Fortnite, the kid actually pays you back with a little respect! Bonds tend to be safer than stocks and are often less volatile, so think of them as the cashmere sweaters of investing—comfortable and solid, but possibly lacking the pizzazz of that glittery disco shirt you might've eyed across the room.

Now, let's not forget real estate, shall we? Real estate is like that relative who shows up to family gatherings dressed in sequins and believes they are the life of the party. Buying property is no small feat, and with it comes responsibilities—maintenance, tenants who may or may not think beasts from the barn belong in their apartment, and yes, the dreaded home repair expenses that spring up like chubby weeds in your garden. However, with patience and a touch of determination, investing in real estate can yield some serious long-term benefits. Just think of it as growing your own money tree, but remember to water it with knowledge, respect, and, if I'm honest, a healthy dose of sweat!

Then, of course, we have mutual funds. Think of them as the buffet of investing. You want a slice of everything, but aren't ready to commit to any particular food (or stock). With mutual funds, you pool your money with other investors, allowing you to buy a diverse range of stocks and bonds while sitting comfortably at the table, chowing down on all the financial delights without worrying about picking just one. It's like having your cake and eating it too, without the added stress of deciding if that triple chocolate cake is better than a classic vanilla! But please, no one expects you to hog the whole cake now—share those funds, my dear friends!

And let's not ignore exchange-traded funds (ETFs), the trendy cousin of mutual funds. They are like the Instagram influencers of investing—similarly diverse but traded on a stock exchange like individual stocks. They can provide great access to a variety of sectors or themes. Want to invest in clean energy or tech stocks from companies that make only eco-friendly shoelaces? You bet they've got an ETF for that!

Finally, there's the world of alternative investments. This can include everything from collectibles (think rare stamps, coins, and, for some wild-hearted souls, vintage Beanie Babies) to commodities like oil and gold, which may add a little sparkle to your financial portfolio. It's like venturing into the offbeat, artsy neighborhood for mysterious treasures that might pop up around every corner! But do tread lightly. While these investments can offer exciting glimpses of worth, they can also be as unpredictable as my Aunt Rose when she decides to take up karaoke.

In summary, whether you want to play the stock market like a jazz pianist or nurture a steady yield through bonds, the type of investments you choose is entirely up to you. So get your superhero cape on, channel your inner Budget Avenger, and let's take responsibility for our financial future with the knowledge that there's a whole spectrum of options just waiting for you! I assure you—there's plenty of fun and profit to be found in this adventure, and investing doesn't have to feel like rocket science. Just remember, whatever you invest in, don't forget to have a little fun along the way!

The Importance of Risk Tolerance

Risk tolerance—a phrase that sounds fancy enough to grace the lips of a Wall Street executive, yet is likely best understood by anyone who valiantly navigates Tuesday family dinners without losing their sanity. In the realm of investing, your risk tolerance is like your inner compass, guiding your strategies and decisions while ensuring you don't end up crying in a corner (or worse—overcooking the meatloaf) after a market downturn. So, how on earth does one determine their risk tolerance? Buckle up, my dear readers, because it's a wild ride!

Let's be real for a moment. Each of us has a different threshold for what we consider "risky" behavior. For some, it's the thrill of bungee jumping off a bridge, and for others, it may be the minor act of tossing sanity aside to buy all the latest kitchen gadgets from an infomercial. I myself—not to brag—have been known to go all in on a three-chip cookie recipe that requires precisely 22 steps, which looks exciting until I realize I've added one too many chocolate chips. Instead of tantalizing perfection, I end up with a melted, gooey chocolate explosion resembling a failed science experiment.

In investing, understanding your risk tolerance sheds light on how you approach stocks, bonds, and those mysterious alternatives lurking in the financial shadows, like artifacts that could be the star of a budget-friendly museum tour. Too conservative? You might feel anxious watching stocks tumble while sticking with stable bonds that pay you like a moderate TikTok influencer. Too aggressive? You could find yourself holding on to risky investments during market fluctuations like a cat trying to stay upright on a rollercoaster. Being aware of your risk tolerance helps prevent making irrational decisions when external circumstances try to hijack your investment journey.

Your risk tolerance is influenced by a couple of key factors: personal finances, time horizon, and psychological makeup. Personal finances are like your investment vitamins—they're essential! If your bank account looks more like a bottomless pit than a prosperous treasure chest, starting with a conservative approach is prudent. You wouldn't walk into a carnival with ten bucks and risk it all on the whack-a-mole game—unless you're feeling lucky, and then you may just end up getting a banana plushie and regretting your life choices all at once. On the flip side, if you find yourself as luxurious as a gold-plated toilet, you might be more open to daring investments that carry a promise of higher returns but come with that spicy edge of risk.

Your time horizon also plays a critical role. Are you investing for a vacation next summer or playing the long game, aiming to retire on a beach in the Bahamas, sipping piña coladas? If it's the former, your risk tolerance probably isn't sky-high, and you'd prefer to play it chill while still eyeing that spa resort. But if you're looking at long-term goals, investing might feel more like an adventurous journey—one where you hop on a moving train without knowing your final destination, trusting the winds of fortune.

Let's not overlook personality traits—some people are born risk-takers, while others are as anxiously cautious as that squirrel that darted across the road in front of your car and caused you to slam your brakes. If the thought of stocks dropping gives you immediate heart palpitations, it might be a sign to tone down those high-flying investments until you feel comfortable with the idea. Alternatively, suppose you remain unfazed by market choppiness (while snacking on popcorn and binge-watching your favorite reality show). In that case, that's a good indication that you can embrace volatility and take advantage of opportunities that come from adjustments and shifts.

So, how do you find the sweet spot that aligns with your unique risk tolerance? Start by assessing your financial situation—be honest with yourself! Ask yourself, "Can I handle potential losses, or will I turn into a pile of worry lines?" There are countless online quizzes about risk tolerance; they're like personality tests but for investors—no one wants to hear they're a "recluse cactus" in the stock market world! But in all seriousness, you must solidify an investment strategy that mirrors both your comfort levels and long-term goals.

By understanding your risk tolerance, you're setting yourself up on the fun and financially sound path to wealth-building, complete with appropriate safety nets to cushion any potential surprises. Investing shouldn't feel like walking a tightrope over a pit of fire while juggling flaming torches; it should be an exhilarating journey where you can frolic freely among market opportunities, confidently knowing that you are walking in sync with your own style and choices! So go ahead, lean into your investment adventures, and remember: the journey is one to be enjoyed, complete with laughter and learning along the way.

Developing a Personal Investment Strategy

Alright, folks! Gather 'round because today we're diving into the craft that is developing a personal investment strategy. Now, I know what you're thinking: "Tumeka, that sounds about as exciting as watching paint dry!" But fear not, my friends! This is less about watching paint and more like creating your masterpiece—a masterpiece that involves your hard-earned money, a sprinkle of risk, and a dash of creativity. Think of it as hosting your very own potluck dinner where the guests (a.k.a. your investments) are all invited, and they might just end up surprising you in delicious ways!

To start, the first step in developing a solid investment strategy is understanding your financial goals. Are you looking to retire early and live out your dreams of beachfront burritos? Ideal! Or perhaps you want to save up to send your kids to the fanciest private school where they claim to teach them how to tie shoelaces in multiple languages? Everyone has different aspirations, and that's perfectly okay! The important thing is to grab a piece of paper (or a matched set of monogrammed stationery if that tickles your fancy) and jot down your financial objectives. Be specific, and don't shy away from dreaming big. Want to buy a yacht? Note it down! Want to ensure you have enough to sprinkle on your grandkids' college funds? Write it boldly! This isn't just about the numbers; it's about painting your future picture vividly.

Now that you've clearly stated your goals, let's talk timeframe! And no, this isn't a race to the finish line with a twisty straw that takes forever to drink out of! When you think about how long you plan to invest, you must consider whether you're in it for the short game or the long haul. Short-term investors might get anxious about daily fluctuations in the market—those little bugaboos that can turn you into a nervous wreck when your stocks drop by a few bucks. If your target is a holiday in Bora Bora within a year, you're likely better off sticking to more stable investments. On the other hand, if you're aiming for a sunny retirement decades away, feel free to take on a bit more risk, with the understanding that it may result in a few surprises along the way, much like Aunt Rose's "surprise" casserole recipe that involves marshmallows.

Next up, let's chat about asset allocation! Now, I know this term sounds like something that gives you an instant headache, but it's basically deciding how to mix your investment "pasta" to create the tastiest dish possible. Picture this: you want to have a balanced diet, so why would you load up on just one type of stock? You wouldn't go to an Italian restaurant and order only fettuccine without even glancing at the lasagna! Instead, as your own investment chef, combine stocks, bonds, and maybe even some real estate into a delightful portfolio that satisfies your hunger for potential growth while keeping your stomach (and your wallet) from going haywire! Your mix will depend on your individual risk tolerance, timeframe, and financial goals—like combining fruit salad with whipped cream and calling for some kitchen magic!

Diversification is a key ingredient in the personal investment strategy cake—in fact, the sprinkles take it from mundane to magical! When your investments are spread across different asset classes, like how you serve various dishes at a dinner party, you can mitigate the risks that come with any one particular investment. So, instead of putting all your eggs into the proverbial chicken basket, throw some of those eggs into real estate, bonds, and even a few of those quirky alternative investments. Not only does this strategy protect you from economical hiccups (because, let's face it, the economy can be as unpredictable as your uncle's dance moves at weddings), but it also positions your portfolio for maximum growth potential—kind of like hiding those coveted snacks in your room during family movie night.

But wait, it doesn't stop there! You need to keep reviewing and adjusting your investment strategy regularly—the same way you wouldn't wear last season's fashion. As your financial circumstances evolve, your strategy might also need to go through a makeover! Life events like promotions, job changes, or hitting the jackpot at the bingo hall can all impact your financial situation, resulting in the need for fresh tweaks to your strategy. Set aside some dedicated "financial salon" time—perhaps with a glass of your favorite beverage in hand—and reassess your goals, allocations, and performance; stay involved with your investments like they're your darling house plants!

In conclusion, developing a personal investment strategy is an exciting journey that bridges your dreams with sound financial guidance. It's about painting your desired life, one investment brushstroke at a time. As long as you're willing to explore your goals creatively, mix and match your options wisely, and do a little housekeeping once in a while, you'll be well on your way to becoming the investment artist of your own financial future! So go ahead and get started—your masterpiece awaits!

Resources for Continuing Your Investing Education

Alright, my aspiring Budget Avengers, let's talk about the golden ticket of investing success—continuing your education! Now, I can already hear some of you groaning at the thought of cracking open yet another textbook or sitting through a dry seminar that sounds like more fun than watching paint dry. But fear not! Your investment education can be as engaging as Aunt Rose's karaoke parties (minus the accidental high notes). The secret? Finding the right resources to keep you informed, inspired, and entertained while diving deeper into the wondrous world of investments.

First up on our educational buffet are books. Yes, those glorious paper-bound packages filled with pages of accumulated wisdom—and let's be honest, some terrible fiction we all love to ignore. There are tons of fantastic books on investing that read more like a thrilling novel than a textbook. For starters, look into classics like *The Intelligent Investor* by Benjamin Graham. It's like having your own Gandalf guiding you through the mystical lands of stocks and bonds while telling you to "remember the fundamentals." If you're looking for something a bit more modern (and whose Spice Girls CD collection isn't?), check out *The Little Book of Common Sense Investing* by John Bogle. It's like your well-meaning friend who's always there to remind you to keep it simple when you're overwhelmed with information. And let's be real; who wouldn't want that in their arsenal?

In this tech-savvy world, podcasts have become the hipster cafes of investment education. You know what I'm talking about—those little nuggets of joy you can munch on during your morning coffee or while trapped in traffic behind the slowest driver in history (I'm looking at you, Grandma!). A few of my favorites are "Smart Passive Income" by Pat Flynn and "InvestED" by Phil and Danielle Town. These gems will fill your ears with valuable insights and strategies without overwhelming you. Plus, nothing feels better than pretending you're super productive while really just sipping your overpriced latte and grooving to financial wisdom.

Now, let's not forget the magical realm of online courses! Yes, my friends, these are the magical portals that take you from "What the heck is a 401(k)?" to "I can calculate compound interest faster than my kids can eat a pizza!" Platforms like Coursera, Udemy, and Khan Academy offer a plethora of courses on investment strategies, personal finance, and everything in between. And the great part? You can learn at your own pace—maybe even in your pajamas after a long Netflix binge. Just think of the excitement of discovering new concepts while surrounded by your beloved snacks, making every lesson feel like a party in your mouth and noggin simultaneously!

If you're more of a social butterfly, consider joining investment clubs or online forums. You can surround yourself with fellow financial nerds who want to share ideas, strategies, and possibly even war stories of the latest market downturns they survived. Don't be shy; it's a chance to make new friends! Check out Meetup.com to find local clubs in your area or participate in online communities like Bogleheads or Reddit's r/investing. Just remember to wear your invisible cape of discernment—sometimes, suggestions can be like Aunt Rose's mysterious casserole: both intriguing and a bit unnerving!

Another valuable resource is financial news websites and newsletters. Staying updated on market trends, economic developments, and investment strategies is integral for those who want to keep their portfolios flourishing like an indoor plant that hasn't yet been named. Subscribe to resources like The Wall Street Journal, Bloomberg, or even good ol' fashioned CNBC. But here's the catch: select your news sources carefully! You wouldn't take fashion advice from someone who's perpetually stuck in the '90s, right? So be sure you're getting your information from reputable outlets—but don't forget your sense of humor while sifting through the serious stuff.

Lastly, let's talk about the beauty of mentorship. Find a mentor—someone who's been through the ups and downs of investing and is willing to take you under their financial wing. This person could be a friend, a colleague, or even a family member who has discovered the magic feather of investing. They can provide personalized guidance, impart killer strategies, and share insights that you won't find in a book. And if your mentor is half as fun as Aunt Rose at karaoke, you'll walk away with more than just financial knowledge—you'll have a few laughs and maybe a new inside joke to toss around at dinner parties.

In conclusion, continuing your investing education is essential as you navigate the ever-changing landscape of finances. By tapping into books, podcasts, online courses, investment clubs, news outlets, and mentorship, you'll build your financial knowledge base to superhero levels—and hopefully achieve your dreams along the way. So grab your cape, and let's conquer that investment education together, one quirky resource at a time! The financial future is bright, and each step you take toward education will help you shine even more on your journey to becoming the ultimate Budget Avenger!

CHAPTER 10
AVOIDING THE CREDIT PITFALLS

Understanding Common Credit Mistakes

Credit scores are like that nosy neighbor you never wanted; they peek into your financial life and judge you based on everything from that fancy latte you splurged on last week to your overzealous use of discount codes at your local department store. But here's the kicker—most of us don't even know how we're accidentally handing over our credit score to that judgmental neighbor, and trust me, they're judging! As the Budget Avenger, it's my duty to help you sidestep the pitfalls of common credit mistakes. So buckle up, folks, and let's dive into some hilarious yet cringeworthy blunders that can sabotage your credit score quicker than a poorly chosen home renovation project.

First on the list is the infamous late payment. Ah, the late payment—it's the "I'll just get to it tomorrow" of the financial world. You know, when you casually toss your credit card bill on the table while thinking, "I'll pay it after I finish this season of that show with the dramatic cliffhangers!" Little did you know, what seems like a minor oversight can send your credit score plummeting like a contestant on a reality show who didn't see that elimination coming. You may think, "What's a couple of days?" but trust me, in the credit world, your credit card company treats every missed deadline like a betrayal worthy of a soap opera love triangle. So, if you don't want to be the Dorothy in a painful credit score rendition of "Wizard of Oz," learn the subtle art of paying on time, even if it means binge-watching your favorite series during commercials.

Next stop on our credit faux pas tour is the oh-so-sneaky credit utilization trap. The premise is simple: the more credit you have available, the more free rein you think you have to splurge. It's like visiting a buffet and thinking it's a good idea to eat three plates of food because it's "all you can eat". While we're all for enjoying a delectable meal, treating your credit limit like it's an endless buffet can derail your credit score faster than I can say "debt disaster." Experts recommend keeping your utilization below 30%. Think of it as a diet for your spending habits! When your credit utilization ratio goes through the roof, your score starts gasping for breath, and that's just not a good look.

Then, there's the absolute clunker of ignoring your credit report. It's like being told that you have a small child in a closet you just forgot about. How can you fix what you don't know is broken? You can't! So, before you find yourself in a horror movie plot twist, grab your annual free credit report and take a good look at what's happening. This is especially crucial because mistakes happen; companies make errors like I make cookies—with a dozen eggs instead of a dozen chocolate chips. Check for inaccuracies and, if necessary, dispute them. The last thing you want is a phantom debt haunting your score like a ghost at a Halloween party.

Now let's discuss the well-intentioned but terribly misguided act of closing old credit accounts. It might feel like decluttering your life, but it's akin to tossing your good china to make room for paper plates in the credit world. Old accounts are like safety nets, keeping your score stable by showing a lengthy credit history. Consider it your financial vintage—you don't throw away that 1995 baseball card that's gathering dust; you appreciate it, hold onto it, and make sure it still has value. By closing old accounts, you're arguably removing the good karma from years of responsible credit management. Please resist the temptation, my friends. Keep those accounts open like grandma keeps her hoard of questionable sweaters—just in case!

Lastly, let's celebrate the importance of building a positive credit history. You might think you can skip this part, but it's vital. Just like you would never ask your relatives to come for a family reunion if you've been absent for years, banks are not enthused to lend you money if you don't have a reliable track record. Make sure you're using credit wisely, even if it means paying off small balances promptly to establish a healthy credit mix. It's your chance to flaunt that budget superpower in the realm of credit, and who doesn't love showing off their superpowers? Use your cards strategically and sprinkle in some responsible behavior.

So there you have it, folks—an entertaining romp through common credit mistakes that can sabotage your financial well-being. Avoid these pitfalls, maintain your credit score like it's your favorite piece of jewelry, and you'll be well on your way to claiming your title as the Budget Avenger. Always remember: a happy credit score is a fantastic sidekick for financial freedom!

How Late Payments Haunt Your Score

Late payments—those sneaky, stealthy creepers that slink into your credit report like a shadowy figure at a midnight snack raid. You think you're safe, that cupcake is calling, and suddenly, boom! You've missed a payment date and triggered a credit score horror story that's scarier than binge-watching a true crime series! Imagine your credit score suddenly sporting a ghost-like appearance, with an "oops" etched in the corner like an unending reminder of that dreadfully forgettable Tuesday you decided to let Netflix take precedence over your financial obligations.

Okay, so here's the deal: Late payments don't just knock on your door—they come barging in with a full marching band! One missed payment can drop your score significantly. If you're super unlucky (or, let's be honest, super forgetful), multiple late payments can unleash a storm that looks like a financial hurricane. Picture it: while you're sipping your morning coffee, your credit score throws a fit, throwing numbers around like confetti after a bad New Year's party. And trust me, no one wants an angry credit score in their life.

Not to mention, late payments can haunt your finances for years, like a former contestant from "The Real World" who keeps popping up in your memories, long after their season has ended. A single late payment can linger on your credit report for a good seven years! Yep, you heard me right. That's over two presidential terms, meaning you might still face the consequences when your child learns to drive. That's not just a mistake; that's a time capsule of your regret! You might think, "A single slip-up isn't a big deal," but it's really like a single potato chip ending up in your lap—you know you'll be having more before the night is over. And that, my friends, is a slippery slope of a financial diet you don't want to begin.

So let's talk numbers. When a payment is just 30 days late, your credit score will likely plummet like a rock thrown into a silent pond—ripple effects included! Some lenders even report it sooner, so your banks and everyone else who plays a role in your financial fate will be ringing the alarm bells. With every missed deadline, you're not just creating an atmosphere of sheer panic; you're also giving banks the ammo they need to shove extra fees and higher interest rates into your face. The horror doesn't stop at your score—it reaches into your wallet! It's like a horror movie where you keep inviting them over for tea breaks instead of escaping the killer.

But hey, I get it. Life happens; sometimes you're juggling more balls than a circus clown with a caffeine addiction. You've got bills, kids, sports practices, and God knows what else pulling you in every direction. Letting a deadline slip through the cracks is easy, but avoiding late payments is harder than solving a Rubik's Cube blindfolded! The best tip I can offer? Set up reminders—digital ones, if you have to. I mean, we're not living in the 1800s, are we? Use your phone, your calendar, or even a sticky note plastered on your mirror (which, let's be real, might be the most artistic option). There's no shortage of apps available to help you keep track of your payments like a personal financial assistant, minus the side-eye you'd get for having cake for breakfast.

And if you find yourself facing a late payment situation, don't throw your hands up in despair just yet! Life isn't over—you still have options. Call your creditor! Believe it or not, they're often more understanding than you might expect. After all, they want your money—even if you forgot to send it earlier. Sometimes they'll let you slide if it's your first lateness, offering you the rare find of "grace periods" like a golden ticket in a banker's game of Monopoly!

So, as I wrap up this thrilling saga about late payments, try to keep in mind that each missed deadline can linger like a bad song stuck in your head. You wouldn't want it playing during dinner parties, so let's make it a point to keep that payment game strong! Late payments don't just haunt your score—they linger like a silly ghost, just waiting for the moment you least expect it. And trust me, when you're on a financial roller coaster trying to achieve that superhero status as the Budget Avenger, nothing is scarier than an unwanted late payment lurking in the shadows. Keep your payments timely, and you'll be swiping left on those cringeworthy moments in no time!

The Trap of High Credit Utilization

High credit utilization—a dark, swirling path in the financial world that can lead you straight to the land of diminished credit scores and financial regret. It's like walking into a buffet with a plate so large you can't even hold it without assistance, and every bite you take just adds to the weight of decisions you'll spend the next decade regretting. Imagine this scenario: you might start with a responsible budget and a solid plan, but one fateful Black Friday, you get sucked into that glittering vortex of "50% off" and "Buy Now, Pay Later." Before you know it, your credit utilization ratio is turning into a monstrous creation faster than Frankenstein on a bad hair day!

So, what is this mysterious creature named high credit utilization? It's simply the amount of credit you're using compared to the total amount of credit available to you. Think of it as your personal credit score's embarrassing bedroom—distant relatives would be horrified if they ever saw it! Experts recommend keeping that ratio below 30%, which is like saying you should only eat three cookies from a plate piled with sixteen. But when the cookie jar beckons, "just one more won't hurt," it all seems too tempting!

The problem lies in the delusions of grandeur that come with having multiple credit cards and lines of credit. You get excited! You think you're king of the world, ready to conquer anything—until the credit card bill arrives, and suddenly your "kingdom" looks more like a junkyard of poor financial choices. Researchers have shown that the higher your credit utilization, the lower your score tends to drop. It's like a seesaw; high utilization takes you flying down, and the only thing that can balance it out is paying down those balances as if they were weighing you down in a swimming pool.

Let's take a moment to talk numbers because, as a self-proclaimed credit guru, I can't resist a good stat. A credit utilization rate of over 30% can cause your score to dip like a diver at a twirling circus show. And when it climbs above 50%, prepare yourself for a plunge worthy of Olympic recognition! It's the perfect recipe for lenders to label you as "risky", and with interest rates soaring higher than a hot air balloon without a passenger, you will certainly find yourself feeling the financial burn!

Now, I know what you might be thinking: "Tumeka, how am I supposed to resist the allure of that sweet, sweet credit when I can barely pay the rent?" The answer lies in a combination of strategy and self-discipline. It's all about making a proactive plan and treating your credit the way Supergirl treats her powers - with both responsibility and style! Start by setting a budget that allows you to live your best life, but also keeps your credit utilization lower than an accordion player during karaoke night.

You know what else can help? Credit cards with lower limits. I know, I know. It sounds a bit counterintuitive, but having a card with a lower limit forces you to budget much more strictly. It's like being put on a diet; you have no choice but to be aware of the snack options. You're subconsciously urging yourself to only use what you can afford, which will ultimately keep your credit utilization ratio healthy and your score soaring like that triumphant melody at the end of your favorite rom-com!

Plus, make friends with your credit report. No, I don't mean scrolling through it like a social media feed. I'm talking about regularly reviewing it, challenging inaccuracies, and maybe even working with a credit counselor on occasion. They can offer you guidance like a financial Yoda who will help you dodge the dark side of debt utilization faster than you can say, "May the credit score be with you." Recognize what you're using and what's available to you, so you can expertly balance your financial creations.

In the grand scheme of finance, understanding high credit utilization is crucial to stepping out of the financial 'trap.' It's all about showcasing your responsible habits and choosing to defeat temptations. High utilization may be the "mean girl" of credit scores, but you can absolutely be the superhero who stands up to it. So the next time you feel the urge to blow through your limit and take that escape with open wallets, remember high utilization is just waiting to trip you up. Treat your credit wisely, and you'll dodge that emotional rollercoaster while balancing that plate of cookies like a pro!

The Dangers of Ignoring Your Credit Report

The credit report—a document so mysterious and shrouded in financial intrigue that it should come with a warning like a crime show on a rainy night. Ignoring your credit report is like ignoring the smoke alarm while making a three-cheese casserole. Sure, it might seem fine until you realize you've accidentally invited the fire department for an unexpected celebration. Credit reports are often treated like diet plans: we know we should pay attention, but sometimes it's just easier to shove it under the proverbial pizza box and forget about it, right? Well, my friends, let's dive into the dangers of ignoring your credit report, because trust me, the stakes are higher than your great aunt Edna's fruitcake at Christmas!

First off, your credit report is a reflection of your financial reality. It's the "Report Card of Adulting," and who doesn't want to ace that? When you're swiping your credit card with confident abandon, it's easy to forget that your credit report is keeping tabs on all your spending sins. Ignore it, and you might just end up with surprises that would make your high school physics teacher's test results look thrilling! More often than not, people discover their score has plummeted due to errors they've never even known existed, like misplaced grades on a report card that could dictate a job offer. And when lenders see those strange blemishes, they won't cut you any slack; they'll raise interest rates and toss fees your way faster than a kid on a sugar rush.

Speaking of errors, let's talk about that little gremlin lurking in your credit report—fraud! Yep, it's a thief's playground out there, and you'd be forgiven for thinking that ignoring your credit report is just a bad idea. Taking a peek at it regularly helps you detect signs that someone might have snuck in through the back door of your financial life, swiping funds like they're picking apples off a tree. One day, your report could be chugging along quietly, and the next, you discover your identity has been hijacked by someone creatively using your credit for their lavish lifestyle. I don't know what will if that doesn't send shivers down your spine!

And if you're digging through all this drama to find those pesky errors, just realize that challenging them can feel like trying to win a game of Monopoly while half your players are trying to flip the board over. It's not as easy as saying, "This isn't mine!" You've got paperwork, explanations, and perhaps even awkward conversations with creditors. Audience, please imagine me with my cape on, rallying the forces to battle financial foes while laughing maniacally in the process. The point is, ignoring your credit report means you could be allowing potential financial disasters to mount, people!

Yet, maybe the scariest thing about ignoring your credit report is how it could immediately impact your future, like those existential crisis moments that creep up on you while you're basing your life's decisions on a really 2010-era internet meme. Let's say it's time to buy a house or a car. The last thing you want is to get the dreaded denial because your credit report is waving a big "STOP" sign right in your face. Suddenly, all those dreams of the Too-Good-To-Be-True-Mansion or That-Dream-Car come crashing down like a toddler running a marathon towards a candy jar. You've put in all this effort to save, only to discover your report is filled with information that screams "nope, not today!"

Finally, let's address the elephant in the room: the emotional toll. Finding out that your credit report is riddled with inaccuracies can be deflating. It's like discovering your prized cactus is actually a six-foot-tall rubber tree that doesn't even belong to you! If you've spent your lifetime in denial about your credit report, figuring out the labyrinth of errors is the first step to reclaiming your inner financial superhero. Ignoring it won't magically make all the problems disappear—they'll just continue to lurk, accumulating like clutter in an attic, waiting for the opportune moment to drop into your life with a nasty surprise.

So, my fellow finance adventurers, let's take a stand against the dangers of ignoring your credit report! With each moment of awareness, you can be your own financial superhero, confronting those mysterious past transgressions head-on. Grab your favorite snack, dive into that elusive report, and embrace the journey! You'll discover a clearer picture of your finances along with a newfound appreciation for ACING adulting—because we all know that managing your credit is just part of the job, and just like grandma's casserole, maybe you'll even learn to love it! Who knows, you might even discover that opening your report is the first step toward a healthy financial future—one where the smoke alarms stay silent, and the only surprises you meet are cake pops at a birthday party.

Building a Positive Credit History

Building a positive credit history—sounds like a delightful fairy tale, doesn't it? A bit like finding that perfect pair of shoes on a frenzy shopping spree and realizing they fit like a glove. However, instead of shoes, we're talking about your financial reputation, a status that floats around in the credit universe like a prized trophy. But let's keep it real: finding that admirable credit history can feel much more like an epic quest in a video game than a simple stroll in the park. So grab your financial map, adjust your cape, and let's delve into the exhilarating world of building a positive credit history!

First things first, it's essential to understand that building a positive credit history isn't an overnight endeavor. Oh no, my friends! It's more like cultivating a beautiful garden where every flower represents a sound financial move. It takes dedication and time to see those blooms smile back at you. If you've knocked on the door to adulthood and found credit waiting on the other side, don't panic! We all start somewhere, and growing that credit history requires a bit of patience, just like trying to get a toddler to eat broccoli—demanding yet undeniably rewarding once achieved!

Now, here's where it gets good. If you're aiming for the best, start by securing that first credit card. Think of it as your golden ticket into the magical realm of credit history. Might I recommend a secured credit card? They're nifty little tools that require a deposit, serving as a credit limit. It's like getting a playdate for your finances! Use that card wisely, treat it respectfully, and pay your balance in full each month. Remarkably, this small act can help build your credit history faster than knitting a blanket for a new puppy you know you shouldn't have adopted. But hey, who can resist those puppy-dog eyes?!

Ah, my fellow financial ninjas, let's not forget the importance of making on-time payments! Much like a reliable friend who never bails on plans, paying your bills on time is a vital part of keeping your credit score afloat. Grab that calendar and designate payment days—treat them like sacred events on your social calendar! You wouldn't let your best friend sit alone at a wedding; likewise, don't let your payments hang in limbo. Each on-time payment builds your positive credit story like pages turning in a page-turner novel—you definitely want to avoid the ending where the mailman delivers bad news instead of delightful surprises.

And while we're on this riveting journey of positive credit history, let's chat about credit utilization. I know, I know—this sounds a little dry, but trust me, it's the spice to your financial meal! Credit utilization is how much of your available credit you're using relative to your total credit limit; keep it below 30%, and you'll be smiling like a Cheshire cat! The lower the number, the better! Imagine inviting friends over for an all-you-can-eat pizza party—sure, you can indulge! But the guilt you feel after devouring the last slice while everyone else is still at it? You want to prevent that scenario in the credit world! Strike the right balance; your credit utilization will keep you in a sweet spot.

Getting your credit mix right is just as crucial. Yes, folks, Variety is the name of the game! Mix it up a bit, like adding chocolate chips to that oatmeal; maybe a credit card here, a small personal loan there—mixing in a mortgage or auto loan if you're living life on the edge. By proving that you can handle various types of credit responsibly, you're not only showcasing your impressive financial acumen to lenders, but you're also building a credit history fuller than Taylor Swift's fanbase! Keep your options open, but remain practical in your pursuits; balance is key, just like that rest day you promised yourself between gym sessions!

Don't forget to monitor your credit report! You wouldn't ignore a mystery book with enticing twists and turns! Check your report regularly, safeguarding your hard-earned credit history against sneaky errors that might derail your journey. Thanks to various websites and credit agencies, it's remarkably easy to obtain a free credit report, so embark on this adventure as if you were opening a treasure chest. And if you do find inaccuracies, dispute them faster than your aunt can ask when you're getting married!

Lastly, patience truly makes a strong, positive credit history bloom. No one gets crowned king or queen of Creditville in a day! Allow your history to grow, learn from your mistakes, and celebrate your little victories. Once you start to see that credit score tick upward like a push-up challenge gone right, you'll feel like a financial superhero who's emerged victorious in the epic battle for creditworthiness.

So, my financial warriors, go forth and build that positive credit history! Treat it like your favorite action movie, kicking down obstacles, dodging pitfalls, and conquering challenges with dazzling finesse. With time, effort, and a dash of humor, you'll establish credit success that makes you shine brighter than a diamond in the financial universe! Grab your cape, take flight, and show the world what this credit saga is capable of!

CHAPTER 11
NAVIGATING THE MORTGAGE MAZE

Understanding Mortgage Basics

Mortgages—the necessary evil that often feels like a bad relationship you can't escape! You know, the kind where you wake up in the morning and wonder how you got tangled in this mess. Understanding mortgage basics is crucial on your journey toward financial freedom, and you bet your bottom dollar I'm here to guide you with a sprinkle of humor and a dash of "what were we thinking?"

First off, what even is a mortgage? Think of it as a marriage contract between you and your bank. You get to "live happily ever after" in a house of your own, while the bank ensures you pay your dues like clockwork or else. In other words, this sweet setup allows you to purchase a home without having to pay the entire sum upfront; instead, you'll pay a monthly fee that feels suspiciously like your Netflix subscription—except no binge-watching on reality shows! Just the reality of adulting.

Now, mortgages come with a lot of lingo that makes you wonder why they didn't just call it what it is: a money loan with a side of stress. "Principal" is the amount you actually borrow to buy a home, and trust me, you'll hear this term so often, it might as well have its own fan club. Then there's "interest," which is the fee for borrowing that money, basically a monthly rent to have permission to live in your own place. It's like paying a cover charge to get into your own home party. And let's not forget about "escrow," which sounds like a fancy spa treatment but is really the place where your taxes and insurance get to hang out before they hit the bank—no aromatherapy involved!

How long do you want to be married... I mean, how long do you want your mortgage? Fixed-rate mortgages are like traditional marriages—preferable for those who want stability (seriously, who doesn't?). Your payment remains the same for 15, 20, or 30 years, depending on your commitment level. On the other hand, adjustable-rate mortgages are like dating someone who refuses to commit. Your interest rate can change after a set period, which means your payment could spike up faster than your heart rate when you see an ex at a party! Spoiler alert: My advice? Stick to the fixed rate, save the drama for your llama.

Now, let's talk down payments—most commonly set around 20% of your home's price, which is the amount you pay upfront. Think of it as the deposit you put down to reserve that coveted pizza on pizza night; no one wants a half-eaten slice when you can have the whole pie! But here's the twist: If you don't have that hefty deposit, you might end up with private mortgage insurance (PMI). It's like paying for an insurance policy that protects the lender—in other words, protection for the one actually getting your money! Such a deal, huh?

Thank goodness that neighborhoods come in all shapes and sizes. When you're considering homes, location is everything! But remember, sheer desire can lead to mortgage heartbreak; don't let your longing for that chic downtown bistro fool you into breaking your budget. It's important to ensure that the location fits your finances, not just your Instagram feed. Nobody wants to be stuck in an "up-and-coming" neighborhood if it feels like it's repping the "north of broke" demographic.

Most importantly, know that mortgages don't just navigate the terrain of home-buying; they'll shape your financial future. Don't forget to check your credit score before you start the process because it's the golden ticket to better interest rates. It's the one time in life where you desperately want to have had fewer late payments—sorry, not sorry to that one pizza delivery guy whose late-night cravings swayed me into spending my entire budget on pepperoni and extra cheese!

So there you have it! Understanding mortgage basics isn't as scary as it may seem. Whenever you feel overwhelmed, just think of it as your financial commitment toward a home sweet home. And like a wise woman (my mom, Rose) always says, "You're not just buying a house, you're buying a neighborhood, some questionable neighbors, and the right to complain about lawn care—what more could a person want?" And trust me, there's no place like home!

Types of Mortgages Explained

When it comes to types of mortgages, let me just say that it's a beautifully chaotic buffet that would make even the most dedicated food critic raise an eyebrow or two. Don't get me wrong, I love a good smorgasbord, but when you're trying to decide how to finance your forever home, it can feel like being a kid in a candy shop at a dentist convention. Choices, choices everywhere, and every step forward can lead to severe indecision—in short, you'd better bring your decision-making muscles and perhaps a therapist!

Let's kick things off with the classic: the fixed-rate mortgage. If mortgages were a family, this one would definitely be Uncle Joe—reliable, steady, and has probably been saving for retirement since the age of five. With this option, your interest rate remains unchanged for the life of the loan, which means you pay the same amount month after month, year after year. It's like blissful marriage: you know what you're getting into and how much you'll be paying during your lifetime in that house (which, let's be honest, might just mean your lifetime of loving every single wall crack! *eye roll*). So if you're looking for stability in the turbulent waters of home ownership, this one might just float your boat.

Next up is the adjustable-rate mortgage (ARM)—or as I like to call it, the "I-don't-know-where-this-relationship-is-going" option. With an ARM, your interest rate can fluctuate based on market conditions. Let's say you start off with a sweet, low interest rate for a couple of years, feeling like you stumbled into the best prom night ever. But hold on! Because the rabbit hole doesn't end there. After that initial period, the interest rate is subject to change, meaning your payment could explode faster than your child's volcano project from last summer—very much like the time I gleefully asked if it was okay to impress everyone by trying "gumbo" for the first time. Spoiler alert: take it from me, that was a confusing adventure, and so is navigating an ARM!

Looking for something more specific? Enter the FHA loan, also known as the "inclusion of everyone" mortgage. Backed by the Federal Housing Administration, this loan is like one of those welcoming parties at the beginning of a new school year, where everyone gets a name tag—because everyone deserves to feel included! These loans allow you to enter homeownership with a lower down payment, generally around 3.5%, which is often music to a first-time buyer's ears. Just keep in mind that the dance floor can get crowded, and you'll be subject to mortgage insurance premiums, but hey, it's a party!

Now, we have the VA loan for those adventurous souls willing to put a little skin in the game. This one's specifically designed for our veterans—thank you for your service! Picture it as the VIP lounge at a celebrity event. You don't need a down payment, and your interest rates might make everyone wish they'd just enlisted instead! Plus, no mortgage insurance, which is like being able to order the lobster special without ever having to look at the price on the menu. What's not to like?

If you've got bigger aspirations—like possibly renting out that glorious property for some cash flow—an investment property mortgage could be your new best friend. This mortgage is for those looking to add a bit of entrepreneurial flair to their lives. But remember, owning an investment property is a little like being a contestant on a reality show—exciting at times, but fraught with unexpected plot twists and the occasional cliffhanger that keeps you awake at night. You'll definitely want to consider additional factors such as property management and tenants—or better yet, how to deal with running into them at the grocery aisle after they mysteriously "forgot" to pay their rent last month!

And last but not least, we have the USDA loan, aimed at those who are ready to pack their bags and head to the countryside. You guessed it, this loan is for rural properties and aims to promote homeownership in those beautiful, serene landscapes. So if you've ever dreamed of a white picket fence and a life free of city chaos, take this route—it's the mortgage lover's version of running away to the countryside like in a cheesy rom-com. Who knows, you might even end up living out your very own Martha Stewart fantasy!

So there you have it! A delightful spectrum of mortgage types to peruse, like a gallery of homes, with all the beautiful chaos involved in choosing the right one. Whether you're a fixed-rate fan or the daring kind with an adjustable rate, just remember to do your homework—because unlike whatever you claim to learn from TikTok, deciding on a mortgage is not just a trendy hashtag; it's a lifelong commitment that will always require the "fine print" reading glasses you've been avoiding!

The Importance of Credit in Mortgage Approval

Credit scores—the mystical numbers that haunt us at night, haunt our dreams, and sometimes outright terrorize our finances. It's like that one relative who always shows up at the Thanksgiving dinner uninvited and critiques your stuffing to no end. When it comes to mortgage approval, your credit score is the main character in this compelling drama, and trust me, it holds more weight than your favorite heavy-duty pot you use for family meals. So, let's dive into why your credit score matters more than your choice of dessert at family gatherings!

First and foremost, your credit score is essentially your report card for adulthood. Remember those red circling marks on an English paper from freshman year? Yeah, that's how your lender sees your credit report—a series of badges reflecting your financial behavior. Scared yet? You should be! Banks and lenders use that score to assess whether you're worth the risk of lending money to. You're in business if your credit score is sparkling like a freshly cleaned diamond. But if it's as stained as last week's leftovers in the fridge? Well, grab your prayer beads, my friend, because you might be in trouble.

A healthy credit score typically ranges from 700 to 850, but let's just say that anything north of 740 basically makes you the prom king or queen of home financing. It tells lenders, "Look at me! I pay my bills on time! I follow the rules! I'm a keeper!" Conversely, a score below 620 might as well have "Send Help" tattooed across it. You'll be facing higher interest rates, higher down payments, and possibly, a few eyebrow raises from mortgage brokers. I can't even tell you how cringey that encounter might feel—it's like trying to grab that last slice of cake right in front of Aunt Gertrude. Not a pleasant prospect!

But what exactly goes into this oh-so-important credit score? Your payment history carries around 35% of the weight like a hamster on a giant wheel, while the amounts you owe (30%) feel like your little brother weighing in on your life choices—also significant! Lenders want to see that you're not swimming in a sea of debt where sharks lurk around every corner. If you're constantly maxing out your credit cards, that's like showing up to the mortgage interview in a T-shirt that says, "I take financial risks!" Spoiler alert: lenders don't dig that vibe.

Now, let's talk about credit inquiries. You know, those nosy lenders who want to keep tabs on your financial habits? If you apply for multiple credit cards all at once, it's like yelling "pick me!" at a crowded job fair without doing any research on the employers. Too many inquiries indicate to lenders that you're desperate for credit, and you know what they say about desperate people—they often make questionable choices (like allowing Aunt Mildred to bring her famous jello salad to Thanksgiving!).

When preparing for your mortgage application, take a good, hard look at your credit report. Think of it as pre-game showtime. Fix those little inaccuracies that can stick out like a sore thumb, like that time I forgot to take off the banana peel before whipping out my latest banana bread recipe. Call me Ms. Forgetful, but I assure you, no one wants to serve rotten debt solutions. Clean it up! Handle those weird pieces of debt like cleaning out your closet before the family arrives. You'd be amazed at how many skeletons can be hiding in there, like those forgotten accounts from your college days that mean nothing but are still casting a dark shadow over your credit life.

Then there's the sweet joy of maintaining a solid payment history. Automate it if you have to—set mythical calendar reminders on your phone or enlist your kids to sing a lovely tune every time the bill is due (trust me, it's hilarious). Budgets are your best friend when tackling your finances; if life feels too hectic, get help! Hire a credit counselor or consult me—your fearless Budget Avenger!

As you assemble your mortgage application, remember that your credit score is like the conductor of an orchestra. It has the power to dictate how beautifully that music plays. A solid score can lead to harmonious mortgage terms—a fixed rate that sings, adjustable rates that play nice, and maybe, just maybe, VIP access to those exclusive loan programs. In the world of mortgages, having a good credit score might just get you a front-row seat and a backstage pass—who could resist that?

So, my friends, take your credit score seriously. Treat it like that friend who helps you navigate the wild world of dating—helpful, perhaps a bit pushy, but ultimately there to ensure you avoid all those bad relationships, whether they're with lenders or a badly rated pizza place. Remember: mortgages are life-changing financial decisions, and your credit score is here to support you on your journey, like a superhero with its own theme music (which happens to be completely uncopyrighted!). So go out there and capture the mortgage of your dreams, armed with the vast power of good credit!

Navigating the Mortgage Application Process

Navigating the mortgage application process can feel like trying to find your way through a labyrinth, with every twist and turn leading you straight to a minotaur named "Paperwork." Don't let that scare you, though! This beast is actually quite tame if you come prepared with your cape on. Think of me as your trusty sidekick—here to guide you through the invisible ink of lender jargon and the swirling vortex of document requests that might otherwise leave you gasping for air (or with a glass of wine in hand). Buckle up, because this is one adventure you won't want to miss!

Let's start with the power move: gathering all necessary documents. Imagine your colleagues at the office on a mission to unearth their summer vacation pics—dedicated, passionate, and, potentially, mildly annoying! You'll need to provide everything from your tax returns (cue the dramatic gasp), pay stubs, bank statements, and employment verification. Lenders want to know every detail of your financial life, like a nosy neighbor who keeps track of when you cut your grass. So, assemble them like a financial superhero squad, ready for battle! And don't even think about hiding that avocado toast expense from last weekend; we'll save those battles for another day!

Next up is the mortgage pre-approval stage. If you thought a marriage proposal was anxiety-inducing, wait until you step into this arena! Getting pre-approved means a lender exhibits interest in your financial worth as if they are eyeing your best friend's new romantic partner. You may even feel like you're being vetted on various dating platforms that offer "100% financial compatibility." Trust me—this is where your credit score reigns supreme. The lender will run a hard inquiry on your report, turning that glimmer of hope into a full-blown reality check. So, don't trip on the red flags; just sit back and enjoy the ride, as lenders will determine how much money they're willing to lend you based on your financial situation.

Now that you're pre-approved (or adequately groomed for potential rejection), one of the most important parts awaits: choosing the right lender. You wouldn't just show up at a potluck, eating whatever your neighbor is serving, would you? Each lender has its own special concoction of loan products, tastes, and fees, so be smart about whom you join forces with! Are they known to respond to emails faster than a cheetah chases its dinner? Or do they make you feel like you're waiting for the next season of your favorite show—an unbearable and agonizing wait? It's essential to pick a lender who can balance your needs with a level of responsiveness that screams "financial superhero." You deserve that attention!

Once you've chosen your lender, brace yourself for the flood of paperwork to come. Yes, there will be more forms than a cereal aisle at the grocery store! Some will require your deepest financial secrets—like your understanding of how long it takes to pay off student loans from your perfect college experience (which, let's be honest, was "better" than scrolling through TikTok all day). Don't be afraid to ask questions! Think of the lender as your personal treasure map curator; request clarification if you don't understand something. They're there to help you navigate the uncharted waters!

Next, you'll be heading towards the underwriting phase, which is like a rite of passage. Underwriting is where the magic happens, but remember, this is also where some legends die! The underwriter will scrutinize your entire financial history like they're an FBI agent trying to solve a case of misappropriated funds. Be prepared for tighter scrutiny on your employment history and credit behavior. Stay calm amidst the storm of requests for even more paperwork or clarifications—think of yourself as a financial warrior standing tall! This is not a time to crumble.

Oh, and let's sprinkle a bit of humor into this process: just know escrow will join the party! You might feel like you've suddenly signed up for adult supervision when in reality, it's just the process where all the financial obligations meet for the final showdown. It's where your down payment and any seller credits land safely until it's time to close. Consider it a stylish lounge for all stakeholders involved, from your lender to the title company—like a classy cocktail party for all things financial, without the weird small talk!

Finally, you'll be greeted with the closing day, the moment you've been waiting for, where you sign on the dotted line confirming your commitment to the house. It's like that wobbly moment when you stand up to make a toast at a wedding—sure, you might trip over a few words, but hey, this is the good stuff! Once you sign that stack of papers thick enough to choke a horse, you'll have the keys to your very own castle, complete with a new fridge that might just eat away at your decorating budget!

So, to sum it all up, navigating the mortgage application process requires preparation, persistence, and a healthy dose of patience—and maybe some flowcharts on your wall to map it all out. Channel your inner detective and house-hunting warrior, and soon you'll secure that mortgage like a pro! This adventure is worth every twist and turn along the way to unlock the door to your home sweet home!

Homeownership Costs Beyond the Mortgage

Homeownership—the great American dream! You get the white picket fence, neighbors who borrow your lawn mower, and an eternal battle with your mortgage provider! Sounds perfect, doesn't it? But like a magician pulling bunnies out of hats, the reality of homeownership comes with hidden costs that show up faster than unexpected in-laws during holidays. While the mortgage payment is often front and center, you better believe there's a cast of supporting characters waiting in the wings, ready to hit your wallet when you least expect it. So, let's dive into the messy world of homeownership costs beyond the mortgage—and add a little laughter to this plot twist!

First up on our surprise roster is homeowners' insurance. Sure, it sounds logical—you want to protect that lovely abode you just purchased, right? Homeownership insurance typically covers your property and personal belongings from unforeseen disasters like fire, theft, and that unexpected meteor strike (hey, stranger things have happened!). But listen carefully—you don't just pay the mortgage; you also pay for insurance. It'll be like that friend who always borrows your snacks without asking, leaving you wondering why your pantry is suddenly bare. These premiums add to your monthly expenses and can vary dramatically depending on your home's location, age, and many other factors. It's like a game show contestant trying to guess the price of cereal on a random Tuesday—who even knows?

Then comes property taxes, which are affectionately known as the "gifts" to your local government. You now proudly hold your castle, but don't be surprised to find yourself paying a portion of your hard-earned money to have nice neighborhoods, public schools, and roads for your cheese-meets-kale lifestyle. Often calculated as a percentage of your home's assessed value, property taxes can snowball into a hefty cost! Think of them as the not-so-cute sidekick that you can't shake off—like that one adult in a superhero movie who can barely keep up but somehow manages to survive every catastrophe. You might even say you're now performing a public service, but who isn't a little bitter about taking out a loan for a new roof only to find out half of it is going to make sure the rubber duck pond at the community park stays afloat?

While we're on the topic of unexpected surprises, let's not forget about maintenance costs—the unsung hero of homeownership! Homeownership is like adopting a needy puppy—you love it to bits, but sometimes you wish you could hit the "mute" button when it starts to demand attention. There's always something that breaks, leaks, or needs fixing, from leaky faucets to faulty air conditioners. And let's talk about upkeep: lawnmowers, gardening supplies, and that ever-present "honey-do" list will keep you busy every weekend until you begin questioning if you've signed up for a second job! If you don't want your neighbors staring at your lawn like it's a science experiment gone wrong, budget for maintenance; your flowerbed's dignity depends on it.

Also, don't forget about the cost of utilities; it's like hosting that no-show friend who shows up at the most inconvenient times. Your gas, electric, and water bills will become a monthly fixture that you can't escape. You'll find yourself staring at those bills while practicing your best psychic powers to foretell how much you can expect to spend each month. And if you throw in things like trash collection and sewer fees, you've got yourself a party that no one invited you to! Together, these costs can run you hundreds of dollars each month, and your utility bills may sneak up on you like an awkward text to the wrong person after a few drinks!

Now, if you want to kick your financial stress into high gear, let's talk about homeowner associations, or HOAs, where your neighborhood becomes its very own governing body. They can establish rules that dictate everything from the color of your front door (because "fuchsia" isn't an acceptable option) to the types of ornaments you can place in your yard (let's face it, no flamingos allowed). HOAs charge fees to maintain common areas, landscaping, and all the fun stuff that gives your neighborhood those Pinterest-worthy vibes. You might think it's an investment in neighborhood quality, but just remember: if you don't follow the rules, you could find yourself facing fines as if you were a rebellious teen attempting to sneak back home after curfew.

If you're planning to remodel or renovate—the "fun" part of homeownership—don't forget to budget for permits and professional help. While the DIY shows on television make it look easy as pie (and why don't they ever have sticky floors?), in real life, you might find yourself grappling with learning curves that leave you gasping for dear life. Expect to fork out some cash for tools, materials, and the wisdom of that sarcastic handyman who wears a tool belt everywhere, even at the grocery store.

So there you have it: homeownership is a grand adventure filled with costs beyond the scope of your mortgage. Dig deep into your pockets, ladies and gentlemen—it's like opening a treasure chest only to find a wild "we do what we want" lifestyle lurking behind the glittering hope of financial security. Approach this journey with humor, patience, and a healthy dose of reality, and you'll learn to embrace the sweet chaos of homeownership! Happy house hunting and may your home bring you as much joy as prancing through fields of daisies—I mean, at least a small fraction of that nostalgia!

CHAPTER 12
FAMILY LEGACY AND FINANCIAL RESPONSIBILITY

The Importance of Financial Legacy

The financial legacy—the one thing we all roll our eyes at until we realize our grandkids are going to spend all our hard-earned cash on avocado toast and the latest iPhone! Seriously, though, when I think about financial legacy, it feels like the adult version of a bedtime story. You know, the parts where we put our kids to sleep with tales of financial witches that cast spells on foolish spenders, turning them into coupon-wielding budgeteers? So, let's dig into why this legacy business is not just a necessity but a superpower for our family's future.

First off, let's face it—money talks. Like, literally. It can whisper sweet nothings in the ears of your heirs or throw tantrums that rattle the very foundations of your family (think a family feud worthy of a soap opera). When I say "financial legacy," I'm not just talking about the cash you leave behind; I'm referring to the lessons, principles, and sheer audacity to take. Charge your finances and live the kind of life that fosters wealth. After all, if I had a dollar for every time I heard someone say, "I don't want to talk about money," well, I'd be living in my own budget-friendly mansion on a beach somewhere sunny!

Creating a financial legacy is like baking a cake. The flour is your financial literacy, the eggs are your budgeting skills, and the icing on top is the generational knowledge you pass down. Have you ever tried to bake without following a recipe? I did once, and let's just say the fire department got involved. That family recipe for financial stability is equally crucial; if you ignore it, you might end up with a hot mess that nobody wants to eat—or inherit. So, teaching our kids the difference between a 401(k) and a 501(c)(3) might just save them from burning their money in ways we never could.

We've all heard the saying, "Money doesn't grow on trees." But guess what? While that might be true, I firmly believe that money can grow if you nurture it, much like my beloved houseplants (although they tell me the secret is not overwatering, unlike my spending habits with online shopping). Your family legacy can foster an environment where financial success is the norm, not the exception. When children grow up in a household that values budgeting, saving, and investing, they inherit not just money but a foundational understanding of how to manage it. It's like sending them out in the world with a financial superhero cape, ready to tackle the budget villains that lurk around every corner!

But wait, there's more! A financial legacy is also about adaptability. The financial landscape is changing faster than I can say "capital gains tax"! With tech advancements, cryptocurrencies, and the impact of global events on the economy, there's always something new on the horizon. Imagine sending your kid off to college, armed not only with a checkbook and a 17-step guide on "How Not to Overspend on Ramen Noodles," but also with a skill set that includes understanding the latest financial tech tools. Now that's a legacy worth leaving! Our job is to prepare them for whatever the finance universe throws their way—like a financial intergalactic space battle!

In wrapping this hilarious exploration of financial legacies, remember that this is about crafting a narrative for your family's future more than just dollars in the bank. It's about instilling values that create a flourishing financial ecosystem where your descendants can thrive. Let's be honest; the only thing worse than your kid showing up to a dinner party without appropriate table manners is them showing up without a clue of what a budget looks like!

So, as we navigate raising budgets brave enough to defeat debt dragons and financially savvy offspring who can say "no" to impulse buying like a superhero facing a villain, I urge you all to think about the legacy you want to leave behind. It might even inspire you to get off the couch, stop binge-watching that Netflix series for the twelfth time, and take charge of that family money dialogue—because clearly, scrolling through social media doesn't teach financial literacy!

Creating a Family Financial Mission

Creating a family financial mission is a bit like orchestrating a family band—if everyone plays their own tune, you end up with a cacophony that rivals a cat fight. But when everyone gets on the same music sheet, it's like The Beatles meets The Supremes, and who wouldn't want that? For many families, conversations about money can be more awkward than discussing your great aunt's foot fungus over Thanksgiving dinner. That's why crafting a family financial mission is not just essential; it's downright revolutionary—like introducing a spoon into the world of forks!

Let me tell you, setting this mission is not about drudging through endless spreadsheets and accounting wizards. No, my friends—this is about creating a vision for your family that even a group of overly caffeinated squirrels would rally behind! Your family's financial mission should encompass your values, priorities, and most importantly, your hopes for the future, possibly with a few whimsical side stories sprinkled in for good measure. Think of it like our personal Grandma Moses painting. Still, instead of quaint landscapes, we're illustrating a financial future that's bright, authentic, and filled with possibilities (and maybe a few dollar signs).

First things first: gather the troops! Consider this your financial family council meeting, akin to the whimsical strategy session the Avengers might have before heading off to battle. Whether it's the kids who partially hear you in between episodes of "Teen Titans" or the spouse who's glued to memes all day, make sure everyone is involved in the creation of this mission. One of my kids thought our family financial mission had something to do with our dog's next crunchy treat, and, you know what? That's valid! But now is the time we lay out the groundwork for our economic endeavors that don't include exploring the wonders of pet gourmet snacks.

Once everyone's assembled, it's time for the brainstorming session. In true family fashion, I recommend diving into the "who, what, where, when, and why" of it all while bouncing ideas around like you're playing a game of financial dodgeball. Ask questions like: "What are our financial goals, and do we want vacations, a house, or a lifetime supply of organic kale?" (Just kidding about the kale, I think we can all agree to leave that out of our mission). Identifying what truly matters doesn't just make for better money habits; it creates a vision everyone can get behind—even Grandma Rose, who has a penchant for penny-pinching.

While we're at it, infuse it with a bit of humor and personality! Your family mission can reflect the quirks that set you apart, like how we have a tradition of taking a vacation that's just a well-pitched tent in the backyard, proving that travel can be inexpensive if you set your imagination free! If achieving the dream of financial freedom sounds like a high-stakes gamble, toss in a few fun ideas like potluck fundraising dinners or "no-spend" months where the kids plan meals around what's in the pantry, which could lead to "inventive" recipes, like canned beans and microwave popcorn casserole!

Once you've settled on your collective vision, it's all about action! A mission is just a piece of paper without a road map. Think of it as your family treasure map: "X" marks the spot where you're financially stable, debt-free, and living the dream! Portion out your financial objectives into manageable bite-sized pieces—this could involve savings goals, a family budget you all agree to, or just setting aside "fun money" for spontaneous family adventures! Most importantly, keep that treasure map visible; hang it on the fridge, and let it serve as a daily reminder of your united front against the financial unknowns.

Now, creating this family financial mission isn't just about the dollars and cents; it's about the heart, soul, and sometimes hysterical mess that comes with family life. From arguments about who really opened the last bag of chips to declaring who's on dishwasher duty, these missions, when crafted together, foster incredible teamwork! So, grab your family, rally their spirit, and embark on this memorable journey where the only thing better than bank accounts and budgets is the shared laughter along the way. Because, let's face it, if your family can't annunciate the term "financial responsibility" with a wink and a giggle, are you really building a legacy at all?

Strategies for Involving Family in Financial Planning

Involving the whole family in financial planning might seem like an ambitious endeavor, kinda like trying to put an octopus in a barrel at a circus! But let me tell you, it can be not only manageable but downright fun—like a circus, minus the tightrope walking (unless you're into that, in which case, be careful!). Opening the dialogue about money can be a little daunting. Still, if you approach it with humor, creativity, and a sprinkle of family chaos, you'll have them all on board faster than you can say "budgeting worksheets!"

First off, we need to establish that the finance talk doesn't have to be filled with realistic projections and dry statistics that could bore even the most energetic toddler. Instead, treat it like planning a family movie night—everyone gets to have a say on what shows to watch! Why not kick things off with a "Family Finance Night" where everyone brings their unique ideas to the table? You could even offer popcorn and candy as bribes to get the kids involved. Mention how budgeting skills are the superheroes of finance, and they'll likely be chomping at the bit to join the celebration—and let's be honest, who doesn't love popcorn?

Next, it's essential to break down the money jargon into bite-sized pieces that don't require a degree in rocket science to understand. I've had sit-down sessions with my family where I tried explaining the concept of compounding interest, only to be met with puzzled looks reminiscent of cats confronted with a laser pointer. Use relatable analogies! Explain compound interest like watering a plant; your money grows if you do it consistently! Conversely, neglect it, and you're left with a dried-up branch—an excellent cautionary tale not just for plants, but also for your savings!

Next up on the agenda—kids love visuals! Why not create colorful charts, graphs, or even a family money "scoreboard"? Kids are motivated by little achievements, and nothing beats a tidy graphic that shows how much closer they are to that coveted trip to the amusement park or their very own video game! On our scoreboards, we proudly display our financial goals next to fun family activities like "movie night" or "pizza party"—because let's face it, money doesn't just go to savings; it also goes to indulging amazing family experiences! So boost their engagement by adding a "fun factor," and watch them brighten up like they just discovered a hidden candy stash!

To get everyone contributing to the family finances, encourage older kids to take on small financial responsibilities, like managing their own savings accounts or planning their own lunch expenses. Not only does it give them a sense of responsibility, but it also makes for some hilarious stories when they miscalculate the budget and try to make a gourmet meal from nothing! Bring them into the conversation by asking them to research prices or create a monthly budget for their projects. Trust me, nothing motivates kids faster than the desire to buy the latest trendy gadget—suddenly they'll become excellent financial researchers!

But let's not forget the most critical aspect: regular check-ins. Finances aren't a one-and-done conversation; they evolve. Just like your kids' taste in music changes from "Baby Shark" to—dare I say it—some cringe-worthy pop song they insist is a "banger," so should your financial discussions!

Schedule monthly family finance meetings to review goals, reassess budgets, and maybe play judge on which purchases were silly. The laughter that follows from arguing about who bought the cringiest item will keep things light, informative, and far from boring!

Now, let's add the cherry on top of our financial sundae—encourage open dialogue. Create an atmosphere where everyone feels comfortable sharing ideas, successes, and even failures without the judgmental foot tapping of a strict accountant behind the desk. By fostering an environment of trust, you'll not only raise a financially literate household but also blissfully avoid the financial therapy sessions we all dread. Make it evident that mistakes are not only allowed, but they're practically encouraged, just as long as they're not made with the credit card!

In conclusion, involving your family in financial planning doesn't require you to craft intricate spreadsheets or hold relentless discussions that sound more painful than a dentist appointment. Bring joy, laughter, and engagement into each session, and turn financial topics into fun family adventures! Because when family members work hand-in-hand to manage money, you can rest easy knowing you not only built a foundation for financial literacy but a legacy that will ensure a delightful comedy of stories sharing just how chaotic yet rewarding managing finances together can be!

Passing Down Financial Knowledge

Passing down financial knowledge is about as important as passing down grandma's secret macaroni and cheese recipe—except this one won't clog your arteries, and it might even save your kid from a lifetime of anxiety in the checkout line of Target! Seriously, if we can teach our kids the nuances of saving, managing their credit, and being smart consumers, we're essentially arming them with a cape made of financial wisdom. And let's face it: we really don't want them entering adulthood armed only with "how to dodge financial responsibility" and "what's on TikTok today?"

To kick off this critical mission, let's talk about the everyday opportunities we slip by when it comes to imparting financial wisdom.

You know those mundane moments we often overlook—like grocery shopping. I mean, it's not just a place to buy broccoli and cookies disguised as "healthy snacks." Nope! When we're at the store loaded down with lists, that's our moment to shine a light on budgeting. I pose questions like, "Which item on the list is the best deal?" or "Can you figure out how much we'll spend on apples if we buy three bags?" You'd be amazed at how a casual trip to pick up milk can close the gap between frazzled parent and financially literate child faster than you can say "discount coupons!"

Next up, let's talk about that oh-so-glamorous realm of chores. If you want to truly pass down knowledge, attach financial incentives to everyday responsibilities and make it more fun than a game show. It's simple—say your kid cleans their room, they earn a dollar. They wash the dishes; they earn another. Eventually, they'll start calculating "How much can I save and what can I do with it?" That moment—the eye sparkles and the light bulb of understanding turning on—is like watching fireworks on the Fourth of July—joyful, illuminating, and a little bit dangerous if you don't keep your wits about you!

However, transferring knowledge isn't just about handing down dollar bills like some modern-day Santa Claus. No, it involves creating open, relatable discussions—like comparing the pitfalls of overspending to eating an entire sheet cake by yourself. Sure, it's delicious, but you might regret it thoroughly later! I've learned to challenge my own children with scenarios that require critical thinking: "If you could spend this $20 on either a new video game or a week's worth of snacks, which would you choose?" This little exercise opens up their minds to weigh options, distinguishing between needs and wants, and helps them understand the pressure of financial decisions without the threat of debit card debt looming over their heads.

Don't forget to share your own tales of financial folly—yup, your embarrassing, cringeworthy money mistakes. My husband, Sims, loves recounting how he bought a "pirate ship" inflatable pool for our backyard during a moment of excitement akin to a kid in a candy store. While it sparked joy for a day, the aftermath—think about all those inflatable pieces floating in our yard like lost sailors—taught him more about the concept of buyer's remorse than any boring lecture ever could. Authentic stories can teach kids lessons that charts and graphs never will because humor allows room for understanding, leading them to think, "Hmmm, maybe I shouldn't be frivolous with money... like Dad!"

Now, let's talk about technology, because today's kids need tools that are as savvy as they are. Introduce them to budgeting apps and financial trackers that can make money management as easy as sending a Snapchat. I remember when we introduced our kids to an educational finance app, their faces lit up more than fireworks on New Year's Eve! They were clearing levels faster than a racing car in a video game and, best of all, they were learning the value of tracking their spending and saving goals without even realizing it!

Finally, make sure that passing down financial knowledge extends beyond just surface conversations. It's about fostering a lifelong relationship with money, akin to the kind of bond I have with my oversized collection of shoes (seriously, if shoes could talk!). Host family meetings where everyone can report back on their money triumphs, alternative budgeting paths, and even the occasional blunder. This provides an opportunity to experience a collective journey while iterating on lessons learned. Let's be honest, nothing brings a family together like laughing about a past financial faux pas while enjoying that secret macaroni and cheese!

In conclusion, passing down financial knowledge doesn't have to feel like a chore or bring images of dry textbooks and monotone lectures to mind. Life is filled with relatable experiences that can be transformed into valuable lessons. When we establish an engaging and funny dialogue around money, we not only prepare our children for a life of financial literacy but make our family stories richer while they do it. So let's put on our financial guru hats, forgo the boring lectures, and embark on this significantly more entertaining journey instead! Who knew imparting knowledge could be as entertaining as binge-watching the latest reality TV show? Now that's the financial legacy we should all strive for!

The Role of Community in Building a Financial Legacy

When it comes to building a financial legacy, let's not forget the unsung heroes of this journey—our community! Picture this: your financial aspirations are like a massive potluck dinner, and the community is the colorful mix of side dishes, desserts, and that one suspicious casserole nobody dares to touch. We can't help but thrive on the support and shared wisdom that surround us because let's face it, navigating the financial world without our neighbors cheering us on feels a little like running a marathon in flip-flops. There are plenty of pitfalls, and we definitely need sturdy shoes!

First off, think of community as an essential toolbox for any financial endeavor. In my experience, networking with neighbors, friends, and local organizations can yield a treasure trove of resources and information. Imagine hosting a backyard barbecue and casually discussing the ins and outs of retirement planning with the neighbor who lives to bake the cookie of knowledge! Who knew that Janice, the same lady always trying to get you to join her knitting club, would also hold financial wisdom hotter than her famous jalapeño poppers? Involving your community not only fosters relationships but also opens doors to new opportunities no one expects.

Now, community initiatives can offer financial empowerment unlike anything we can do alone. Local workshops, seminars, or classes often pop up, teaching everything from budgeting to investing in stocks. Colleagues aiming for financial independence usually host such events to encourage growth and knowledge sharing. You could waltz into an event featuring a special guest speaker who offers insights you never knew existed, like the fine art of negotiating interest rates or how to ask a bank for a better mortgage deal without sounding like a nervous penguin. Trust me, attending these events will have you walking out with both a wealth of knowledge and the oddest desire to bake something extravagant afterward!

Additionally, community involvement provides a support system that rivals your favorite social media group! Sharing struggles, successes, and occasional financial blunders with neighbors can feel refreshing. While you're sitting around your patio, sipping lemonade, why not compare stories about that one online shopping spree that went wildly off the rails? Emphasizing relatability helps break the financial taboo around discussing money, paving the way for genuine conversations. That shared laughter can help to transform the "money talk" from tension-filled to as soothing as a Spotify chill playlist you can't turn off!

Don't forget the power of collaboration! Many communities offer resources like co-ops that connect families for bulk buying. Who doesn't want to save on groceries while fostering local camaraderie? Just as we feel excited as children when we see the ice cream truck approaching, pooling resources allows families to enjoy more while spending less! Your purchasing power could rival that of a small army. It's like establishing a mini-micro-economy right in your community—and yes, you can treat yourself to ice cream without feeling guilty about those high prices!

Speaking of ice cream, mentoring is another powerful asset in building a financial legacy. Sharing experiences is like concocting a delicious sundae where everyone can feel included and tasted. Establishing mentorship programs to equip younger or less experienced community members can yield benefits for all involved! Can you picture hosting a workshop for high school students where you teach them why saving for college is cooler than spending money on the latest smartphone? Those sessions could inspire kids as future financial experts, and let's be real, it'll likely boost their appreciation for the age-old tricks of budgeting and credit scores! They might just turn into dollar-saving superstars who arm themselves with financial knowledge they pass it down to their peers.

Of course, let's not overlook the importance of supporting local businesses. As we build the community's financial legacy, it's crucial to boost sustainability! By shopping local, not only do you keep your local economy thriving, but you also get a sense of fulfillment that spells out community spirit! It's like casting our votes for economic growth and creativity while forming relationships that often lead to barter systems; I mean, who wouldn't want homemade jam for lawn mowing services, right?

In conclusion, the role of community in building a financial legacy is both inspiring and practical. Like peeling back the layers of a well-baked lasagna, the community pulls together resources, ideas, and support to nourish our financial dreams. We can weave an intricate tapestry of financial success that stretches across homes and families by fostering connections, sharing invaluable knowledge, and supporting one another's endeavors. So, let's shake hands with our neighbors, attend a few local events, and maybe even host a potluck with a side of money talk! After all, the more we involve our communities, the stronger our financial legacies will become—casseroles and all!

CHAPTER 13
TAX STRATEGIES FOR THE EVERYDAY HERO

Understanding Tax Basics: What You Need to Know

Taxes! The one thing we all must face—even more confidently than a toddler facing a broccoli. As a self-proclaimed Credit Guru, I like to think of myself as the Financial Avenger, swooping in to save the day from the evils of financial ignorance. I mean, let's face it, a good tax understanding is just as important as wearing your superhero cape when facing down debt. So, let's take a dive into the fabulous world of tax basics! This isn't just boring numbers on a piece of paper; it's the winning ticket that can keep your budget from looking like a sad, deflated balloon.

First, let's make sure we're on the same page about what taxes are. Think of taxes as a necessary, albeit annoying, contribution we make to keep our government functioning, similar to how one might feel about sharing their last slice of pizza with a friend—grudgingly necessary! We pay taxes on our income (yes, that includes that side hustle selling "vintage" Tupperware), some commodities we buy, and property we own. Each dollar funneled to taxes is intended to pay for things we all use: schools, roads, defense systems, and, of course, a hefty budget for the annual Capitol Hill office party. It's only fair.

Now that we're acquainted with taxes, let's discuss the essential tax terms that you absolutely must know—consider this the "Basic Tax Vocabulary for Dummies" section. First up, we can't avoid the word "deduction." No, it's not the latest dance move making waves at family reunions, but rather an amount you can subtract from your taxable income. Think of deductions as that magical friend who always brings dessert to a gathering—everyone loves their presence! Itemized deductions include things like mortgage interest, charitable contributions, and medical expenses. If you can correctly identify your deductions, you could save a pretty penny. Look out, because Uncle Sam isn't the only one who can hustle. Get to work on maximizing those deductions!

Next, we move on to "credits"—and let me tell you, it's not the type you receive on your credit card after a successful spendathon. Tax credits are even better! They reduce your overall tax bill dollar-for-dollar. In simpler terms, a tax credit is like winning the lottery without even having to pick numbers, and you just get handed cash at the end. Potential credits include the Earned Income Tax Credit and Child Tax Credit—so whether you're a new parent or just someone who enjoys buying children's toys for yourself, you could be eligible!

It's also vital to grasp the difference between "aggressive tax planning" and "tax evasion." The former is essentially you being smart and strategic, while the latter lands you in a really difficult-to-escape situation (think jail time and maybe a snazzy orange jumpsuit). Trust me, nobody wants to be the star of that show! Your goal here is to seek ways to legally reduce your tax bill while basking in your financial glory's rise.

Also, let's talk about filing statuses for a moment—because choosing yours may feel like a Facebook relationship status: single, married, head of household, or filing jointly. Each has its own implications, especially when it comes to your tax rate or eligibility for specific credits. There's nothing worse than realizing too late that you could've saved more if you had simply checked the right box! So, always ensure you choose your status wisely; it can save you from a financial mid-life crisis.

As tedious as tax forms may appear—look at them like you would your bizarre Aunt Betty's cat pictures. They might seem daunting and nonsensical, but once you decode the hieroglyphics, you'll find they hold the potential for savings near and dear to your heart (and wallet). Think of taxes as the proverbial game of Monopoly—navigate the board cleverly, avoid going bankrupt, and always invest in properties you can later improve for maximum returns! So, roll those dice wisely, and remember that even the IRS can't steal your fun... unless you let it!

Whether you're plotting your deductions or eyeballing those fabulous tax credits, understanding tax basics is the first step on your path to financial freedom. Taxes don't have to be all doom and gloom—they can be an adventure! So put on your superhero costume (with plenty of pockets for your tax returns) and get ready to save the day!

Deductions and Credits: Finding Hidden Money

Let's talk about deductions and credits—those magical little nuggets of financial goodness that can smooth out the rough terrain of your tax return like a good moisturizer on an overcooked turkey. It's the difference between thinking you owe the IRS a small fortune and discovering that you're entitled to a treasure chest of hidden money. I once heard that taxes are like a game of hide-and-seek: most people just think they're being hunted down by the taxman, but if you know where to look, you'll find loads of money just waiting to be claimed!

First, let's dive into deductions, which are akin to finding a fifty-dollar bill stuffed in the pocket of last year's winter coat. Imagine you're mindlessly scrolling through the news, and suddenly, BOOM—there's cash! Deductions are the amounts you can subtract from your taxable income, lowering the overall figure that Uncle Sam will have their greedy hands on. Some well-known examples include mortgage interest (ah, the sweet smell of homeownership), student loan interest (thank you, degree!), and medical expenses. If you've forked out some dollars for health-related needs—and by "health-related," I mean that time you bought ice cream to cope with your crippling existential dread—you might be eligible! Just remember to have those receipts handy, like they're an emergency stash of chocolate hidden in your desk drawer.

But let's not forget that there are two types of deductions: the standard deduction and itemized deductions. Think of the standard deduction as that steadfast friend who can be counted on to provide a shoulder to cry on but is also totally fine with binge-watching a show instead of going out. Using it is straightforward—just claim it and move on! The itemized route, however, requires a bit more effort, like trying to put together IKEA furniture without swearing under your breath. With itemized deductions, you're breaking down all those expenses line by line to justify your potential refund. Crafting your tax return like a work of art may feel tedious, but hey, if it nets you some extra cash, that's the kind of masterpiece I can support!

Now let's shimmy over to the glitzy world of credits! These are the live band playing all your favorite songs at a wedding, making everyone positively giddy. Credits are even more coveted because they reduce your tax bill dollar-for-dollar, like being handed free tacos with no strings attached. You could practically walk out of that tax season with your head held high and your pockets jingling! Two of the most common credits are the Earned Income Tax Credit (EITC) and the Child Tax Credit—perfect for people working hard to support their families. Just imagine the EITC as a financial hug that wraps around low- to moderate-income taxpayers, offering a boost that makes tax season feel a little less like a horror movie.

While diving into all this, be cautious—untamed excitement can lead to significant blunders! Whether you mistakenly forget to claim a credit or fail to gather your documentation for those deductions, inconsistency could lead to serious headaches later on, like when you tried to assemble that IKEA shelf and ended up missing parts! Make sure you have everything documented, just like you would for your Instagram influencer account—everything should look pristine and ready for the world to see!

And speaking of documentation, the elusive task of keeping records cannot be overstated. Your receipts, bank statements, and expense logs should be treated like precious artifacts. You wouldn't shove your mom's heirloom jewelry in a shoebox, would you? No, you'd keep it polished and insured! So go ahead, draft up that budget with pride, and stash it away like a dragon hoarding treasure. Remember, the better your records, the easier it will be to claim those deductions and credits, turning that sad, cold tax return into a vibrant party of possibility!

So go forth and conquer the realm of deductions and credits! Armed with this newfound knowledge, you're now prepared to find hidden money like the financial wizard you are. Whether you're laughing in the face of high tax bills or feeling the thrill of good fortune when filing your return, remember that knowledge is power—and with great power comes great responsibility (and, of course, a couple of really great tacos). The quest for financial mastery is a challenging adventure, but when you uncover those hidden treasures, you'll be glad you put in the time and effort. Happy treasure hunting, my fellow Budget Avengers!

Filing Strategies for Maximum Refunds

The quest for a maximum refund—the Holy Grail of the tax world! We've crossed the seven seas of deductions and credits and are sailing toward the glittering oasis of refunds. Picture yourself as a tax-savvy Indiana Jones; you've got your fedora on and your heart set on finding treasure buried within those complicated financial statements. But fear not, my fellow adventurers! I'm about to impart some strategic wisdom that'll have you flipping through your tax forms like they're confetti at a party. So, tighten your seatbelt and get ready for a rollercoaster of filing strategies to maximize that sweet, sweet refund!

First things first: timing is everything! When it comes to filing your taxes, you have a window of opportunity that can make or break your refund. Sure, you could procrastinate until the very last minute, only to find yourself frantically sorting through receipts like a raccoon in a dumpster. I mean, who doesn't want to experience the sheer thrill of last-minute panic? But let's be real—it's far better to file earlier. Not only does it minimize stress, but it may also catch the IRS on their toes, which might lead to a faster refund. And who doesn't want to feel like a tax ninja, stealthily slipping your tax return into their mailbox way before the rush?

Now, let's talk about maximizing those deductions. If you think about your taxes as a buffet, you're going to want to pile that plate high! The more deductions you're eligible for, your taxable income is lower. And with that, hello larger refund! Be strategic! If you've made charitable contributions—like giving your cousin's thrift shop that extra bag of clothes or donating to your favorite pet rescue—make sure you keep those receipts handy, because they count! And if you think you're missing out on something, dig deep into your memory banks (and your filing cabinet). Take a walk down memory lane, and remember things like mortgage interest or medical expenses! Every little deduction counts; you want to make the tax gods proud.

Speaking of gods, let's sprinkle some credit magic on this filing party! You wouldn't believe the number of people who overlook available credits. Seriously, it's like walking past a pile of cash and saying, "Nah, I'm good." The Earned Income Tax Credit, Child Tax

Credit, and education credits can be the parthenon of your tax filing strategy. I suggest you become best friends with the IRS website or an amazing tax software, which can pinpoint credits you may not have realized you could claim. And just a pro tip: if you've got kids, turn them into your financial sidekicks! They love being helpful and might be able to remind you of things you might have forgotten, like that summer camp expense that seemed cute but still cost an arm and a leg!

Prepare yourself for an astronomical adventure with your filing status! Choosing the right one can significantly impact your refund. Many people are oblivious to the power of the "married filing jointly" option. It's like when you realize that pairing certain foods can create a culinary masterpiece—avocado on toast, anyone? So if you're married, look at the possibility of filing jointly with your spouse to scoop up more credits and deductions than you could individually. But if you're single, never fear! The head of household could be your shining ticket to a larger refund. I mean, who doesn't love empowering titles accompanied by validation from the IRS?

Don't forget to keep those records tidy! I'm talking about a filing system that would impress even Marie Kondo. If you're a clutter-bug, I recommend grabbing some folders, coloring them, and treating them like trophies you've earned throughout the year. Breathe life into that shoebox overflowing with receipts, and establish a system. When it comes time to file, having everything at your fingertips makes it seamless! Plus, if the IRS were to play detective, they'd appreciate your attention to detail... or at least not decide to audit you for a DIY financial thriller.

And let's end with embracing the digital age! Filing taxes online is like getting your favorite fast-food meal delivered to your door—quick, easy, and probably a little greasy at times. It's smart to leverage technology to speed things up. Tax software solutions can help you navigate filing, maximize deductions, and calculate credits. Plus, these platforms often provide step-by-step guidance, and you don't have to squint and decipher if you accidentally filled out Form 1040C when you needed the 1040-A!

So there you have it. Armed with these filing strategies, you're now a certified refund-hunting ninja, ready to attack that tax return field like the fierce Budget Avenger that you are. With a little bit of timing, organization, optimization, and a whole lot of charm, you'll transform that extra tax refund into financial empowerment. Your mission? Go forth and get that refund, and may your financial future be as bright as a fireworks display in July! Happy filing!

Common Tax Mistakes: Avoiding Pitfalls

Tax season! The glorious time of year when people everywhere unleash their inner accountant, only to discover they have the financial prowess of a squirrel trying to open a nut. As a seasoned Budget Avenger, I've seen my fair share of tax mishaps, and trust me when I say avoiding these blunders can save you from unnecessary fines, headaches, and possibly even an embarrassing family dinner discussion. So, grab your sharpened pencils and maybe a cup of coffee (or a strong cocktail, your choice), as we take a light-hearted yet serious look at some common tax mistakes and how to dodge those pitfalls like a ninja on roller skates!

First up on our list of blunders: forgetting to report all of your income. You'd think this would be a no-brainer, right? Yet, somehow, people act like it's the best-kept secret, hiding income like they're concealing a poorly written diary. Listen, if you worked for it and earned it, it needs to be declared! If you tried to slip by reporting only your paycheck but forgot about your side gig selling artisanal cat sweaters on Etsy, consider this your wake-up call! The IRS has access to super-high-tech systems, and they definitely know about your income streams, whether they come from a paycheck or weird hobbies. So don't be that person trying to convince your accountant that "no, I absolutely did not get paid for those karaoke performances." They'll laugh, and then they'll probably place you on the tax "nice list" which is actually just a euphemism for "we'll be auditing you soon."

Another common blunder involves claiming deductions or credits you simply don't qualify for. This goes beyond just scouring Pinterest for tips on how to make your life look better than it is; it involves serious financial repercussions. You wouldn't walk into an exclusive club with a borrowed ID, would you? Similarly, just because you wish it were true doesn't automatically make it legit! Misrepresenting your deductions could put you head-to-head with the taxman, and there's nothing sexy about a tax audit, I assure you. Ensure you do your homework, understand eligibility requirements, and consult reliable resources instead of your cousin Larry, who once claimed he could own a private island because he found a two-dollar bill. Make sure your intentions are pure and your claims are legitimate!

Then there's the classic case of filing using incorrect information. You may be shocked to learn there's no secret tax code that allows for a creative interpretation of your Social Security number or address! So, please tell me that you aren't one of those brave souls who think numbers are interchangeable. You have a unique number, and if you use your best friend's birthday by mistake, the IRS will put you on a list faster than you can say, "auditioning for an episode of *Lost*." Take that extra moment to verify everything—your name, social security number, and bank account details. Missing one digit could leave you stranded on a desert island of confusion!

And speaking of being stranded, let's chat about procrastination. Nothing screams "I'm ready for tax season!" louder than the image of someone filing their taxes the night before they're due. It's like deciding to run a marathon without ever training—pain and regret are inevitable! You'll be scrambling to gather receipts while eating Cheetos at 2 a.m. and wondering if you should've just become a tax advisor instead. Avoid the last-minute stress and start preparing early. Stay organized! Not only will you improve your chances of a bigger refund, but you'll also be the envy of your friends and relatives when they catch wind of your diligent tax prep efforts. Consider hosting a "tax-season party" where you all gather to check off tax tasks while snacking on copious amounts of pizza and avoiding actual work! Sounds fun, right?

Now let's touch on record-keeping because, oh boy, is this one important! If you treat your receipts like they're in the witness protection program, you're going to run into trouble if you're on the ball and keep meticulous records, finding that health expense deduction will feel like scoring a touchdown in the Super Bowl. Hooray! Conversely, if you lose those receipts or fail to keep up with expenses, you may as well hand over your good old-fashioned folders to help track expenses; this will keep you from having "Lost in Receipt-land" nightmares.

Lastly, let's not forget about the dreaded confusion over filing status. For many, choosing whether to file as "single," "married," or "head of household" can be akin to choosing which flavor of ice cream to indulge in during a mid-life crisis. But trust me, picking the right filing status is crucial. It can put you in debt or bless you with a sweet refund. So take a deep breath—do some research, and get it right. You have the power!

In conclusion, navigating the tax landscape is no picnic: it can quickly become a treacherous journey. Avoiding these common tax mistakes can save your sanity and maybe even score that cherished tax refund. So, tighten those bootstraps, suit up in your best financial armor, and go forth knowing you're armed with tips to avoid any pitfalls. Let's make this tax season a victorious one! Happy filing, my financial champions!

Resources for Ongoing Tax Education

Let's kick off our exploration of ongoing tax education! You might be thinking, "Why on Earth would I want to dive deep into tax knowledge when I could binge-watch cat videos instead?" Well, dear reader, allow me to enlighten you! Tax education is like finding the "secret sauce" to transforming you into a tax-savvy superhero, minus the spandex, although I won't judge your wardrobe choices. With the right resources, you can navigate tax season with confidence, fend off fiscal predators, and occasionally throw in an eye-roll for good measure when TurboTax gets a little too "techy." So grab your explorer's hat because we're about to embark on a thrilling quest for the best tax education resources!

First and foremost, let's chat about the majestic, all-knowing Internet! Yes, it has its fair share of memes and conspiracy theories, but the web is also chock-full of invaluable financial resources. In all its governmental glory, the IRS website is a treasure trove! Here, you can find the latest tax forms, publications, and—my favorite—a glossary of tax terms that sounds like it was written by a very serious robot. While navigating the IRS site can sometimes feel like trying to read Shakespeare in another language, I assure you that sifting through this information can equip you with the tools to demystify taxes, understand regulations, and become an expert in deductions. A nifty tip? Bookmark it for quick access, especially during tax season when your last pizza delivery guy counts as a financial advisor!

You can't overlook the power of tax-focused podcasts and YouTube channels either! Yes, that's right; there are some talented tax wizards out there spreading their knowledge like peanut butter on toast. Whether you're chowing down on breakfast or ironing a shirt that you've ignored for too long, listening to tax professionals sharing their wisdom can turn mundane household chores into enlightening moments. Podcasts like "The Tax Guys" or "Tax Girl" provide a blend of humor and insight, making tax topics accessible while ensuring you chuckle at least once or twice. And YouTube is filled with charismatic tax experts who can explain provisions with the flair of a Broadway performer! Who knew taxes could be entertaining?

In addition, let's pay homage to good old-fashioned books. Yes, those delightful paper tomes still exist! You can't blame a person for wanting to avoid staring at a screen while sipping coffee, right? Take a stroll through your local bookstore or library, and you'll find a plethora of categories ranging from basic tax principles to advanced strategies for investing. Titles like *J.K. Lasser's Your Income Tax* or *Tax-Free Wealth* are amazing doorways into the vast world of taxation and are the perfect companions for your evening relaxation. Trust me; there's nothing like cuddling up with a good book while sipping a glass of wine, soaking in contingency tax methods instead of fictional drama!

Community workshops and local tax education programs are fantastic resources for ongoing understanding as well. Many communities offer free or low-cost workshops focusing on taxes, especially when tax season approaches. Local credit unions, libraries, or nonprofit organizations might host volunteers who can give you the lowdown on navigating your tax journey. Plus, these workshops often create opportunities to network with fellow taxpayers who can share their experiences, such as that one relative who always seems to land the jackpot when filing taxes (seriously, what's their secret?!) Talks over coffee can lead to insider knowledge that's just as useful as the IRS handbook, but way more fun!

Moreover, let's recognize the social media platforms, which have morphed into dynamic educational resources! Believe it or not, there's a whole world of tax professionals spilling the tea on Twitter, TikTok, and Instagram. They break down complex topics into bite-sized nuggets of information combined with witty humor and engaging visuals. Just follow the right influencers specializing in tax education, and your feeds will be filled with enlightening content that feels like a good cheat meal: satisfying and easy to digest! You'll no longer be wandering in the dark, wondering what a "Schedule C" is—you'll have a squad of financial superheroes at your fingertips.

And finally, don't forget the classic approach of finding a trusted tax professional or advisor for personalized learning! This is where you can go from knowing what a deduction is to understanding how to make it work for you, all while enjoying the comfort of a one-on-one conversation. Tax advisors are, likewise, mentors in the financial world, guiding you through the nuances of tax regulations, and they often offer educational sessions or seminars to deepen your understanding.

So, there you have it! An arsenal of resources awaits you in your quest for ongoing tax education. Whether you're tuning into podcasts, browsing through books, or attending workshops, actively seeking knowledge about taxes will empower you to tackle financial hurdles like a true Budget Avenger! Knowledge is your cape in the daunting world of taxation, and with the right resources, you'll soar confidently into the future. Happy educating, dear readers! May you forever seek wisdom and dodge tax season like a pro!

CHAPTER 14
THE ENTREPRENEURIAL MINDSET

Adopting a Winning Mindset for Financial Success

When I first stumbled into the world of finance, it felt like I had accidentally walked into a monster truck rally instead of a serene Sunday picnic. There I was, surrounded by numbers fashionably flying at me like ninja stars, the sound of calculators getting ready to rumble in the background, and alarm bells ringing every time someone mentioned "debt." It didn't take long for me to realize that the key to taming this chaos wasn't just knowing how to manipulate figures or deciphering credit terminologies. No, the real game-changer was something far more elusive: adopting a winning mindset for financial success.

Let's face it, attitude is everything! The moment I decided that I wouldn't be just another victim of financial despair but rather a superhero in my own right, things started to change. It might sound corny—like some motivational speaker's anthem—but let me tell you, the brain isn't just a sponge; it's also a powerful control center for the rest of your financial universe. And like any Marvel superhero worth their salt, I knew I had to start with a mission statement better than "Save my pennies and hope for the best." Instead, I adopted a mantra that would resonate through my entire financial life: "I am the master of my money, not the other way around!"

First and foremost, to cultivate this winning mindset, I had to kick my negative self-talk to the curb. For too long, I was that person who avoided financial discussions like dogs avoid the doorbell—getting up and running as soon as the topic even hinted at "budget." I had convinced myself that financial literacy was only for "those people" who wore suits to brunch, looked chic with briefcases, and shared PowerPoints as a hobby at their family get-togethers. Oh, how misguided I was! What I discovered was that the only difference between them and me was that I had been hiding behind my own excuses. Once I learned to smile in the face of numbers, instead of cringing in horror, my confidence began to bloom like the first flowers in spring.

Next, I realized that cultivating curiosity about money could actually be fun—who knew? I started engaging with financial concepts like I were unraveling the latest plot twists in a juicy soap opera. I turned on my detective skills and dissected the 'why' of investing, budgeting, and saving—not just the 'how.' Sure, it sometimes felt like I was deciphering ancient hieroglyphics, but hey, who doesn't enjoy a good treasure hunt? Plus, every time I cracked the code of a new financial puzzle, it was like winning an Oscar, complete with my imaginary acceptance speech. "I'd like to thank my checking account for always believing in me and, of course, my credit score, for reminding me of what could've been..."

And just when I was starting to feel like a finance ninja, reality hit me like a two-ton brick. It dawned on me that while my self-motivation was fabulous, surrounding myself with other like-minded financial enthusiasts was just as vital. Humans are social creatures, after all! So, in my quest to conquer this financial landscape, I brought along my gemstone family and pals who were equally tired of living paycheck-to-paycheck, not so much for the snacks but for the mutual spirit of being broke... together. Enter the "Financial Avengers," my trusty sidekicks who could meet every money-related dilemma with more humor than you could fit in a clown car! Together, we cheered each other on, shared ridiculous budgeting fails, and supported one another in this newfound willingness to adopt a winning mindset.

Finally, let's not forget the importance of infusing our journey with laughter. After all, life gets too serious with bills that show up like clingy exes, trying to suck the joy out of life. Whenever I faced a daunting financial task, I'd put on a superhero cape—or more accurately, a frumpy bathrobe—and remind myself that failure doesn't mean defeat; it's merely a plot twist in the epic saga of financial empowerment. The truth is, a winning mindset means allowing myself the freedom to mess up and then pivot like I just stepped on a barrel of slippery bananas!

So, as I emboldened my financial spirit, I found clarity and purpose in a place I never expected. Winning isn't just about balance sheets; it's about passion, resilience, and an undeniable belief that, like superheroes, we can all learn to harness our unique powers—including the power of a winning mindset—one swipe of a credit card at a time. So here's to us—the money warriors in pajama suits, dancing through financial challenges, and wielding our superpowers like they're hundred-dollar bills!

Overcoming Limiting Beliefs About Money

The pesky little beliefs about money that snugly burrow into our brains like unwanted guests at a party! You know the type—the ones that show up uninvited, wear their shoes on your pristine carpet, and regale you with tales of financial doom and gloom. I, too, was once a proud owner of these limiting beliefs, and oh boy, did they make my life miserable. I would lie awake at night, staring at the ceiling, imagining my credit score plunging like a contestant on a game show where the grand prize was a lifetime supply of ramen noodles. If only I had known then what I do now: that these beliefs were nothing more than lies I had told myself.

To kick things off, let's take a moment to acknowledge the classic limiting beliefs that plague many unsuspecting souls. You know, the real knee-slappers, like "money doesn't grow on trees" or "rich people are just lucky." As they ricochet around our minds, they create a fog so dense that we can't see the financial opportunities lying right in front of us, waving their hands and chanting, "Pick me! Pick me!" The reality is, I had to dislodge these notions before I could shift my relationship with money into high gear. It was time to start pulling weeds out of my financial garden, rather than just sprinkling some water on them and hoping for a miracle.

One day, as I was sipping my morning coffee (the nectar of the gods), I had an epiphany while staring into my cup. I realized that limiting beliefs about money had the same validity as a spaghetti monster lurking under my bed—totally fictitious! This was my moment of clarity, stronger than a double espresso. Just because I had grown up hearing my parents fret about bills didn't mean I had to perpetuate that cycle! Instead, I could rewrite my money script, filling it with comedic adventures and superhero triumphs rather than the same tired old lines of despair. Sounds amazing, right? Just picture me, cape billowing in the breeze, standing atop a mountain of financial knowledge with a megaphone, shouting, "I AM IN CHARGE HERE!"

Over time, I put myself through a crash course in overcoming these thoughts—sometimes by sheer force of will, other times by sheer denial (you know, the good old "I refuse to engage with that nonsense" strategy). I started engaging with money mindfully. I'd catch myself thinking, "I'll never be able to afford that," and quickly counter it with "I can create a plan that allows me to afford it!" I mean, if you've ever tried to convince yourself that buying a luxury car is out of reach, only to watch your neighbor's dog wear a diamond-studded collar, you'll understand how ridiculous that is! Let's focus on reality: money isn't a villain; it's a tool—an extension of our power, if you will.

Additionally, I learned to rewire my brain to view money as a game rather than a battleground. Instead of endlessly chasing after "more" and becoming a money-motivated monster, I embraced the joy of making strategic moves to reach financial goals. Think of it as Monopoly—but without the betrayal and sibling rivalry. I took the time to celebrate my little victories, whether it was a successful budget or actually remembering to put gas in the car without breaking the bank at the pump. I would dance around the living room, channeling my inner Beyoncé, shouting, "I am a financial champion!" It was as if I had been reborn like a butterfly emerging from a cocoon, only this butterfly was adorned in cashmere and had a killer portfolio.

I also tuned into affirmations because, if I was going to alter my belief system, I might as well do it with some flair! I slapped sticky notes with messages like "Richness isn't just a number, it's a mindset!" on my bathroom mirror. So, every morning while brushing my teeth, I'd gaze into my sparkling, toothpaste-smeared reflection and remind myself that yes, I could manifest abundance just like I could manifest edible leftovers from my refrigerator. And isn't that the dream?!

In the end, overcoming these limiting beliefs was less about who had the biggest pile of cash and more about discovering the potential already festering in my soul. I found freedom in smashing those self-imposed walls into bits. I became a resilient money warrior, charging relentlessly through negativity like a bull through a china shop—only with a bit more grace and a lot less broken crockery. So, tell those pesky beliefs to take a hike! Let's blaze our own financial trails, buy our own financial kaleidoscopes, and watch the world transform and unveil before us in a whirlwind of prosperity, laughter, and maybe a little bling-blings for good measure. After all, who wouldn't want a touch of sparkle while navigating the exhilarating journey of life?

Goal Setting: From Dreams to Achievable Targets

Goal setting—going from dreamy "what ifs" to actionable "heck yeahs!" You know, life is a lot like a buffet. You can't just stare bewildered at the spread of options and hope someone brings you the mashed potatoes. No, my friends, you must take the initiative, grab a plate, and start serving. I used to think that goal setting was as intimidating as trying to fold a fitted sheet (seriously, who can ever get that right?). Still, I found out that setting goals can be refreshingly simple—and sometimes, downright amusing!

Initially, when I thought about my financial dreams, they felt as useful as a chocolate teapot—exquisite, yet entirely impractical. I would daydream about lavish vacations in remote islands, the kind where the cocktails flow faster than my bank account could ever keep up. But I had one major flaw: my dreams floated like fluffy clouds in the sky without any substantial foundation beneath them. I realized it was time to turn those airy fantasies into tangible targets, much like a suspenseful movie plot, where they rise from the ashes for the "Avengers Assemble" moment.

First, I had to start small—baby steps were a must! Instead of vowing to become a millionaire overnight (also known as planning to take an extraordinary leap into the realm of the absurd), I began with practical, bite-sized goals that wouldn't send me careening down a mountain of regret. These were not your average run-of-the-mill, "save a dollar a month" aspirations, either. No, I decided to set radical targets like "save enough for a spa day" or "invest in a tornado of experiences rather than just things." Honestly, the thought of basking in a massage while listening to soothing music made those faster-paced life goals feel like candy-coated chocolate. Who wouldn't want that?

Next, I infused my goal-setting journey with the power of humor. It was all fun and games until I realized I was half-serious about my goal of owning a llama (an actual llama, people!). Instead of retreating to "realistic" territory, I decided to scale it down to "own a well-groomed houseplant." Ah, yes, the exotic houseplant, the ultimate goal that requires minimal responsibility and maximum bragging rights! This creativity led me to intertwine fun with practicality, making the whole goal-setting fiasco far less overwhelming than standing in line at the DMV on a Monday morning.

While I crafted my goals, I discovered the significance of the SMART framework (or as I like to call it, the "Super Marvelous Achievable Realization Template"). It's basically a fancy way of saying that goals should be Specific, Measurable, Achievable, Relevant, and Time-bound. Think of it as molding a pancake with a unicorn-shaped cookie cutter; you want it to be cute, yet functional! Instead of "I want to save money," I refined it to "I will save $50 a month for the next six months for a spectacular, Instagram-worthy getaway to the beach." Plus, "beach" just has a more sensational vibe than "staring at the wall in my living room." As soon as I framed the goal, it felt like creating a treasure map, marking "X" for every little victory along the way.

Let's not forget accountability—it's an essential ingredient in this recipe. I enlisted my family and friends to hop on the goal-setting bandwagon with me. Together, we became the "Dream Team of Financial Awesomeness." We met regularly, like a support group with a twist of fabulousness, where we cheered each other on, asked about our progress, and even concocted silly bets to push ourselves further. I mean, there's nothing quite like the exhilarating rush of having to do the cha-cha in a grocery store if you dare fail to stick to your budget! Picture it—a whole food aisle vibrating to the rhythm of my poorly executed dance moves, all because I chose to tempt fate instead of sticking to my plan. It was worth the giggles!

And finally, as I continued down the road of goal setting, I learned to celebrate my wins, no matter how small. After all, even a tiny bit of accomplishment deserves a parade! Each month's savings led to another thrilling photo before jetting off to that imaginary beach, even if the only sand I was lounging on was in the litter box. Those moments filled me with joy, and I rewarded myself with treats like ice cream, a new book, or, you guessed it, a random llama-related item from the magical world of online shopping!

So, my fellow aspiring budget avengers, the secret to conquering that daunting realm of goal setting is a mix of delight, strategy, and creativity. Break those dreams down, turn the mundane into the whimsical, and approach them with as much laughter as you can muster. Trust me, you'll never look back once you treat your financial goals like a funky carnival ride—amusing, slightly disorienting, yet totally exhilarating. Together, we can navigate this journey of goals like the wizards we are, twinkling stars in our eyes, armed with dreams, and eagerly chasing every silly llama we can find along the way. Onward, my dream-chasers!

Embracing Risk: The Power of Taking Chances

Risk—the notorious friend in the room that most people pretend to ignore like a karaoke enthusiast belting out show tunes at a formal dinner party. When I first ventured into the world of finance and entrepreneurship, I thought risk was the villain of the story, lurking in dark corners, sowing chaos like an over-caffeinated squirrel with a penchant for mischief. But as I grew wiser (and maybe just a tad less terrified), I realized that embracing risk was not only necessary for financial success; it was an exhilarating rollercoaster ride that added joy, thrill, and a sprinkle of "what on Earth was I thinking?" to my journey.

Let's face it: most folks view risk as a one-way ticket to financial ruin. I used to think the best way to avoid taking risks was to hoard my pennies and play it safe, like a conservative tortoise peeking out from its shell. The truth hit me, however, like a nail gun at a carpenter convention: life's biggest rewards come when we take those brave leaps forward. It's like the person who dares to taste a fried cricket at a state fair. Yes, you could end up spitting it out while making horrified faces, but what if, just what if, you discover that it's actually… not half bad? That tiny act of bravery could lead you down a path of endless possibilities, perhaps including a lucrative side business selling cricket-flavored snacks! Okay, maybe not the best example, but you catch my drift.

The first time I purposely stepped out of my comfort zone was when I decided to invest in my own business. At the time, the idea terrified me more than binge-watching an entire season of a detective show where I was 90% sure the butler was the culprit. But I realized that without risks, there would be no rewards. With the love and support of my family, who supposedly enjoy my company even when I'm contemplating my financial choices, I made the plunge. And let me tell you, the thrill of seeing my business take off felt like I had just discovered the true meaning of freedom, like when you finally find the TV remote that had been lost in the couch cushions for three weeks!

But of course, not all risks lead to glorious victory. Along the way, I encountered my fair share of setbacks that would tremble even the stoutest hearts. It felt like a reality TV show episode where the main character had to endure chaotic challenges, only to stumble upon compulsory cooking with rubber chickens as a twist. But, as I discovered, we become beautifully resilient in these moments of apparent failure. I decided instead of wallowing in pity like a sad puppy who just lost a game of fetch, I'd sit down, eat a slice of pizza (because pizza cures all), and examine what went wrong. Those instances proved to be learning experiences, full of humor and wisdom, the kind of nuggets you could serve up over coffee with friends who continually ask, "What was that about rubber chickens again?"

In embracing risk, I also learned the critical skill of assessing my decisions. You know that feeling of realizing that your backseat-driven companion is a bit too eager with their "go for it" attitude? I avoid making impulsive choices like buying a car that shouts "sports model" while my bank account whispers "grocery budget," a delicate dance of financial sanity. I have grown fond of weighing my options and asking myself, "What's the worst that could happen?" – a mantra that has become as uplifting as a motivational cat poster. Making informed decisions helps me sift through what would be a risky venture versus an overly ambitious faceplant.

Another reason to embrace risk: it encourages growth, not just in your bank account, but also in your character! Stepping into the unknown often transforms us into fabulously confident versions of ourselves. Every risk I took felt like launching a new flight on a paper airplane. Sure, sometimes my trajectory was rattled by prevailing winds, but other times, I soared high into the clouds, eliciting "ooohs" and "aahs" from the admiring crowd. And those delightful moments of unexpected success—that's where you find your financial superpower! What happens, my friends, when you start taking those leaps? Suddenly, you wake up, look in the mirror, and realize you've turned into a "can-do" machine. You start seeing opportunities where others see obstacles, distinctly hearing the whimsical music score in the backdrop as you confidently glide forward.

So, as I sit here spilling the beans about embracing risk, spreading financial cheer with giggles, I say this: life is too short to shack up with safety and avoid the fantasies of what could be! Risks were not meant to be feared like villainous soap opera characters; they were designed to be tackled with the finesse of a ballerina – elegant and brave, simultaneously! So, invest wisely, pursue passions, and leap fearlessly into the great unknown. You never know—the immense delight waiting on the other side may turn your life into an adventure worthy of a blockbuster sequel! Now, let's go make some fabulous financial memories that'll have us laughing over pizza for years to come!

Learning from Failures and Pivoting for Success

Failures—the kindred spirit of every entrepreneur! Picture them as that unwanted guest at a dinner party, who arrives uninvited but somehow manages to suck up all the air in the room while regaling the crowd with tales of their spectacular flops. Once upon a time, I thought failures were the end of the line—a dark tunnel of despair with no light at the end, like being lost in the aisles of IKEA without a map. But as I embarked on my financial journey, I soon discovered that failures are not just brick walls; they are actually pesky speed bumps, crafted to make us laugh (eventually) while nudging us toward success.

Let's take a nostalgic trip down memory lane, shall we? I vividly recall my first foray into entrepreneurship—a fabulous plan that revolved around creating a gourmet dog treat business. I fancied myself a culinary genius, firing up the oven and channeling my inner Martha Stewart. I whipped up delectable peanut butter biscuits that would make any Pooch drool. But did I mention I mixed up the salt and sugar? That's right—there's nothing quite like presenting your products to a group of half-hearted customers who politely nibbled on what tasted like devilish paperweights with sprinkles. Talk about a flop! To make matters worse, I ended up with furiously barking pups creating a scene as though they had just been betrayed by Sir Mix-a-Lot himself.

Instead of curling up in a ball and declaring that I'd never bake again, I embraced this culinary catastrophe as an opportunity for growth. With a delivery of strength reminiscent of a plot twist in a daytime soap opera, I began dissecting my failure. What went wrong? Was it merely poor ingredient selection? Or perhaps my charismatic marketing couldn't counteract the culinary horrendousness of a dog's worst nightmare? I jotted down lessons learned and ensured that I wouldn't repeat that salty blunder. So, I pivoted, refocused my mission, and began exploring the world of human-style, dog-friendly treats that actually tasted pretty darn good. Who knew that mint-flavored biscuits could be a hit when sprinkled with love, attention, and a sleigh of witty marketing?

With each subsequent venture, I realized that failures come gift-wrapped with invaluable life lessons. They're like those hidden compartments in furniture where people stash their valuables—it takes some digging to find the gems. If you don't trip up occasionally, you'll miss out on discovering something truly wonderful. So, I embraced failure with open arms and started looking for patterns. Every time I stumbled, I picked myself up, brushed off the imaginary dirt, and asked, "What else can I learn? How can I turn this into a moving forward?" I playfully dubbed it "the art of graceful falling," like a clumsy dance that only I could perform with majesty!

Then came the realization that failure is all about perspective. You may view it as a dead-end street, but what if it's actually a detour to someplace magical? I began to treat every setback as a comical plot twist, where the cock-eyed hero finds themselves in ludicrous predicaments and somehow emerges victorious. When I once lost track of time and missed a client meeting because I was engrossed in a riveting episode of a reality show about competitive foam sculpting, I realized that instead of panicking, I could simply own up to it, laugh about the hilarity of my choices, and reschedule while bringing a bouquet of foam flowers as an icebreaker.

But knowing it's all about perspective doesn't mean the journey is ever simple, oh no! With each pivot comes the necessary courage to embrace change, and change can feel just as jarring as a surprise jolt in a horror movie. Balancing ambition and inventive strategies often leads to moments that make you ponder, "What have I gotten myself into?" Yet, if you treat each pivot as a grand adventure—like leaping off a cliff and sprouting wings mid-fall—the fear becomes invigorating instead of paralyzing. I began exploring fresh ideas, experimenting like a mad scientist, and surrounding myself with cheerleaders who lifted me even when my own faith waned. After all, even the fiercest warriors need a squad!

As I journeyed through various entrepreneurial adventures, I kept collecting "failure trophies"—I still channel some inspiration from that ill-fated dog treat launch—but this time, it's a framed picture hanging proudly in my office. It acts as a whimsical reminder that the pathway to success is as unpredictable as an amusement park ride; there will be ups, downs, and sometimes even loop-de-loops that leave you breathless.

So remember, dear reader, that failures are but stepping stones along the journey filled with laughter and lessons. Don't shy from tripping over obstacles; embrace them, learn, and smile. When life serves you a dodgy plate of salt-laden dog treats, don't just toss them away—transform them into something spectacular! After all, life is the ultimate comedy, and you, my friends, are the stars of your show. Every time you stumble, take that chance to look around, laugh at the absurdity, and show up as the witty comeback kid—a magnificent blend of brave adventurer and savvy entrepreneur. Strap in, hold on tight, and get ready to pivot your way towards success!

CHAPTER 15
RAISING MONEY-SAVVY KIDS

Why Financial Literacy Matters for Kids

Financial literacy isn't just for adults with graying hair and a mountain of bills to pay—oh no, my friends! It's crucial for our kiddos too. You wouldn't let your child run a race without teaching them how to tie their shoelaces, right? So why on Earth would we let them venture into the wild world of adulthood without understanding money? I mean, have you seen what happens to folks once they step into the boots of financial responsibility? If you haven't, let me tell you, it's like watching a scene from a horror movie, with wild-eyed people clutching their credit cards like they're golden tickets to the financial theme park of doom.

Now, let's dive into why this matters. First and foremost, teaching kids about financial literacy is equipping them with survival skills for a world that's designed to perpetually say, "Surprise! You owe another bill!" Whether it's credit cards, mortgages, or those pesky little subscription services that eat away at your bank account while you binge-watch another cooking show, these are all topics that kids need to grasp before they can say, "Can I have another slice of pizza?" Knowing how to manage money effectively will help them make conscious choices rather than ending up as the unsuspecting victims of financial vampires—those baffling, breathy monsters that lurk around every corner, whispering, "Just one more purchase."

Can you imagine sending your kid to college without a clue about how debt works? It's like sending a deer into the headlights of a speeding truck! They'd graduate not only with a degree but also with a three-ton boulder called student loans strapped to their back, wobbling like a toddler trying to walk. Imagine them on graduation day, tossing their cap in the air, only to feel the crushing weight of their financial future come crashing down like a bad sitcom episode. Kids need to learn not just the difference between a debit card and a credit card, but also that budgeting doesn't mean sacrificing joy! It means knowing that one must save smartly before diving into spontaneous late-night trips to Taco Bell!

You might be thinking to yourself, "But Tumeka, how on Earth do I teach my little darlings about finances without boring them to tears?" Easy peasy! Start young! Make it fun! Why not introduce a pretend play game called "Baby Shark's Budgeting Bonanza"? This involves ruling the fridge and creating shopping lists for snacks while discussing the budget. You can throw in quirky financial terms, picnic-style! "Well, lil' Jenna, you can buy the gummy bears for our movie night; however, that means no more ice-cream while we play Monopoly, and we all know how 'monopoly money' doesn't help with groceries!" That way, they'll learn that making choices can be both fun and educational.

Let's not forget the social aspect! Financial skills will build a solid foundation for teamwork and collaboration. Teaching children how to set goals together—like saving up for a family trip to Disneyland—is not just about money; it's a bonding experience! Picture this: your kids huddled together, cutting coupons or setting up a lemonade stand while practicing their sales pitch: "Get your refreshing lemonade here! It's sweeter than grandma's hugs! Pay in cash or risk sharing the flavor of a credit score!" Just imagine the chuckles and the valuable lessons that come with it—where mixed math skills are learned, and common sense is honed through actual practice.

Lastly, let's talk about societal impact. As family money gurus, we have to recognize that financial literacy extends beyond our own little ones. When kids learn about finance now, they grow into responsible adults who are less likely to contribute to the cycles of debt and financial despair plaguing society. They can emerge as bright superheroes of fiscal responsibility, casting light in a world where overspending has become the norm. I can just visualize my grandkids' future; they'll be the shining examples for their peers, turning budgeting into a trend like avocado toast.

So, all of the arguments come down to this: teaching your kids about financial literacy is not just a good idea; it's a fantastic investment in their future—a future where a credit score is more than just a number at the bottom of a report; it's a symbol of freedom, opportunity, and yes, a lifetime supply of Taco Bell adventures without any regret!

Age-Appropriate Money Lessons

When it comes to teaching our children about money, there's only one rule you need to remember: age-appropriate lessons are key. Yes, nobody wants to crash-land into any deep financial philosophies when your kid is still in their dinosaur phase—although, believe me, some might think opposing raptors are better with a budget than some adults! Teaching kids about money should be as fun as letting them run with a pack of puppies that don't bite back. The trick here is to toss aside the adult-sounding jargon and make everything relatable, like turning a boring math class into an exhilarating game show episode.

Let's start small, shall we? If you're the proud parent of a toddler who's still mastering the fine art of identifying each color in the crayon box, you can gift them a piggy bank—yes, the classic! Your kid will see this wonderful, often cartoonishly designed bank as a beloved friend that eats their precious coins instead of just being a metal box that reverts savings to its original state (like turning snacks into a calorie count—major bummer). Catch their attention by calling it a "treasure chest" and explain that every shiny coin is one step closer to their own personal treasure map, which I assume can lead them to a mountain of candy.

As they grow and enter the realm of elementary school, dive into basic budgeting lessons while allowing them to control a modest allowance. This could entail teaching them to say, "Hold on! I can't get that trampoline until I save, because a trampoline is a BIG DEAL!" Plus, make it interactive! Set goals with them, like saving for that colossal bouncy castle, and watch the excitement as they cycle between choices and consequences. Nothing says "financial literacy" louder than seeing your child eagerly counting their coins with a fierce determination that rivals true athleticism. This moment's critical for their future, trust me. They learn that being responsible with money means they won't end up at a birthday party without their very own bouncy castle.

Now, transition them into that delightful middle school age where they can grasp the concept of wants versus needs and realize that cereal isn't just a glorious breakfast; it also comes with a price! At this stage, mount the challenge of understanding the beauty of saving versus spending, just as if you kindly introduced them to the craziness of watching bills pile up faster than socks in a dryer. Encourage them to set up a mini business, like a car wash for the neighbors, which is basically a creative way of saying "Let's wash your dad's old, rust bucket and charge him $5.50 while soaking your best friend's shoes." Here's where they can learn the inflated value of a quarter, along with the spectacular art of negotiation.

As your financial little warriors transition into high schoolers, things start to get a bit more serious. They need to know what a credit score is—and heaven forbid if they still think it's a cool math game! It's time to brush up on bank statements, credit cards, and the glorious world of interest rates. Suppose they aren't ready for the serious-sounding financial lingo. In that case, simple games like Monopoly (not the one where you constantly get sent to jail) can become a crash course in real estate, allowing them to see the glamorous life of owning properties versus landing face-first into bankruptcy! The more you engage them in real-life discussions about finances, whether it's family budgeting for vacations or discussing high-stakes decisions like "Should we buy that ridiculous inflatable flamingo?"— the better they grasp those financial lessons.

Around these times, equipping them with earnings from part-time jobs or side hustles is imperative. They'll learn the hard truth: not every penny is going to come from the tooth fairy. Encourage them to put a percentage of their income into savings (and let them feel fancy about their "emergency fund" while avoiding that "emergency" pizza order). Throw in some light-hearted reminders about taxes or monthly bills, perhaps with silly stickers—after all, nothing creates a memorable lesson like visual aids with cartoons attached!

At every age, meet them where they are, and sprinkle in financial wisdom while avoiding the more terrifying adult reality for as long as you can. And observe that money conversations can be entertaining and jovial instead of fraught with seriousness. If your young ones can learn about money in a way that resonates, they'll be well on their way to becoming financially savvy adults who don't get puzzled looking at their first pay stub. They won't just avoid being that friend who asks, "Wait, credit cards need to be paid back?"—because they'll have been schooled by the Budget Avenger (that's me, just in case you forgot!), sparking the next generation of fearless financial crusaders!

Getting Kids Involved in Budgeting

Budgeting—the magical world where numbers come together to help you figure out how to pay for both grandma's birthday present and your kid's obsession with the latest superhero toy that's inevitably going to be tossed into a corner and forgotten within a week. Getting kids involved in budgeting can seem like tackling the world's largest pizza; it's messy and a little uncomfortable, but the rewards are totally worth it! Just imagine how proud your mini-me will feel being involved in the adult-ish world of budgeting—it's the mental version of wearing socks with sandals, but eventually, it somehow becomes trendy!

The first step toward inviting your kids into the budgeting fold is to show them it's not some boring exercise in constraint. You've got to jazz it up! Kids aren't blind; they see the nuances of the world, from the joy of ice cream to the hair-pulling agony of those credit card statements. Make budgeting an adventure! Present it as a treasure hunt: "Your money is our map, and it's leading us to find the best deals, saving us coins for a rainy day, or in our case—saving up for that deluxe family trip to the aquarium where they'll witness the biggest fish flopping enthusiastically for the crowd!" This way, they'll engage in the process rather than thinking of it as some punishment system enforced by their arch-nemesis, also known as 'The Parent'.

When it comes to creating a budget, don't just draw up spreadsheets and keep all that valuable information to yourself: Involve your kids. Break down methods like "50-30-20" into kid-friendly versions, where 50% goes to fun and treats (yeah, that means the extra-large pizza), 30% goes to savings, and the remaining 20% can tackle future investments—aka, the latest action figure they'll need for their next caught-in-the-crossfire superhero battle. They'll learn that budgeting isn't just about saying "no" to fun but rather finding a balance between their desires and responsibilities.

Now, let's spice things up with some gamification, folks! Who does not want to turn budgeting into a game where your kid can win and lose? Set up a fun competition, akin to "Survivor: Budgeting Edition." Lay down some ground rules—such as earning pointable rewards for budgeting wins, like successfully sticking to the grocery list or showcasing imaginative skills while scavenging for discount coupons. You could even involve family members in this hilarious show of budgeting prowess. Just picture this: "Momma Jinks wins the sparse trophy for saving from that super-fluffy yet overpriced pillow!" Suddenly, budgeting becomes important, and everyone has their role, like a cast member in a financially savvy sitcom!

And guess what? Letting your kids fail is vital—yes, you read that right! Imagine letting your child "overspend" their allowance instead of saving for their desired electronic toy. This is the moment for gentle guidance! It'll teach them through experience how spending beyond their means leaves them without the new things they actually wanted. Don't worry, they'll learn real fast that money disappears faster than their favorite shows on Netflix. As they come to understand their financial decisions, they'll start thinking, "Hmm, maybe buying five coffees in one week isn't sustainable, even for my 'business' where I sell friendship bracelets!"

Moreover, as they hold their budgeting reins, they steer their focus towards real-world expenses. Take them grocery shopping alongside you and let them weigh the merits of buying organic bananas versus regular ones. Do they want to chip in by saving money as a family? As you open the conversation, you'll lead them to realize that budgeting is all about power and choice. They could become the maestro of finances that enables the family to eat healthier, and ensure they have enough leftover to cover Saturday's special movie night. Talk about learning by doing! They'll develop a keen sense of value early on.

Last but not least, celebrate your kid's budgeting achievements—because every victory deserves to be recognized! Dramatically award them the "Budgeting Superstar of the Month" trophy, complete with confetti and a cheesy ceremony. Whether it's a high-five when they keep expenditures under budget or just getting praise for being diligent, positive reinforcement goes a long way in cementing their understanding of money management. Over time, they'll grow into financial warriors, equipped with skills that help them tackle the adulting world without the anxiety of being caught off guard by a surprise bill, because they've been practicing since their innocence!

So, my fellow Budget Avengers, let's make budgeting a family affair! Together, we can turn budgeting pitfalls into priceless life lessons for our little financial heroes—one pizza and coupon at a time!

The Importance of Saving from a Young Age

Saving money—the adulting lesson that often feels like trying to convince a toddler to let go of a half-eaten lollipop. No one wants to give up the instant gratification of spending those hard-earned coins on a shiny new toy or the latest trendy gadget, especially when their friends brag about having the coolest stuff. But let me tell you, teaching our children about saving from a young age is like giving them a compass for life—a glorious compass that can guide them through the thicket of financial mismanagement. Plus, let's be real: no one wants to be that adult who still has to beg their parents for help after budget mistakes could leave them binge-watching cooking shows in debt!

So why is saving important? Well, picture this scenario: your adorable 7-year-old wants a new bike. They have their heart set on it, but you quickly toss in, "How about we save up to get the ultimate racing bike of your dreams?" Suddenly, they are facing an epic adventure—saving for something substantial rather than impulsively buying just any bike that comes along. It's like discovering a hidden treasure chest underneath your couch, packed with old coins! Teaching them how saving allows them to afford larger, more gratifying purchases leads to the mental realization that not every penny needs to be spent right away. They'll learn that life is not just a rollercoaster of instant gratification; instead, it's also about worthwhile, long-term goals that come with the waiting game—this is where the real wins occur!

Can we take a moment to appreciate the absolute thrill of watching your children save their allowance for weeks just so they can buy that elusive item they've been drooling over? It's captivating! Kids can begin to understand the satisfaction of delayed gratification by experiencing it firsthand. So when that magical day arrives, and they finally hand over that perfectly counted stack of bills for their long-coveted treasure, you can bask in the glow of their achievement. They'll experience that sweet, sweet joy of reward; it's the ultimate sugar rush without a sticky mess to clean up! They might even stop and ask you, "Is this how American Express feels when they say, 'Don't leave home without it'?" Now there's a word about saving they'll never forget!

Next, let's not forget the rookie mistake many young savers tend to make: forgetting their savings exist. It's like kids holding a cookie in front of them, totally forgetting there's a room full of other cookies waiting to be devoured. Regularly checking on their savings and goals helps paint a clearer picture of progress. It transforms their saving efforts into an exciting project with tangible milestones! Try keeping a colorful chart or a goal thermometer on the wall where they can add stickers as they save up from their allowance. One sticker equals a little chip towards that shiny bike! It becomes an educational family art project and truly joyful as they see the thermometer bursting with colors like a bottle of soda shaken too hard before opening.

Now, to sprinkle in a dash of humor, let's just admit that saving can become a bit of a family affair! Create a competition between siblings. Whoever can save the most money or sticker count at the end of the month earns a homemade trophy or a fun night out. I mean, who wouldn't want to strut around the house with the title "Saving Princess" gleaming on their proud little heads? You'll find yourself facing a frantic rush at the dinner table filled with wildly fluctuating tables—both pasta and savings might end up in a chaotic dance, but foster a little sibling rivalry! Just ensure it stays light-hearted; the only thing flying around the room is positive energy and support!

And let's not skip the inevitable lesson about emergencies. As kids grow older and begin to understand the complexities of life, help them create a mini-emergency fund of their own. Let them know that saving isn't just about purchasing; it's also about preparing for the unexpected, like a surprise pizza party or finding out the car's engine went bonkers! With good ol' pandemic vibes still lingering in our memories, they'll appreciate the importance of digging deep to cover unplanned expenses without covertly raiding their piggy banks.

In conclusion, instilling the importance of saving from a young age empowers our kids with financial awareness that sets them up for life! It'll help them create that strong financial foundation to build their dreams on, and the thrill of that bike waiting to be ridden will surpass anything they hurriedly bought along the way. In their lives, they'll have the wisdom to differentiate between "want" and "need," and a savings account will become their ultimate ally rather than a distant fantasy! So let's create the next generation of savers, educators, and superheroes who remember to value every penny, one glittery sticker at a time!

Encouraging Philanthropy and Financial Responsibility

Alright, my fabulous fellow Budget Avengers, let's dive into the importance of teaching our kids about philanthropy and financial responsibility! You might be thinking, "Philanthropy? Isn't that just a fancy term for giving money to rich people to look good in front of cameras?" Well, I'm here to deliver the truth sandwiched between two slices of fun—it's so much more than that. Teaching kids the art of giving while being financially responsible sets them up for life. It transforms them into little superheroes ready to tackle any financial challenge while also spreading kindness like confetti at a parade!

First off, let's talk about why it's essential to introduce the concept of giving. View it as nurturing a sense of social awareness that, ironically, our self-absorbed screens often neglect to teach. We live in a world where our kids are bombarded with flashy commercials tempting them to buy the next coolest gadget or wear the trendiest sneakers. But let's be real; how often do they get that warm, fuzzy feeling of actually making a difference? Imagine the impact of channeling those "I want" desires into "I can" initiatives! Encourage them to donate part of their allowance to a cause close to their heart—whether it's supporting animals, education, or saving the octopus in that cool aquarium. It enables children to grasp the idea that their dollars can create waves of change, no matter how small.

Now, let's spice up philanthropy with creative projects! I'm talking about turning the process of giving into a family bonding affair that everyone will find delightful. Want to build a little compassionate camaraderie? Start a family charity jar! You can designate a specific percentage of each person's allowance to drop into this jar. Then, make a family meeting out of it every month, complete with plenty of snacks, to discuss where to send that treasure. Picture it—a cozy living room filled with laughter, as everyone realizes that they are making a collective difference in the world! The joy of presenting their chosen charity with their hard-earned funds will be a memory they cherish. Plus, let's not forget how a well-placed snack can sweeten any deal!

Speaking of memories, here's a hilarious nugget of wisdom: host a "When Life Gives You Lemons" lemonade stand! If your kids are itching to save for something special, encourage them to host their own stand with a thrilling twist—50% of the profits go into their savings jar, and the other half can be donated to a local cause! It's like the ultimate party where everyone walks away with smiles, a refreshing beverage, and a feeling of goodwill! Plus, what kid doesn't enjoy squeezing lemons and yelling out, "Lemonade for sale!" at the top of their lungs—only to see an old neighbor look amused while pretending not to hear? It's a win-win scenario all around!

As they grow more connected with philanthropy, don't shy away from discussing the lighter side of finances and responsibilities. Create fun financial challenges! For every amount saved towards their goals (let's say a new skateboard or a gaming console), they can add an additional increment to their donation fund. As they get more room to wiggle their philanthropic wings, they can realize that giving does not always have to come at the expense of their desires. They could end up supporting fellow whiz kids trying to achieve the same flashiness themselves!

While we're on that delightful path, let's instill the concept of budgeting part of their allowance for charitable giving. Teach them to create a mini-budget that includes "Every Little Counts." If they budget $10 monthly, explain that it accumulates over the year. Soon, they'll see how their financial responsibility plus their desire to give transforms into a mighty force of goodness! They'll witness the magical combination of caring for their own needs while also looking beyond their circle of self-interest. It's like wearing a superhero cape while carrying a bag of groceries—getting things done with style!

Finally, instill the value of consistent giving. Make it easy for them to understand that giving doesn't have to be a bank-breaking endeavor. Involve them in family volunteering days where they are giving back to their community instead of buying the latest toy. Let them see the joy in helping others, whether it's organizing a beach cleanup or wrapping gifts for families in need during the holidays. They'll experience the rewarding feeling that comes with helping people up close and personal, forming a lifelong habit of compassion that resonates far beyond a single contribution.

So, dear readers, empowering our kids with the principles of philanthropy and financial responsibility can be both enlightening and wonderfully entertaining! Let's strive to cultivate a generation that not only knows how to save and invest but also embraces the joy of giving. By planting those seeds early, we help them create a cornucopia of kindness, financial awareness, and significance in their lives, preparing them to spread waves of compassion. At the same time, they navigate the exciting journey of adulthood. Because, let's face it, life is much sweeter when you can share it with others.

CHAPTER 16
FINANCIAL FREEDOM THROUGH COMMUNITY

The Importance of Community in Financial Growth

Community. It's one of those words that conjures up images of neighborhood barbeques, group hikes, and (let's be honest here) awkward potlucks where that one lady always brings fruit salad with marshmallows. Gross! But here's the kicker: community is not just about sharing stale pizza and complaining about your property taxes. Nope! It's way juicier than that—it's an underappreciated engine of financial growth that can supercharge your journey toward debt-free bliss!

Let's face it, folks, when you're navigating the treacherous waters of personal finance, having a solid crew around you makes all the difference. Remember that one time you tried to assemble an IKEA furniture piece, and somehow, it turned into a modern art installation? That's life without a support system—chaotic! But when you have a community to lean on, even the hardest financial battles feel like child's play. Your neighbors, friends, and fellow financial warriors can provide insights, encouragement, and occasionally pizza (the non-fruit salad kind) when all else fails!

But how does this transformed support system become a goldmine for your financial growth? Well, let me spill the beans. First off, we all know that money can be a bit of a lonely business. You work hard, keep your credit score as pristine as an untouched slice of cake, but honestly, who wants to sip that financial tea alone? By reaching out to your community, you create an accountability network. Want to save more? Join a savings challenge with your pals. Can't figure out how to invest? Have a community book club that tackles finance-related reads! Having a partner (or ten) can make all that brain crunching a lot less daunting.

And don't even get me started on the treasure trove of resources just waiting to be discovered! Your community is brimming with knowledge and expertise. It's like having a personal library full of characters who have overcome financial struggles themselves. Ever needed a web designer? Your neighbor's kid probably knows a thing or two because they run a TikTok page about gaming. Or maybe you're thinking about flipping houses? Your great-aunt Lucy might have some wild stories about how she turned a decrepit shack into a cozy cottage—and let me tell you, her stories are the stuff of legend. Pro tip: Never underestimate a woman who has successfully evicted a raccoon.

Furthermore, local businesses often have free workshops or classes that can help you hone your financial skills or learn about budgeting and saving techniques. Sometimes, they throw in free snacks as a bonus! Trust me, there's nothing like sipping on a cup of sparkling water while learning about interest rates to make you feel like a million bucks—well, unless you end up staring at your budget and suddenly realizing you spent a fortune on avocado toast last month. Ah, the irony!

You see, financial education isn't just something you find in books—it lives and breathes in your community, too. Whether it's through relationships, shared experiences, or just bonkers discussions over coffee, your neighbors can provide insight that books and seminars sometimes can't. Real-life scenarios, differing perspectives, and even the occasional rant about why saving is impossible when there are sales every week can lead you to light-bulb moments, where you suddenly grasp financial concepts that once felt like algebra! A community can help identify money-saving hacks, career opportunities, and investment ideas faster than you can say "retirement fund."

Ah, and what's more? Volunteering! Yes, good old community service offers a valuable lesson in reframing your financial mindset. By working on community projects, you'll inevitably learn the nuances of budgeting, resource allocation, and even negotiation. Plus, you'll meet a bunch of folks who are likely as hilarious and eccentric as your Aunt Edna. I mean, where else can you find people who think that scoring a deal at the thrift store is a legitimate Olympic sport?

In the grand scheme of financial growth, the bottom line is simple: you can't do it alone. So, dust off that old casserole dish, show up at a neighborhood gathering, and start building those relationships. The money lessons, resources, and built-in support systems you gather along the way will prove infinitely more valuable than a lifetime supply of marshmallow fruit salad, which, to be honest, sounds like the worst idea ever! Embrace your community, folks, because together, we'll all rise from the ashes of financial mediocrity to the glorious heights of financial fabulousness!

Building Connections: Networking in Your Neighborhood

Networking! The delightful art of shaking hands, exchanging awkward smiles, and collecting business cards like they're Pokémon—gotta catch 'em all! But let's be real, folks. The networking world can feel like being thrown into a kiddie pool filled with Jell-O: messy, unpredictable, and mostly just sticky. Still, if you can navigate this slippery landscape in your neighborhood, you'll find it's one of the most rewarding adventures for your financial life—and trust me, it's far better than struggling to assemble a shelf from IKEA.

In a world where digital connections often overshadow face-to-face interactions, neighborhood networking is like that vintage pair of jeans hanging in your closet—timeless and utterly irreplaceable. Think about it: you're surrounded by a treasure trove of friends, entrepreneurs, local talent, and maybe even that eccentric guy down the street who collects lawn gnomes like they're trophies. Your neighborhood is full of potential allies who can help you expand your professional network, share valuable resources, and kick-start new financial opportunities. The only thing you've got to do is muster up the courage to step out of your comfort zone and, you know, not trip over your own feet during introductions.

Here's an essential tip: breaking the ice doesn't have to be painful. Try starting with something as simple as asking someone about their favorite local restaurant—or, better yet, boldly inquire if they have any culinary secrets for making vegan kale salad taste like a five-star restaurant dish. This gives you a common ground to build on and saves you from awkward silences that ultimately lead to gazing longingly at your phone. Newsflash: nobody wants to discuss how you meticulously planned your outfit for this gathering while looking lost in a sea of strangers!

Now that you've taken that first step, it's time to explore what your neighbors can bring to the table—and no, I don't mean the salad bar! Your circle may include accountants, marketers, retired bankers, and even freelance artists who can offer support or advice to elevate your financial game. Trust me when I say, the conversation will flow much smoother than when you tried to talk to your cat about your budgeting woes. I can spot a financial wiz a mile away; however, if you don't even know what their profession is, how will you get to that life-changing money tip hiding just beneath the surface?

Host casual gatherings! Organize get-togethers where you can invite your neighbors, and let's spice it up with themed listening parties where everyone shares "The Worst Financial Decisions of Their Life." Believe me, you'll have them laughing and bonding over their own Pip's moments faster than you can say, "Do four credit cards really count as a 'collection'?" These casual interactions will foster friendships, strengthen connections, and create a knowledge-sharing platform, eventually leading to networking without the stuffy, formal atmosphere typical of corporate events.

For those who fancy a more strategic approach to networking, joining local business groups or attending community meetings can be beneficial. Not only do you get a chance to learn about community resources, but you'll also be able to engage with local entrepreneurs who understand what it's like to hustle in your own backyard. Imagine how powerful it would be to have access to a group of savvy individuals who've successfully navigated the financial mazes of your area! With their insights, you'll be sharing hacks faster than a dog can chase its tail.

Let's also not forget the power of social media! While online interactions can feel less personal, platforms like Nextdoor bring that neighborhood charm right to your screen. You can ask for recommendations, share knowledge, and engage with locals who may have the golden nugget of wisdom you never knew you needed, like how to dodge late fees at your local utility company. Plus, it's perfect for connecting with individuals who may not live right next door, but are still part of your larger community!

In the end, building connections in your neighborhood may seem intimidating. Still, it's as important to your financial journey as finding that perfect balance between avocado toast and ramen noodles (which, let's be honest, is a genuinely great life hack). So, go out there, charm your neighbors with your unparalleled wit, bring your most impressive dish to the next neighborhood potluck (after googling "easy recipes" of course), and watch your network multiply faster than the gnomes in your friend's yard! With every conversation, you're not only expanding your financial horizon but also getting an exclusive backstage pass to the incredible stories and lessons that can transform your financial life! What's better than that?

Understanding Community Resources for Financial Education

Financial education—sounds fancy, doesn't it? It's like the diploma you wish you had for binge-watching YouTube finance tutorials in your pajamas. But let me tell you, folks, when I say community resources can turbocharge your understanding of finances, I mean it! Your neighborhood is a hotbed filled with opportunities, programs, and services just waiting for you to uncover its financial gold. Picture it like a scavenger hunt, complete with treasure maps, only instead of X marking the spot, it's probably Grandma Ethel's living room, where she offers free Financial 101 seminars over cookies. Sign me up!

To kick things off, let's talk about libraries. Yes, that place where the old Nancys and Bobbies huddle over encyclopedias and where you develop some serious skills in shushing. Libraries are not just tombs of dusty books—oh no—they're financial resource powerhouses! Many local libraries host workshops on everything from budgeting and saving to investing and tax filing. The best part? No one's charging you an arm and a leg for this education. In fact, the only thing you might lose is a favorite pen when you accidentally poke your friend while illustrating how to create a budget (trust me, it'll happen).

Now, let's not forget about community centers! These vibrant hubs are often packed with knowledgeable staff members who are eager—and I mean EAGER—to help you along your financial journey. They offer workshops, seminars, and often even one-on-one counseling sessions for anyone looking to learn about managing money better. Whether it's a self-help program to tackle debt or a class on the latest budgeting apps (because heaven knows we all need a little tech help once in a while), the staff at community centers are there, offering guidance and an endless supply of coffee to fuel your financial awakening. And if you ask nicely, they might even share with you their secret coffee stash and how to make it taste just like Starbucks!

Ever heard of non-profits? They're the superhero community resources that swoop in to save the day, especially for folks feeling trapped in the vicious cycle of debt. Many offer free financial coaching sessions, workshops, and resources to help you take charge of your finances. Think of non-profits as the wise aunts of the financial world, guiding you to financial freedom, though maybe with fewer snacks.

As you poke around your community, keep your eyes peeled for local vocational schools and community colleges that might offer financial education classes. These institutions sometimes provide courses that equip you with the practical skills you need to manage your money and understand the ins and outs of investments, all without the eye-watering price tags associated with fancy universities. (Though, let's be honest, the only thing eye-watering at those places might just be the price of their coffee.)

And let's also talk tech! I know technology can feel as daunting as wrestling an alligator when you only wanted to be left alone with your favorite rom-com. Still, community resources often feature local tech programs that teach digital literacy with respect to financial education. Find a mentor who can help you navigate budgeting apps, online investment platforms, and even community webinars that connect you with experts who drop gems of wisdom about personal finance. Think of it as a TED Talk, but one where you can also sit in your pajamas—instead of awkwardly pretending to be interested in that guy in the corner who insists he's also a special effects artist.

Lastly, don't overlook all those financial fairs and expos your community throws together at various times throughout the year! These events often combine with local vendors eager to provide free samples of their financial expertise (and sometimes snacks, let's be real). You can chat with professionals, attend sessions, and leave with a bag of free goodies and knowledge you didn't know you needed. Who can resist walking away from an event with an abundance of pens and notebooks, all while acquiring valuable financial insights? Honestly, I'm pretty sure the only thing better than that exists solely in the realm of unicorns!

The bottom line is simple: Understanding community resources for financial education should be treated like a treasure hunt, only way more amusing (and definitely less sticky). When you tap into the wealth of knowledge and opportunities around you, you're setting the stage for a brilliant financial transformation. So, my friends, don your 'financial sleuth' hats, embrace the quest, and delve into the robust resources just waiting for you to discover them! With a little curiosity and creativity, financial liberation is within reach—and a sprinkle of humor goes a long way too!

Collaborating with Local Businesses for Mutual Benefit

Local businesses—the unsung heroes of our neighborhoods, keeping us fueled with coffee, sustenance, and, let's be real, all the fantastic oddities you only find in that hidden garage sale down the street. You know what really tickles my financial fancy? The idea of "collaborating with local businesses for mutual benefit." It's about transforming that casual "Hi" to your favorite barista into a beautiful financial partnership! Seriously, folks, collaborating with local businesses is not just a stroke of genius, it's a financial strategy even more solid than Grandma's secret recipe for biscuits (which we both know contains love, butter, and maybe an alarming amount of sugar).

First things first: let's demystify what it means to collaborate with local businesses. It's simple! It's about leveraging each other's strengths to create a win-win situation. Picture yourself as Batman and your local bakery as Robin. Together, you could promote each other's services, throw community events, or support each other's marketing campaigns. Trust me, no one will complain about a tasty brownie sample at a finance workshop. In fact, I dare say it might even turn those dreary budgeting conversations into euphoric celebrations. "Yay, I actually saved this month—in between bites of chocolate fudge!"

Let's not underestimate the power of strategic partnerships. For instance, imagine if a gym owner teamed up with a financial advisor to host a monthly "Fit and Financial" meetup. Attendees could work on their squats while listening to fun tips about getting rid of credit card debt. I mean, who knew burpees could be paired with budgeting advice? Together, you could attract an audience consisting of fitness buffs and financially naïve folks just trying to figure out how to afford their green smoothies. You'll spark genuine interest and inevitably create an environment where knowledge is shared, bodies get fit, and those green smoothies finally make sense (nutritionally, at least)!

Another method to create synergy is through the age-old phenomenon of discount deals. Local businesses thrive on community loyalty—ever wonder why your favorite cafe offers you a "loyalty card" after that one enthusiastic espresso binge? Collaborate with local businesses to create deals that benefit their customers AND yours. For instance, if you own a tax office, why not join forces with that new yoga studio on the block? Offer their members a special discount on tax consultations in exchange for their promoting your services. It's like the perfect financial salsa dance—two businesses twirling around each other while their customers are so blissfully unaware, munching on breadsticks in the corner!

And let's not forget the tremendous marketing potential that collaboration creates. By teaming up with local businesses for events, you increase visibility and awareness for both parties. Imagine throwing a "Community Health and Wealth Fair", where local artisans offer wellness products, while I share the best budgeting tips since Scott used pennies to buy a Volkswagen. The locals get a buffet of options while you share your financial wisdom, plus they leave with free samples and your contact information. You can't put a price tag on that!

In this whimsical world of collaboration, everybody wins! Local businesses gain traction, customers fall in love with the ease of accessing bundled services, and you, sweet reader, get to wear the crown as your community's financial guru. Soon, your neighborhood will chat about how you and the local florist have joined forces to declutter their homes for tax write-offs while providing personalized flower arrangement tutorials. Who remembers when finances were boring? Certainly not us!

But please keep in mind—the secret sauce for these collaborations is communication and creativity. Approach local businesses with a genuine desire to elevate each other, and you'll be amazed at the opportunities that will unfold. Don't be shy! Your barista might just whip up a sweet deal for you in exchange for financial literacy on the side. It's like pairing coffee and donuts, but you know, far less detrimental to your waistline in the long run! So go forth and seek out those ordinary folks running local establishments and show them the possibilities—you might just be sparking a delightful financial revolution right in your community, one delicious pastry at a time!

In wrapping up this delightful collaboration carnival, remember, it's all about fostering relationships and keeping that neighborhood spirit alive. So, whether you're aligning with local businesses to create dynamic opportunities or transforming mere acquaintances into lifelong partnerships, never underestimate the power of mutual benefit. Trust me; it's way more enjoyable than standing alone at a networking event with a lukewarm cup of bad coffee! Together, let's dance our way to financial success while enjoying a side of humor and community love. Let's make those collaborations happen and have a blast doing it!

Creating a Supportive Community for Financial Wellness

Creating a supportive community for financial wellness is like whipping up a delicious family recipe: it requires the right ingredients, a sprinkle of love, and a dash of understanding, preferably paired with a good sense of humor. You see, folks, when we band together as a tight-knit community, we can transform the challenging landscape of personal finance into a lively potluck where everyone leaves a little richer, in spirit and in knowledge. So grab your favorite casserole dish and let's feast on the concept of financial support together!

First off, let's acknowledge the elephant in the room: talking about money can feel more awkward than that time you accidentally waved at a stranger who turned out to be your neighbor. But what if I told you that creating an environment where open conversations about finances flourish can be as easy as cultivating your very own garden? It all starts with transparency and trust. When we begin to share our financial struggles, successes, and yes, even our embarrassing moments—like that time you thought "compound interest" referred to a mixture of ingredients—you pave the way for authentic connections. The more you advocate for open discussions, the more others will feel comfortable sharing their experiences, creating a ripple effect of empowerment.

Now, a supportive community doesn't just magically appear; it requires orchestrating engaging conversations and continuous learning experiences. So why not harness the power of workshops and group meetups? Picture this: a gathering where people swap budgeting tips over coffee, share their latest frugal finds at the dollar store, and emerge with a shared commitment to crush their financial goals. Perhaps someone shares their secret strategy for meal prepping, ensuring dinner is handled without breaking the bank. You'll leave not only with new acquaintances but with a treasure chest of knowledge to navigate the financial whirlpool!

Furthermore, let's not overlook the value of mentorship, because who doesn't love a wise elderly neighbor who could school you in the art of thriftiness while providing excellent cookie recipes? Finding passionate individuals to act as mentors within your community can solidify a financial wellness culture. A seasoned entrepreneur who's faced their fair share of misadventures can provide invaluable insights and guidance. Think of this as assembling a financial Avengers team, where everyone uses their superpowers to uplift each other. Your neighborhood can morph into the ultimate think tank for financial wisdom, and soon you'll be declaring, "Move over, Wall Street; we've got this!"

Now, here comes the fun part: leveraging community resources! Extend your collaborative endeavors by forging partnerships with local organizations and businesses that support financial literacy. Host events in community centers with guest speakers who bring their expertise to the table, like financial educators or local entrepreneurs who can share their experiences. Perhaps they'll regale you with tales of their many financial catastrophes, providing the ultimate relief that you're not alone in this chaos. Mix in a healthy dose of humor to make everyone chuckle and realize that learning about finances can be both entertaining and enlightening!

Additionally, developing programs specifically geared toward financial health and awareness can create the foundation of this supportive community. Establishing a "Financial Wellness Committee" is an excellent way to create opportunities for group discussions, facilitate workshops, and share resources. You might even introduce a dedicated "Frugal Friday" in which the whole community sketches out their financial goals while eating homemade snacks featuring a "bring your own dish" approach. Because honestly, who wouldn't be inspired by creative avocado toast recipes while discussing the intricacies of retirement savings?

Also, consider creating a platform for success stories within your community! Celebrating victories—both big and small—bonds you together in the journey toward financial wellness. The person who just paid off a hefty student loan or reached a savings goal deserves the biggest pizza party imaginable, while the person finally facing their credit card debt inspires others to take charge of their own challenges. Trust me, there's nothing quite like a celebratory feast to unite your community over financial triumphs!

Lastly, always remember that the heart of a supportive community lies in unwavering encouragement. A financial journey can feel daunting, laden with ups and downs. But when you've got a group of cheerleaders shouting "You've got this!" alongside you, it becomes all the more manageable. A little humor goes a long way in keeping the atmosphere light, and soon, nobody will consider financial wellness a dreary topic. Instead, it will become a joyous celebration filled with camaraderie, laughter, and lots of open discussions.

Creating a supportive community for financial wellness is both an art and a science: it requires patience, creativity, and perhaps an oddball like me to keep things light and engaging! Embrace the journey, gather your friends (and neighbors) to discuss the ins and outs of managing finances, and together let's build a community that fosters financial growth, resilience, and joy. With the right connections and a heart full of laughter, you'll soon find that financial wellness is not just a solitary pursuit—it's a fabulous group project, and everyone is invited!

CHAPTER 17
OVERCOMING FINANCIAL SETBACKS

Understanding Financial Setbacks

Understanding financial setbacks—it sounds like a term designed to put a real damper on a party, right? Well, I assure you, it's not as boring as it seems. In fact, financial setbacks are like those surprise guests who show up at your door with a six-pack of soda but no food at the potluck. They may cause a little confusion, but they can also be an unexpected source of conversation. Whether it's unexpected medical bills, a job loss, or that infamous moment when you accidentally forget to pay the car insurance and end up with a lovely letter from the DMV—the world of financial setbacks is wide and wild!

You see, as a self-proclaimed "Budget Avenger," I've had my fair share of run-ins with these financial faux pas. Picture this: I'm out there, cape billowing behind me, attempting to save my family and friends from the clutches of debt, when suddenly—BAM! Life decides to drop a financial bomb. I mean, who knew that appliances could break at the same rate that my relatives invite themselves over for dinner? One second, I'm confidently guiding my clients through mortgages, and the next minute, I'm staring at a broken fridge. No, I don't think it's funny either, but that's life for you!

Understanding financial setbacks starts with recognizing that they are part of the grand scheme of adulting. If you expect your financial journey to be a smooth ride, let me hand you a pair of virtual reality goggles so you can feel the roller-coaster rush. Trust me, roller coasters are all fun and games until you drop unexpectedly and feel the wind knock right out of you, much like when that unexpected expense hits your budget. I'd say we all need to arm ourselves with a healthy dose of humor and constructive denial. After all, who doesn't need a laugh when they realize they're going to have to live off ramen for the next month?

So, let's break down why these setbacks tend to smack us upside the head like a toddler with a juice box. First, realizing that our financial lives are not entirely within our control is essential. I can preach all day about budgeting and savings, but life doesn't always follow my script. The universe has a funny way of messing with our best-laid plans, almost like how Tiler, my 15-year-old, messes with my plans for a peaceful evening by inviting his friends over to "hang out" without telling me. And let me tell you, nothing screams financial setback like an impromptu pizza party for ten teenagers!

Second, let's not forget the facts of life—sometimes, unexpected things just happen, and they all seem to occur on a Tuesday around 3 PM. A combination of faulty wiring, techno-mania (you think you've got Wi-Fi but really it's just a mirage), and your doctor's office calling with a "we need to discuss your last test results" can all turn a perfectly calm day into financial mayhem. Unfortunately, when the "money gremlins" invade, that's when you start to learn just how strong your financial foundation really is. Spoiler alert: if you haven't reinforced that foundation with some solid savings, you're in for a bumpy ride.

But fear not! Financial setbacks aren't the end of the world. In fact, when well-managed, they can lead to growth and unexpected life lessons. One day, I found myself knee-deep in debt, with a surprising amount of ice cream in my freezer. Is ice cream a food group? Let's just say that allows me to sleep a little better at night during difficult times. Each setback became a lesson, an opportunity for "Vintage Tumeka" to elbow her way back into the spotlight and show the world that challenges actually build character (and extra layers of ice cream) if you approach them correctly.

At the end of the day, understanding financial setbacks is not about wallowing in self-pity or trying to pin the blame on Uncle Fred, who sweet-talked you into that risky investment. Instead, it's about getting comfortable with the uncomfortable and recognizing the resilience you possess. Financial setbacks can transform you from a novice into a seasoned pro, and if you can learn to laugh at the chaos along the way, then you're not just surviving, you're thriving! And who knows, you may just find your own version of the "Budget Avenger" cape, allowing you to soar above it all while shouting, "Not today, debt!"

The Power of Resilience

The power of resilience—now that's a topic that deserves a fanfare! If there were a superhero league for personal finance, resilience would be its fiery, unstoppable leader, zooming in with a cape made of dollar bills and a sassy attitude that could make even the most miserable accountant crack a smile. Seriously, resilience is like that superhero sidekick that you never knew you needed but ends up saving the day more times than you can count. When it comes to navigating the rocky terrain of financial setbacks, having resilience in your corner is not just beneficial; it's downright essential!

Think of resilience as your financial backup plan, the one you didn't realize was brewing in the oven while you were busy stressing about burnt cookies. When life throws its curveballs—job loss, unexpected expenses, a surprise visit from your mother after 15 years of blissful avoidance—resilience is the quality that helps you bounce back and emerge victorious, like a bounce house during a particularly wild backyard party. And let's face it: if you've just faced the financial equivalent of a growing pile of dirty laundry after a family gathering, you need that bounce-back power!

Now, I'll let you in on a little secret—I didn't just wake up one day wearing a cape and saying, "Call me the Budget Avenger!" Oh no, my friends, I had to work for it! Being in the business of finance and mortgages, it's a bit like being a teacher in a room full of hyperactive toddlers. There's constant chaos, surprises around every corner, and just when you think you've got things under control, the crayons end up in unexpected places! So, I've learned that resilience is less about achieving perfection and more about embracing the deliciously messy journey of life as it comes.

Let's meander down the memory lane of Tumeka's life for just a moment. There was a time when I was knee-deep in financial chaos—bad investments, a budget that felt like a raccoon on a sugar high created it, and a general idea that finances were strictly meant to be hidden under the bed like dirty laundry. That's when I discovered the magic of resilience—a power that allowed me to crawl out from under the piles of misunderstood PDFs and questionable purchase receipts. It's that very same resilience that's helped me guide others through tricky financial situations, like a Jedi master with a lightsaber made of spreadsheets.

But let's address the elephant in the room—resilience also requires a good sense of humor! Why? Because rolling with the punches is much easier when you're giggling about it along the way. I mean, who hasn't felt like they're starring in a bizarre sitcom when your bank account hits an all-time low just as you decide to treat yourself to a splurge? I remember the time I was eyeing those fabulous shoes, and my inner warrior had a meeting with my conscience, which went something like this: "Girl, those shoes could either make you the queen of the streets or knock you out of the reigning budgeting champion of the month." Spoiler alert: I didn't buy the shoes, but I got a great story out of it, and I still laugh about it today while rocking my trusty old sneakers.

Another nugget of wisdom is that resilience is not an isolated quality; your support system amplifies it. Much like how a superhero often partners up with their sidekick, I found my community of fellow money warriors in my husband, Sims, my family, and, of course, my beloved clients. When the going gets tough, sharing stories of financial trials can feel remarkably cathartic. It's like opening a bottle of vintage wine—only instead of a sophisticated discussion about flavors, you end up bonding over tales of catastrophic purchases, epic budgeting fails, or how your toddler managed to book an online shopping spree. At the same time, you were busy playing the role of "Supermom." Resilience becomes contagious, inspiring others to face their challenges head-on, and you end up creating a shared bank of "you won't believe what happened" stories.

Through my journey of discovering the power of resilience, I've learned that it's not about avoiding setbacks altogether. Instead, it's about how you respond when life hurls the equivalent of an unexpected water balloon at you! When financial setbacks arrive, trust me, there's a moment of shock. But then, in true resilient fashion, it's your chance to face the wild side of financial chaos with laughter and wit. So, next time life slaps you with an unexpected bill or financial challenge, don't forget to take a deep breath, pull out your invisible cape, and declare, "Challenge accepted!" You might just find that even in the messiest of moments, you have the strength to bounce back, and you may very well decide that your resilience deserves its very own Netflix special.

Creating a Recovery Plan

Creating a recovery plan—now that's a phrase that should come with a side of popcorn, because it's a thrilling journey filled with plot twists and unexpected characters, just like any good movie! When life unceremoniously throws you into the financial deep end, it's time to grab your floaties and get ready to paddle your way back to shore. Let's be real here: no one wants to tread water, praying for a miracle while their finances look like a tornado has hit them. So, pen in hand and a sense of humor at the ready, let's go over how to create a recovery plan that would make even the toughest financial crisis tremble in fear.

First things first, let's start with a reality check. A recovery plan isn't just about closing your eyes and wishing away your debt like I wish away my aunt's unsolicited life advice during holiday dinners. No, it's about taking a cold, hard look at your financial situation, analyzing every nook and cranny like your overzealous aunt scours a buffet table. Start by detailing what went wrong. Perhaps it was the case of the "oops, I did it again" syndrome, where you thought a spontaneous shopping spree was a harmless exercise in retail therapy. Or maybe the unexpected emergency dental work felt more like being mugged by a toothbrush! Identifying the root cause of your financial woes sets the stage for an effective recovery plan.

Once you've assessed the damage, it's time to dream big—well, in a sensible, budget-friendly kind of way. Just because you now have an amazing plan doesn't mean you're ready to dive into the deep end again without a safety net. Here's where we create the "Budget Avenger Recovery Fund"—a shiny, new savings plan. I'm talking about that euphoric feeling of seeing money accumulate without it mysteriously evaporating faster than soda in a hot car! Set a specific target for how much you want to save each month, and channel your inner tortoise: slow and steady wins the race! Whether it's $25 or $250, the beauty is in the consistency. And believe me, once you begin to see that money grow, you might just start strutting around like you won the lottery!

Next, let's get real about budget cuts—no, I'm not talking about those awkward conversations about appearance at family gatherings! It's time to scour your expenses with the precision of a hawk! Check your monthly subscriptions—do you really need five streaming services? If you're watching "The Office" for the seventh time, maybe you could hit pause on that subscription for a bit? And can we talk about the excessive takeout? When you realize your diet consists of more pizza boxes than vegetables, it's time to shift gears. Turn cooking into a fun family activity! And let me tell you, if my husband, Sims, can put on an apron and make a mean spaghetti that doesn't resemble the sauce from the bottom of the pot, then you can do it too!

Then there's the part about setting realistic goals, which means I need to take a moment to face my arch-nemesis: time! Break down those big goals into bite-sized pieces when plotting this recovery plan. You wouldn't enter a marathon without first completing a 5K, would you? Similarly, if you're aiming to pay down a significant credit card balance, take it one payment at a time. Create milestones, and when you reach them, celebrate! I'm talking about spritzing on your favorite perfume, indulging in homemade muffins, or treating yourself to a night of binge-watching your favorite series, without any guilt. Because, after all that hard work, you deserve some joy!

And don't forget about accountability—this is not a solo journey! Share your recovery plan with someone you trust, whether it's a friend, family member, or that one dramatic cousin who'll make a tutu out of the bowls for your budget plan. Having someone to support you means you're far less likely to splurge on those "I might just really need these sparkly shoes" moments. I mean, every time I even *consider* those shoes, I just picture my husband's expression, and poof—back to sensible sneakers I go!

At the end of the day, creating a recovery plan is all about remembering that it's perfectly fine to stumble and trip along the way. Life may be filled with plot twists, but with a solid plan, plenty of humor, and a dash of resilience, you can bounce back like the fabulous financial hero you were destined to be. So wave goodbye to those nagging financial woes and set your sights on a future where you're the star of your own money management movie—complete with confetti and, if you're lucky, a few free snacks!

Learning from Mistakes

Learning from mistakes—now there's a delightful concept that dances on the fine line between emulating a wise tortoise and going full-on cartoon character slipping on a banana peel! Honestly, if I had a dollar for every financial misstep I've made, I could single-handedly fund my own sitcom, "Tumeka's Terrible Money Choices." Picture it: newscasters reporting financial blunders while I sing my personal financial theme song in the background—what could be more entertaining?

Mistakes in our financial journey are bound to happen; after all, we're no different from toddlers learning to walk. Except, instead of landing face-first on the carpet, we land face-first in a puddle of debt or an ill-fated investment decision. For me, it was that blushing moment when I tried my hand at day trading. I thought I was the next stock market prodigy, waving my metaphorical wand, only to discover that I was better off trading my allowance for a pack of gum. Spoiler alert: I lost more than just my training wheels on that financial bike! The important thing is to shift from a mindset of shame about these blunders to viewing them as teaching moments—a sort of crash course in what not to do (even if it is at the expense of your dignity!).

So, how do we embrace the art of learning from our mistakes without becoming emotionally paralyzed by our past choices? First, we need to own our mistakes like a true superhero would. This isn't about wallowing in regret; instead, I'm talking about taking that leap into accountability like it's a refreshing pool on a hot summer day! Allow yourself to analyze what went wrong: Was it impulse buying? Did your budgeting skills resemble a toddler's crayon artwork? Or perhaps it was trusting, at face value, a friend's not-so-great financial advice who proclaimed they were a "money guru" just because they bought that shiny new car. You know the ones!

Next, let's talk about making a list of lessons learned—imagine a giant scroll unfurling like a declaration of independence from your financial faux pas. I mean, if you're going to put yourself through the experience of learning from your blunders, you might as well capture those style lessons! Create a mistake ledger, complete with colorful doodles and humorous commentary. Did you ever buy that 48-pack of overpriced avocado toast because everyone was doing it? No? Just my husband and me? Well, then let's applaud the collective madness of very trendy choices! Highlight what that experience taught you—perhaps avocado toast symbolizes a need to limit my brunch budget!

Once you've made your colorful list of learning experiences, it's crucial to transform those lessons into actionable steps. This is where the magic happens! Instead of recoiling from that past mistake like a cat avoiding a bath, take a positive turn. For instance, implement a waiting period if you've learned that impulse purchases tend to leave you with more clutter than cash. I suggest at least a week of waiting to see if that shiny object still has your heart racing, or if you'll end up cringing like a bad karaoke singer!

Don't forget about the value of sharing your money misadventures with others! There's something breathtakingly liberating about pulling back the curtain on your blunders and letting others marvel at the absurdity of it all. Offer up your tales of financial woe like a seasoned storyteller, and watch as others nod in agreement, perhaps laughing hysterically because they too have been there, but likely without the embarrassing photo evidence! Sharing stories doesn't just help you process your own mistakes; it also creates a supportive community where everyone can learn together, armed with knowledge, humor, and maybe even a few cringeworthy tales thrown in for good measure.

Lastly, let's not forget that mistakes are what make us interesting! They add color to the otherwise dull black-and-white world of budgeting and finance. Embrace the quirks that come with your misadventures in finance! After all, if I hadn't made that fateful decision of attempting to become a day trader, I never would have created the term "Tumeka dollars," which I now reserve for budgeting setbacks that we all face when life decides to prank us.

Aligning our minds with a growth-focused perspective fosters an atmosphere of empowerment where mistakes become our greatest teachers. So, next time you find yourself face-to-face with the aftermath of a less-than-stellar financial decision, slather on a layer of self-compassion, do a little dance, and shout from the rooftops: "I'm learning here, folks! And I'm fabulous!" Mistakes make you richer in wisdom, laughter, and, ideally, a whole lot smarter with your finances moving forward.

Celebrating Small Victories

Celebrating small victories—oh, my dear friend, this is where the magic happens! Picture this: you've just paid off that teeny-tiny credit card balance, or perhaps you resisted the urge to buy yet another quirky kitchen gadget (sup, avocado slicer!). It's not just about the big wins, folks; it's about recognizing and honoring those glorious little moments that pave the path to financial success. Think of them as stepping stones, glittering with potential as you walk towards your financial goals. And what's not to love about a little celebration? Because trust me, if we wait for the big wins to roll around, we might be waiting longer than some of my relatives waiting for my kitchen pies to cool!

So, why bother with the small victories, you ask? Well, let me tell you, acknowledging these small wins is akin to sprinkling pixie dust on the long and often tedious journey to financial freedom. Celebrating them keeps our spirits up! It's like having a virtual high-five on an epic quest, reminding us that we have the power to make progress, no matter how incremental. Remember that time you resisted the impulse buy for that fancy new tech gadget? Give yourself a round of applause, and break out the confetti! It's little moments like these that boost our motivation and keep us focused, because if I'm not allowed to indulge in a performative dance party when I knock out a budget meeting, what's the point?

Now, how can we effectively celebrate these small victories, you might be wondering? First and foremost, let's ditch the notion that celebrations always need to be extravagant or expensive. Sometimes, it's the humble gestures that strike the biggest chords. After all, I once celebrated trimming my monthly grocery bill by making a delightful pasta dinner from that random assortment of pantry items I could find. I mean, who knew old canned tomatoes and a pre-old chunk of Parmesan could create gourmet magic? So, whether that means treating yourself to a bubble bath, hosting a fun family game night, or indulging in a fancy cup of coffee, the key is making those moments feel special!

And if you need ideas, allow your recently respected friend and Budget Avenger to chime in with a sprinkle of inspiration! Keep a "Small Victory Journal" where you jot down your achievements, big or small, that contribute to your financial goals. Don't be shy to embellish it with doodles, glitter pens, or even stickers because let's be real: adulting needs a splash of whimsy! You can design an entire page dedicated to that week where you skipped dessert after dinner, #AdultingGoals. Or that time you didn't get distracted by the clearance section at Target but walked out with only toilet paper. Visuals help us track progress and can become a cheerful reminder of our steady journey toward financial wellness.

Let's also emphasize the impact of bringing friends and family into the celebration! It's much easier to bask in the glow of victories when your cheerleading squad surrounds you. I mean, who wouldn't want a dance party in their living room for reaching a savings milestone? Invite your pals over, crank up some tunes, and eat celebratory cake (because why can't cake be a key player in financial victory?). You'd be surprised how motivating it can be to share those milestones—who knows, it might even inspire your friends to embark on their own financial quests! Just please ensure you've got a cake-cutting plan; no one wants to turn a celebration into an accidental wrestling match over the last slice!

On the flipside, don't neglect to raise a toast (with your budget-friendly sparkling water, of course!) to yourself in those quiet moments when it's just you. Acknowledge the steps you've taken, ridiculous though they may seem to others. Maybe you fended off that tempting sale or managed your budget like a financial ninja! Give yourself a verbal high-five, because if you don't, who else will? And let's face it: most of our friends just think we're "that budgeting person" until they feel the excitement of celebrating the same triumphs!

Celebrating small victories contributes to a healthy mindset around finances by reinforcing the idea that progress is possible—and it's totally worth it. Just like how I hype myself up to finally beat my own records at the local arcade (even if the neighbors can hear my war cries!), it's crucial to treat your financial journey like the adventure it is! Self-encouragement can fuel your motivation and remind you that every small win is one step closer to bigger goals.

So, as you dance your way through the ups and downs of financial living, take a moment to slow down and appreciate those milestones that may seem like a mere blip on the radar. Break out the glitter, gather your friends, and let those small victories turn into celebrations that empower you to strive for more! Because life is too short not to frolic through the rainy days while basking in the glory of all your achievements, no matter how small they are. Your financial journey deserves to be celebrated, and when you do it right, those small victories will build a budget bridge strong enough to get you across to a secure, limitless future!

CHAPTER 18
CELEBRATING YOUR FINANCIAL WINS

The Importance of Celebrating Small Wins

As I sit here sipping my herbal tea (which, between you and me, is really just fancy water), I can't help but think about how crucial it is to celebrate those small wins on our financial journey. You might be wondering, "Tumeka, why should I throw a confetti party just because I saved five bucks on a grocery bill?" Ah, my friend, therein lies the secret to not just surviving but thriving in the wild world of finances. You see, when we don't acknowledge our achievements, no matter how minuscule they may appear, we risk becoming the financial version of a grumpy cat—forever frowning at our bank statements and wondering why our accounts resemble a sad version of Monopoly money.

Now, I know what you're thinking: "But Tumeka, who really throws a parade because they paid off a credit card with a balance of $15?" Well, let me tell you! Or rather, let me shout it from the rooftops! For every penny you shove down that debt hole, you're heroically punching your financial woes in the face. It's like giving a roundhouse kick to your old self who was too busy picking up fast food because "cooking is overrated." You've crossed a threshold, my friend, and you deserve to reward yourself. So why not splurge on a celebratory cupcake? I mean, who doesn't deserve a little frosting after scoring a personal victory?

You see, celebrating small wins is important because it builds momentum. Think of it like exercising. The first time you manage a single push-up (assuming you can still feel your arms afterward) leaves you feeling like "I AM INVINCIBLE!" You're not just getting buff; you're crafting a superhero out of your former self—one who can conquer their finances! Those small victories stack up like pancakes at an all-you-can-eat breakfast buffet, leading to big changes over time. Before you know it, you'll be lifting heavier (in terms of your savings) and flexing your financial muscles. Your credit score will thank you, and you'll be one step closer to your dreams of financial freedom—and that pair of designer shoes you keep eyeing on sale.

But let's take a moment to acknowledge the absurdity of adult life. Do you know those moments when you finally spot that extra quarter rolling around in your couch cushions and feel richer than Bill Gates? Well, my dearest readers, that's the spirit! Picture yourself hosting a lavish celebration over finding a quarter; you could invite your family over, serve them chips, and toast with sparkling water. It's basically like a financial gala! And why stop there? You could theme it; call it "The Great Couch Coin Fetch," or "The Realm of Revealed Pennies." Seriously, embrace the theatrics! Remove that hefty weight of disdain for your finances and replace it with a childlike excitement that would make even Willy Wonka jealous.

Not celebrating small wins might just lead you down the treacherous path of self-doubt and financial despair. I mean, I've been there! Picture me, five years ago, deep in the trenches of debt—a real-life cringe TV show. I was so focused on where I was failing that I lost sight of the victories I was achieving! I kept saying things like, "Oh, I didn't pay down my mortgage this month; I'm such a failure." Meanwhile, I was scoring small wins left and right: refinancing a student loan, reducing my electricity bill by switching to energy-efficient bulbs, and navigating the grocery maze without losing my sanity or money! If only I had a mini party every time I saved a dollar, my living room would have looked like a Times Square New Year's Eve extravaganza!

And if you think seeing family smiles and high-fives from loved ones doesn't count, you're only half right. It totally counts, but it should come with a caveat. Make celebrations a family affair. It's an opportunity to instill a sense of accomplishment in your kids. You want them to understand that financial literacy is a thing worth celebrating, like a birthday, but with no regret attached when the cake is devoured! Trust me, my grandkids, particularly Tiler and Tristan, have learned quickly that every time Grandma saves money, she does a little dance. I still have questionable moves, but that's not the point. The point is, they see that budgeting can come with joy!

So, my fabulous financial warriors! The next time you find a forgotten coupon or manage to cut costs on something you didn't use to think about, remember to celebrate. Transform momentary triumphs into celebrations that'll give the Kardashians a run for their money. Because in the end, those small wins are the bricks paving the path to your financial castle! And who knows? One day, it might just lead to you discovering a tremendous pot of gold at the end of your budgeting rainbow!

Setting Milestones for Financial Progress

Setting milestones for financial progress is much like charting out a road trip—you've got to know when to stop for snacks, stretch your legs, and most importantly, avoid driving into a metaphorical ditch. I mean, nothing says "life goals" like joyfully achieving a milestone while simultaneously stopping at the all-you-can-eat buffet right off the interstate! Am I right, or am I right? So, let's dive into the riveting adventure of setting those glorious financial milestones!

Now, establishing these landmarks in our financial journey is essential because without them, we're basically just trying to find our way through a funhouse. Picture me in a clown wig, experiencing a serious existential crisis as I keep bumping into mirrors that make me look a lot fatter than I really am. Yes, without those milestones, those mirrors are our debt, our endless bills, and the ominous feeling that we're on a runaway roller coaster we never wanted to ride. Milestones act as stops along the way—confirmations that you're headed in the right direction, plus a handy little reminder to do a victory dance while waiting for your Uber.

Let's talk specifics, shall we? Every incredible journey starts with a budget. I know—yawn, right? But budgeting is essential, just like putting on those stretchy pants we all pretend we don't own when heading to a "dinner party" (you know what I mean). It sets the stage for everything else. Start with some simple financial goals that can be measured in real time. For instance, "I WILL save $1,000 in three months!" You're not only giving yourself a tangible target but also invoking every bit of your inner superhero self to leap over hurdles like the amazing Budget Avenger you are! And once you hit that milestone? Time for the celebratory confetti, my darling!

But wait, let's not stop at one milestone; it's all about progressively building the obstacles. Think of this financial game as leveling up in your favorite video game. You don't just complete the tutorial, grab a victory snack, and call it a day—oh no! You face increasingly challenging missions. Maybe your next triumph is to pay off a credit card or save for an annual family vacation. When you obliterate that credit card balance into dust, you deserve not just a snack but the entire cheese fondue fountain!

Now, speaking of fondue, let's discuss something we all dread: hiccups in our financial journey. Life, my friends, is about as predictable as a cat on roller skates. So why not use milestones to create a nifty safety net? Set a milestone to save for an emergency fund—because let's face it, when life throws you a curveball (or a wildly unexpected car repair), nothing's better than the satisfaction of knowing you've conquered that mountain without having to raid your cousin's "emergency fund" born out of her "secret savings jar" that she probably stole from a remote corner of her attic.

As these milestones begin to stack, similar to how I stack old receipts in my desk drawer (don't judge, I swear they're sentimental!), you'll start to recognize how they interconnect. One win fuels another; it's the Wal-Mart of goal-setting! For me, paying off a credit card catalyzed other achievements like refinancing my mortgage and organizing a family budget (which, I might add, is a whole circus act in itself). Setting these milestones creates a domino effect, and before you know it, you're pitching glitter-filled confetti parties for all the financial achievements without breaking a sweat—or your bank account.

It's vital to remember that milestones can also be personal. I may not be flying first class to any tropical destination, but gosh darn it, I can treat myself to a surprise pedicure after hitting a certain savings amount! Life's too short to deny ourselves the pleasures of soft, sandal-ready feet. Your milestones don't just have to be grand; they can be as simple as finally decluttering that closet, because who knew your old winter coat had a stash of money hiding in the pockets? I imagine that was just the coat's way of saying, "Put me back in rotation; I have financial goals too!"

So, whether it's saving $50 per paycheck for a long-overdue spa day or avoiding potholes in the budget, setting milestones is your way of saying, "I'm taking charge!" And remember, sprinkle some humor along the way; after all, who wouldn't crack a smile at an unexpected bucket of fried chicken in the face of financial doom? Celebrate these milestones, laugh off the slip-ups, and keep moving forward with an unapologetic style! Life's too good, and budget's too wild to settle for anything less than a fabulous leap on your financial path! So let's hit the road with flair and confidence, my friends!

Creating a Financial Achievement Journal

Creating a financial achievement journal feels about as revolutionary as finally getting around to folding that pile of laundry that's been turned into an abstract art installation in my living room. You know the one I'm talking about, right? It's a precarious tower of socks, shirts, and maybe the occasional pair of pants that could be mistaken for a lost garment from "The A-Team." But I digress—what I'm really excited about is how this journal can be a game-changer in your financial journey. It's a creative sanctuary where you can throw your monetary triumphs, goals, and yes, even those occasional bubble-wrapped disasters!

Picture this: you sit down, whip out some classic stationery (because every superhero needs their secret lair), and jot down all your financial goals, big and small. Want to save for a dreamy vacation? Write it down! Paid off that pesky $20 parking ticket you've been avoiding for months? GUESS WHAT? That's a win and deserves a glossy sticker in your journal! This isn't just any ordinary journal; oh no, my friends, this is the sacred tome of your financial adventures—a jumping-off point for you to tap into your inner Tony Robbins while letting your creative juices flow!

Now, I know what you might be thinking. "But Tumeka, isn't keeping a journal kind of old-fashioned?" Well, let me tell you, it's hipster chic and trendy in ways you can't even imagine! When I pull out my financial achievement journal, it's like releasing a confetti explosion at a graduation ceremony. Every page is infused with hope, laughter, and my undeniable determination to conquer my finances! It's a celebratory manifesto of accomplishments, where I can list everything from saving a dime to completely making over that hideous old credit card debt.

As you fill up those pages, resist the urge to be overly serious; sprinkle in some humor! Write about the time you carpooled with questionable friends to save gas money, or how you snagged that incredible deal on organic avocados (which you promptly forgot in your grocery bag until they transformed into a science project). Embrace your highs and lows with open arms. Financial accountability is not about perfection—it's about progress and resilience. You'll find laughter has a way of lessening the weight of budgetary despair; it's like detoxing with a cocktail of giggles!

Once you've filled out your financial achievement journal, it becomes a living archive of your struggles and victories—a scrapbook of sorts that celebrates who you are and how far you've come. When you look back at your entries, reminisce about your junior-year financial choices (like that "Buy One, Get One Free" coupon for ice cream that somehow spiraled into a 12-pint frenzy). You might even find yourself laughing until you're doubled over with the realization that adulthood is like navigating a never-ending maze with shoelaces tied together.

Now, here's a fun little twist: make your journal a collaborative masterpiece! I mean, why keep it to yourself when your family can join the fray? Invite your children to doodle, scribble, or even craft their "spending-free" weeks in the margins. Every kid needs to know they too can be a Money Magician, conjuring savings out of thin air! Plus, this gives you the chance to highlight those moments that matter—working together to stay financially accountable while surrounded by glitter, stickers, and love.

It's crucial to revisit this journal regularly. As ridiculous as it sounds, I sometimes find myself flipping through its pages, and just like that, I'm giddy as a schoolgirl, plotting my new financial conquests. Each new entry signifies a fresh start, an invitation for you to dream bigger than ever before. So don't let that 1.5% interest rate on your savings account hold you back. Instead, jot down your aspiration to get a dog, start a podcast, or buy that "you-only-live-once" karaoke machine!

So, dust off your favorite pen, channel your inner Hemingway, and let your financial achievement journal become the sacred ground for your ambition and whimsical laughter. The key is to celebrate every victory, no matter how big or small, and acknowledge yourself for every step taken along this magnificent journey. And who knows? With the right mix of humor and determination, your financial achievements may very well be the beginnings of epic tales that could inspire others to transform their financial lives, while tickling their funny bones! Grab that journal and let's make magic happen!

Involving Family in Your Celebrations

Involving family in your celebrations is like a good pot of gumbo—everyone brings something different to the table, and together, you create a masterpiece that warms the soul! Financial victories are no exception. When you manage to pay off a bill or inch closer to that savings goal, it's only right to gather the clan and have a little shindig. Who says money management has to be all serious spreadsheets and grim faces? My family knows how to crank the fun dial all the way up, and we celebrate our financial wins like we're throwing a surprise party for the Queen!

I'll never forget the time I finally tackled that ever-dreadful student loan debt. Picture me, beads of sweat on my brow, whipping through the last payment like I was a contestant on a game show. I could practically hear the theme music blaring as I hit submit. Naturally, my first instinct was to grab a combo platter of chicken wings and a cake (because why not mix healthier food choices with a sprinkle of sugar-coated euphoria?). I called up my husband, Sims, who arrived like a superhero with his cape made of kindness and a side of slightly burnt garlic bread. Within minutes, the scene unfolded—a hilarious family dinner that could outshine any birthday bash!

Involving family in your celebrations not only amplifies your joy but also fosters a sense of collective achievement. It's a reminder that our financial journeys aren't solitary but woven into the fabric of our relationships. My grandkids, Bristiniey's little whirlwinds, take on the role of "Chief Cheerleaders," brandishing pompoms made of old T-shirts (I'm an entrepreneur, not a magician, so let's repurpose here!). When they hear that Grandma paid off her credit card, they erupt in a cheer worthy of the Super Bowl! It energizes the household and instills in them the importance of financial accountability—all while surrounding them with an educational, engaging, and totally fun atmosphere.

Now, don't just stick to shouting victory chants and munching on celebratory snacks; make it a theatrical affair! I remember a time when I surprised the family with certificates for "Most Outstanding Supporter of Grandma's Budget Goals." I might've even thrown in a "Best Snack Provider"—a nod to my some days stellar, some days questionable, snack choices. Watching my husband present these faux awards, dressed absurdly in our dog's Halloween costume, was the perfect mix of pride and ridiculousness. Financial conversations suddenly transformed from dry discussions into a community celebration, where we not only recognized the wins but turned them into laughter-filled memories.

And let's not overlook the viral trend in our family: the "Savings Dance" ritual! Yes, you read that right—an actual dance! Every time we hit a milestone, we gather and bust out our best dance moves (or, in some cases, questionable flailing). Each family member has their own unique style—I fancy myself a suave disco queen while Tiler's moves are reminiscent of a perplexed chicken. The teamwork radiates joy and laughter; we even film the shenanigans, inevitably leading to future family roasting sessions. Those dance videos? Gold!

Moreover, celebrating together as a family reinforces open communication about finances. Kids often hesitate to discuss money matters, but through our jovial celebrations, we've created an environment where they feel comfortable chatting about money basics. It allows us to weave financial literacy into our gatherings. During our celebratory dinners, we often take turns discussing our personal budgeting goals. When they hear how we're all collaborating toward shared milestones, they're more likely to engage, collaborate, and set their financial goals. If my son-in-law can pitch ideas for a "Buy-Your-First-Home" goal while wearing goofy glasses, we're onto something special!

So, don't wait for that elusive moment when everything's perfect. Instead, celebrate your financial wins with the people you love, however minor they may seem. Make it a priority to involve your family in your triumphs! From spontaneous dance parties to ridiculous awards, the joy multiplies when shared. It solidifies your strength as the Budget Avenger—and you know what? You owe it to yourself and your family to share the laughter amidst the numbers! So fire up those celebration engines, transform your home into a financial fiesta, and let the good times roll like confetti thrown in the face of a grumpy accountant! Who knew being financially savvy could be this much fun? Let's get cooking!

Turning Financial Wins into Motivation

Turning financial wins into motivation is like harnessing the power of a double espresso shot—once it kicks in, you're unstoppable! The key to sustaining momentum on your financial journey is to transform every small victory into a turbo boost that propels you toward your ultimate goals. It's all about channeling that victorious energy, strutting like the fabulous peacock you are, and letting the world know you are the boss of your finances. Trust me; I've been there, and believe me, it feels downright sparkly!

Let's break it down. Every time I achieve a financial win, whether it's slashing a bill, saving for that dreamy vacation, or even simply outsmarting my grocery list, I take a moment to embrace that feeling of success. It's like when you finally find out that Paula Deen's recipe doesn't require hidden traps of butter—you feel enlightened! So rather than just saying, "Oh, that's nice," and moving on, I blow up the moment and throw myself a one-woman celebratory jam session! Yes, lady, I'll admit that I've busted out my finest dance moves in the kitchen, twirling and humming to the musings of my triumphs.

Transforming these wins into motivation means keeping the celebratory vibes alive. It's not just about one small victory leading to another; it's about cultivating an entire garden of goodwill toward yourself. By celebrating each win as its own milestone, you become your own cheerleader, chanting "Go, Team Me!" instead of that tiny, pessimistic voice shrieking "But it's not enough!" Believe me, the world doesn't need more of that negativity, and neither do you. Commit to being your own hype squad, and watch as your drive skyrockets! The next time you conquer a savings goal, sprint to your nearest dance floor (i.e., your living room) and shimmy like you just won the lottery!

Now let's chat about making those victories visual. I can't stress how important it is to create a financial vision board—a dazzling masterpiece filled with glitter, colorful pictures, and probably a few embarrassing photos of you from last summer's BBQ. Each time you cross off a financial victory or add a new accomplishment, you reinforce a sense of pride and motivation that'll keep you marching forward. This board becomes your action-filled gratitude list, where instead of staring at the refrigerator like a lost puppy, you stare at your fun, energy-infused creation of progress. Every glance ignites that spark to keep pushing for bigger and bolder goals, guiding you toward financial greatness one glittery star at a time!

If you're anything like me, you might've been driven by competition (even if it's mostly imaginary against other family members). Use that! Create a fun family challenge or a friendly competition with friends centered around financial savings targets. When we teamed up to save for debt repayment a while back, it was as if we entered a treasure hunt—songs sung, laughter shared, and goals crushed together. We celebrated each achievement with food, hilarious stories, and "you better watch out; I'm coming for your savings crown!" kind of playful bragging. Turning these wins into a motivation fest will not only propel you forward, but it'll also take the mundane chore of budgeting and save-slogging and toss it out the window like confetti!

Speaking of celebration, remember to reflect on your journey regularly. Grab that financial achievement journal we talked about before and flip through those pages. With every success you define, you'll find validation and encouragement, and surely you'll smile at the memories of your growth alongside the hysterical moments along the way. Spend an afternoon reading about your fabulous financial accomplishments instead of scrolling through social media like a caffeinated sloth! With each reading session, a renewed sense of motivation will fuel your financial ambitions, reminding you why all those efforts were 100% worth it.

Lastly, don't forget to share your success with others! Talk to your friends, family, or even that neighbor who still believes half a loaf of bread is a balanced meal. Sharing your victories not only makes them real but also offers you a network of encouragement that seems to blossom with possibility. You'll find that every story shared will motivate not only you but likely inspire those around you to acknowledge their victories too. Our lives are interconnected; when you start uplifting others, it'll roll back into your motivations like a magic boomerang of good vibes.

So, as you continue conquering your financial journey, remember to turn every win into a wind in your motivational sails. Celebrate! Dance! Create! Share! Turning your achievements into motivation is your personal superpower, and no one can take that from you! So gear up and let's dive into a world of wild success, where financial achievements are recognized, cherished, and danced upon like confetti being launched at a parade! Because, darling, only you can create the life that shimmers with financial freedom!

CHAPTER 19
A DAY IN THE LIFE OF A BUDGET AVENGER

My Morning Motivation Rituals

Every superhero starts their day with a proper warm-up, right? Well, I like to think of my mornings as the pre-game show before I tackle the day as the Budget Avenger! Picture it: I roll out of bed in the morning, eyes half-open, hair resembling a bird's nest, and a last night's pizza slice lingering on my breath like an unwanted guest. But don't let that fool you—I'm about to unleash my morning motivation rituals, which would put even the most enthusiastic yoga instructor to shame.

First, we have the ritual of "the wiggle." This is where I do a little dance to shake off the sleep and remind myself that I'm not just a mortgage facilitator but a financial warrior armed with a pen and an excellent credit score. I put on my favorite (and slightly questionable) playlist that consists of everything from '90s hip-hop to whatever the kids are listening to these days. My husband, Sims, claims I make the most unusual moves, but I prefer to think of them as avant-garde choreography. Who knew getting the blood flowing could also entertain the family? My 15-year-old, Tiler, often records me and jokes that I could be the next viral sensation on social media. Little does he know that my credit score could go viral, too, if I ever decide to make a dance about it!

Once I've successfully woken up the neighbors with my energetic performance, it's time for the "Coffee Conference." You see, I can't function without some good old-fashioned caffeine. I pull out my trusty coffee maker, which looks more like a laboratory experiment gone wrong than a kitchen appliance, and brew the strongest cup of coffee known to humankind. I like to call it "Java of Justice," because it fuels my morning heroics! As the smell wafts through the house, my family members start rising like zombies summoned by the scent of brains. We gather around the kitchen table, bleary-eyed, and I take that moment to remind them about our family financial goals for the day. Yes, coffee AND budgeting talk. My daughter Bristiniey claims it's a pleasure and a pain rolled into one. If we're going to have a financial superpower, we must start early!

Now, we don't just sip coffee idly. Oh no! This is when I infuse the day with vibes from my favorite financial gurus. I have an intricate system I like to call "Inspirational Podcast Roulette." One moment, I'm enthralled by Dave Ramsey's fierce banter about being debt-free, and the next, I'm nodding along to Suze Orman's charming wisdom. It's like being in a financial TED Talk, except I'm in my pajamas, and my audience includes a playful cat that couldn't care less about my credit score! Each morning, I make notes about the potent advice I gather and try to figure out how to incorporate it into my family's budget discussions. Can you tell I'm on a mission?

Of course, I have to sprinkle in the occasional absurd affirmation to really get the blood pumping. The hilarious part is how I gather my kids for a round of "Affirmations with Attitude." Picture this: Tiler doing push-ups while I chant, "I am the Budget Avenger! My financial skills slay!" I'm sure the neighbors think we're either preparing for a heist or getting ready for a family talent show. Even though it's silly, I firmly believe that chanting wild affirmations helps set a positive tone for the day. I refuse to let my financial setbacks define me. After all, in the world of personal finance, being upbeat is half the battle—you can't fight debt with a frown!

Finally, as I prepare to conquer the day, I carve out a few precious minutes for gratitude journaling. I know—it sounds dreadfully serious, but it's genuinely entertaining! I jot down things I'm thankful for, like my fabulous husband, my glorious coffee, and of course, my high credit score, which I sincerely hope is still soaring high after a wild weekend of spending. If I'm feeling particularly cheeky, I might scribble down that I'm grateful the microwave didn't blow up while I was reheating leftovers for the third time this week. A cheerful spirit can move mountains-or at least debt- especially when armed with a pen!

So, my mornings are a wild concoction of wiggles, coffee, financial podcasts, wild affirmations, and gratitude. It's a quirky routine, but hey, it works for me! As I strut out of the house, ready to tackle the world, I remind myself that I'm not just Tumeka Jinks; I'm on a mission to help others become budget superheroes too! And with that, I strut out, confidence on high, ready for anything that comes my way, whether it be crushing debts or flexing the power of my credit score!

The Power of Daily Affirmations

When it comes to wielding the power of positive thinking, I can only compare it to choosing the right outfit for your superhero persona. It's all about confidence—and trust me, when you're standing in front of a mirror declaring that you're a financial powerhouse while rocking mismatched socks, you better believe you're halfway there! Daily affirmations have become my secret weapon in this wild world of finance, and I'm here to share the hilarity that ensues when they become a part of your morning routine.

Every morning, after my joyous wiggle session, before I tackle the family financial discussion, I grab my trusty mirror—yes, the same one that reflects my "Budgets in Progress" message board and the occasional spot of toothpaste. With a determined nod, I get ready to unleash a series of absurd yet empowering affirmations. Imagine this: the brave, unapologetic Tumeka Jinks stands proudly before her reflection and starts yelling, "I am a magnetic force of prosperity!" Honestly, saying it loudly while wearing my bathrobe provides me the boost I need. If only my bank account could hear me through the mirror; I'd be a millionaire by now!

One of my favorite affirmations has to be, "Money flows to me like water! I am wetter than an inflatable kiddie pool!" It's bizarre, sure, but I genuinely believe that visualization plays a critical role in shifting our mindset to attract what we desire. And you know what? I don't know what I would do if I didn't frighten the cat when I say it out loud! Imagine my husband, Sims, waking up to me splashing around like I'm some sort of aquatic finance goddess. The neighbors probably think I'm practicing for a role in a whimsically odd finance pantomime. But here's the kicker: with every silly affirmation, I feel lighter, empowered, and ready to tackle anything—even that pesky credit card bill lurking in the corner!

Now, let's not forget the affirmations that double as role-playing exercises. They can get wonderfully ridiculous, especially when I enlist the "help" of my family. I have a brilliant plan that involves a family chant where we summon the "Financial Powers." Sometimes, Sims plays along and yells, "I am the Maestro of Money!" while holding his spatula like a conductor's baton during pancake brunch. Don't be surprised if I suddenly burst into prophetic speeches about good budgeting practices, topped off with an arm wave or two, to make our community proud. I'll tell you, nothing says "I've got my financial life together" quite like a family burst of inexplicable enthusiasm.

On days when self-doubt dares to spiral into my mind like that unyielding rogue debt, I quickly snatch my trusty notebook, where I've recorded a treasure trove of affirmations. It's filled with goofy lines like, "I dodge debt like a master ninja!" or "My credit score sparkles brighter than my grandma's rhinestone collection!" There's something empowering about writing down my affirmations, even when I sometimes sound utterly absurd. Clearly, I'm a full-fledged financial dork, and I wear that badge with pride!

Writing it down helps solidify that positive energy in my mind so I can channel it throughout my day.

My family enjoys participating in "Affirmation Olympics," which is just a fancy title for our breakfast ritual. We sit together, playfully shouting various affirmations while exaggerating our gestures to the point of theatrics. Bless their hilarious souls, the kids get carried away, reciting lines like, "I'm richer than a Kardashian!" and "My savings account is fancier than a yacht party in the Mediterranean!" If someone were to walk in, they might think we're training for the world's most cheerfully dysfunctional championship, but the laughter that ensues is priceless. At that moment, we're not just a family—we're a team of financial affirmers united against the common enemy: doubt!

Incorporating daily affirmations into my life has resulted in far more than just humor; it's allowed me to ground my financial aspirations in positivity. I wrap up my morning ritual enveloped in laughter, self-love, and a fiery commitment to keep conquering our financial challenges together. Who knew that standing in front of a mirror and proclaiming one's financial prowess while sporting pajama pants could be so empowering? So, whether my credit score remains steady or faces a minor setback, I strut onward with the mighty power of daily affirmations propelling me forward. As the Budget Avenger, I'm convinced that my laugh, positivity, and sheer determination are just as vital, if not more, than any financial degree!

Juggling Family and Finances

"Alright, Tumeka, you can do this!" I tell myself on one fine morning, fully determined to juggle family, finances, and the assorted chaos that comes with raising three kids. Picture it—my daughters' school projects slapping against my budgeting spreadsheets, with Tiler, dear old Tiler, somehow managing to turn a simple grocery run into an Olympic event! If you think being an entrepreneur and a tax office owner is tough, try doing it with the added challenge of keeping track of who borrowed the last of the snacks and when I last yelled at someone for leaving dirty socks around. Fact: Juggling family and finances is like doing acrobatics on a tightrope while balancing a flaming torch—you never know when you might get burnt!

The first rule of juggling family and finances is recognizing that you're entering a circus-like environment. My husband, Sims, lays the foundation as the "Ringmaster." He often pipes in with "creative suggestions" on how we could save money, like cutting down on our grocery budget or shopping at discount stores that look suspiciously like they haven't seen a health inspector in years. I mean, who wouldn't want a shopping cart full of mystery meat and questionable yogurt?! Meanwhile, I grapple with calls from the mortgage company and family members simultaneously, as an array of voices drowns each other out. I sometimes feel like I'm in a game show called "Who Wants to Refinance Their Home?"—front and center, of course!

Managing our finances as a family requires teamwork, and we've simply turned it into a comedic production complete with rehearsals! We have our regular "Financial Family Meetings," which, let me tell you, start off with everyone feigning interest in the topic and end with laughter and a quotes-from-their-favorite-sitcom response competition. At best, they offer me hopeful nods while flushing down any adult conversation on finances with "Did you see that viral cat video?" How an impromptu cat video can somehow emerge in a critical discussion about saving for college will always baffle me—and somehow, it turns out to be essential! It lightens the mood, paving the way for our family brainstorming ideas on how to save for that new gaming console. Honestly, I let them have their moment of distraction, as long as it prompts ideas about budgeting in the end.

Then there's the ongoing mission of "Operation Cook a Budget-Friendly Dinner" at the Jinks household. If I've learned anything about family and finances, it's that my kitchen is the ultimate battlefield. My creative cooking techniques make me feel like a financial wizard when I whip up a "pantry surprise", which is just a fancy term for tossing random ingredients into a pot in hopes it will resemble something edible. Nothing says "family bonding" like passing around a bowl of questionable casserole that gives everyone a sense of bravery as we all take our first bites! Standing proudly, I'm convinced I'm earning some serious financial street cred while avoiding the financial burden of a costly restaurant dinner.

Now, let's not forget not-so-forgotten chores! As the "Family Money Guru," my methods for getting my kids involved in chores are borderline ninja-like, complete with a point system based on financial chores. It could be anything from taking out the trash to organizing the disaster zone that is their rooms. Bless his heart, Tiler once took an old sock and stitched it into a pillow, proclaiming it his "DIY Financial Savings Cushion." Even though we may have different definitions of saving, I commend his creative efforts! By turning mundane chores into a competition, I ensure they're as engaged as I am while instilling a sense of financial responsibility in our daily lives, with a healthy dose of humor.

Despite the hectic atmosphere, I am eternally grateful for these entertaining moments. Each chaotic day brings the inevitable reminder that juggling family and finances isn't just a duty; it's a genuine adventure! My children's giggles echo through me, reminding me that we're not merely a family dealing with finances, but rather a dynamic team of financial jokesters learning to make memories together, one odd meal at a time. I may not always get everything right, but I've learned that laughter—a delightful concoction of love, patience, and a pinch of absurdity—can tackle any financial challenge thrown our way. So watch out, world! The Jinks family is here to juggle, and we'll do it with style!

Setting Financial Goals Every Day

Setting financial goals every day feels a bit like dodging flying rubber chickens in a circus act. You've got goals flinging themselves at you from all angles while you're trying to maintain your balance and not trip over your own ambitions! As the Budget Avenger, I embrace this delightful chaos. Seriously, though, what could be more fun than rounding up the family every morning to lay down a few spectacularly outrageous financial goals? I like to think of it as a daily game of "How Financially Fabulous Can We Be Today?" Somehow, it's always a great way to start our day—even if it gets hilariously messy!

Every morning, I gather my trusty crew after I do my fabulous wiggle and sip on my "Java of Justice" (that's coffee for the uninitiated). My husband, Sims, my kids, Tiler and Tristan—which, I assure you, is a mixture for chaos—and we huddle around our kitchen table like we're about to break ground on a new amusement park. Our morning ritual involves a collective huddle where I unleash my grand vision on financial goals for the day. "Today, we're going to eliminate one unnecessary expense!" I declare triumphantly, like a game show host announcing the grand prize. As Tiler stares blankly and Tristan shoves breakfast cereal in his mouth, I can't help but wonder whether I've bitten off more than I can chew.

I introduce a scientific point system to make goal-setting more entertaining (because life without laughter is like a cake without frosting). The kids have to propose ridiculous ways to save money, and for each idea, they earn points. "Let's wash cars for free and hope that someone tips us!" Tiler suggests, and I'm left trying to stifle laughter while wondering what kind of money-making scheme this is. I applaud their creativity, and the point system morphs into a comical debate about who can craft the most absurd yet somehow feasible notion! My kids see me scribbling down these ideas, and before long, they're brainstorming ways to flip it on me, like declaring a "No Spend Day" for the family. Who knew my simple coffee-fueled enthusiasm for finance would morph into a full-on circus of hilarity?

We sometimes focus on more specific goals, like budgeting for our wild pizza obsession. Trust me, feeding three growing kids with an unyielding appetite doesn't come cheap, and I want to avoid breaking my budget like an acrobat on a tightrope! We sit around the table and open Google, only to discover that my favorite pizzeria is running an "All-You-Can-Eat Pizza Night" promotion. We plan strategically, eliminating extraneous spending on snacks or impulse buys because, let's face it, if I can redirect our pizza fund, we can enjoy the pinnacle of cheesy goodness without guilt! Turning ordinary goals into moneymaking challenges becomes part of our budgetary tapestry, and they end up having a blast!

Sometimes, we engage in wildly ambitious plans, like establishing an emergency savings fund—well, I say ambitious for the kids, who may view it as a mere annoyance. When I introduce the idea at breakfast, they practically erupt: "Mom, you mean we could have money for video games instead of saving?" I assure them that this is precisely the point and try to explain the value of having a safety net, while simultaneously stammering through a comparison about the benefits of financial preparedness versus spontaneous karaoke night tickets. You can see how well that went! Tiler shrieked, "Why save for tomorrow when we can party today?!"

In the spirit of hilarity, I've even started using some colorful stickers to track our progress. My kids get competitive, sticking a glittery star on the chart for every small goal we check off the list, as if we're suddenly transformed into kindergarten students during fun learning time! "Look, Mom! I'm richer in stickers than in actual savings!" Tristan shouted, showing off his "We Did It!" sticker awarded for not pestering me on the way to the supermarket. It's fantastic how a bit of sparkle can light kids' enthusiasm for something as dry as budgeting!

As we reflect on our newfound "Financial Fabulousness," I remind them that each little goal contributes to a larger dream, turning our household into a dynamic machine buzzing with inspiration. Every morning holds the potential for our quirky family traditions—each one a stepping stone to inspire us to be more financially savvy. So, as I navigate this wildly entertaining circus of juggling financial goals amidst my family's antics, I am ever grateful that laughter, teamwork, and a sprinkling of chaos can form the foundation of our financial journey! Adventures await around each corner; it's all about setting those delightful goals and savoring the ride together as a family!

Reflecting on Progress and Growth

The exhilarating art of reflecting on progress and growth! As the Budget Avenger, I can assure you that tracking our financial journey is akin to gazing into a funhouse mirror—sometimes you see your wonderful reflection staring back, and other times, you question if you just accidentally wandered into a circus tent. However, taking the time to contemplate our financial escapades has proven invaluable, filled with lessons, surprises, and most importantly, laughter.

To embark on this reflective journey, our family has established a tradition aptly named "Financial Reflection Fridays." Picture this: a cozy family gathering in our living room after dinner, armed with pizza (obviously, a great motivation), where we huddle cozily like penguins to share our thoughts. How can we not indulge in a delicious meal paired with eye-rolls and giggles as we explore how our finances have fared over the week? Sure, sometimes progress feels more like it's trotting at a snail's pace, but I emphasize that it's okay; even snails make fabulous garden companions, right?

Within our weekly meetings, I like to emphasize a themed approach. One week, we might focus on the glorious wins. "Kids, let's talk about how we managed to save twenty bucks on groceries without resorting to a weird, vodka-infused shopping trip!" And just like that, we strike a triumphant pose, celebrating this glorious achievement with exaggerated jazz hands. My daughter, Bristiniey, often quips, "Can we also applaud ourselves for surviving another week without dining on dollar-store ramen?" Yes, darling, we're the champions of taco Tuesday and hard-earned frugality!

However, a sense of humor becomes essential as we tackle the flip side of our reflections—the setbacks. You know, those nights when I realized I accidentally bought an oversized inflatable flamingo instead of a practical vacuum cleaner? My kids seem to adore sharing this moment every week—probably too much; I can see a "Tumeka's Misadventures" highlight clip forming in their eyes! But hey, laughter is the best way to transform embarrassment into teachable moments. "Mom, did you think the flamingo would double as a vacuum?" they tease. While I want to imagine the absurdity of a vacuuming flamingo, I remind them that these slip-ups are stepping stones, inviting us to learn and adapt as we navigate our financial journey.

Setting the stage for growth through our reflections is like being in a never-ending comedy act. I encourage the kids to identify not just what we did right, but how we can make our goals even more impactful. Perhaps it's finding creative new ways to save or developing new strategies that aren't budget binders but instead resemble mint condition comic books! In all his teenage wisdom, Tiler once proposed a goal to "not buy overpriced energy drinks" while aiming to enhance hydration by simply filling our reusable bottles with water and adding fruit—adulting at its finest! We embrace these little changes, recognizing that they pave the road to sustainable, longer-lasting habits.

As proud as I am of our accomplishments, I always urge my family to look beyond the monetary progress. The relationship we build while gaining understanding about finances truly stands out! Each week, we bond over shared stories, silliness, and the thrill of navigating this strange, wild world together. We celebrate those not-so-obvious victories, like moments when we catch our kids reminding each other to save receipts for budgeting. Seeing them actively engaged spurs a joy in me that perhaps we're doing something right, even if my credit score looks like it's still recovering from a rollercoaster ride.

At the end of our reflection session, we express gratitude. Each week, we all share what we're thankful for, whether it's the ability to enjoy a delightful pizza night, finding creative ways to save, or simply having each other's backs. I cannot stress how cathartic it is to hold space for gratitude amid financial calculations. As I glance around my family, I realize that our triumphs and trials have intertwined our hearts and taught us invaluable lessons. The very act of reflecting can have hilarious consequences—like promising to never allow me to order anything online sight unseen again—but these are the moments that fuel our growth.

In reality, reflecting on our progress and growth is a bit like starting the journey all over again. It's perspective and laughter infusing our journey with purpose, as we embrace the ups and downs of financial adulthood together. So, as we cultivate joy in our everyday victories and face financial setbacks with irreverence, we promise to raise our glasses high, filled with that overpriced energy drink we resisted, of course! We salute our experiences with humor and unity, proudly declaring that we are truly thriving, one ridiculous goal at a time!

CHAPTER 20
YOUR JOURNEY BEGINS NOW

Setting Your Financial Goals

Setting your financial goals is a task that seems simple enough, like baking a cake from a box mix. Just add water, stir, and voilà! Except, if you're anything like me, you wind up with something that looks like a pancake and tastes like disappointment. You see, establishing financial goals shouldn't be approached like you're following a recipe that a hedgehog wrote while riding a unicycle. It requires thought, clarity, and maybe some shouting at your bank statements (which isn't a goal, but can be strangely therapeutic).

So grab your favorite notebook (or one you found under the couch that has a suspiciously smudged coffee stain), and let's get serious about your financial dreams. First things first: start with the "why." Why do you want to set financial goals? Is it to retire in a beach house with a margarita in hand, or is it just to finally buy a decent pair of pants that fit without requiring you to perform a yoga pose to put them on? Whatever your motivation may be, write it down. When you can clearly outline your driving force, it creates a beautiful compass that will guide you through the wilderness of financial uncertainty, kind of like Dora the Explorer but with less singing and more spreadsheets.

Next up, let's talk about specificity. You wouldn't say, "I want to travel," and leave it at that. Instead of the vague longing for an all-expense-paid trip to the Bahamas (which may never happen if you keep swiping right on every shiny item at the store), narrow it down.

Say, "I want to travel to Europe and eat my weight in pastries within the next two years." That's a goal! Goals need to be as clear as my mother's instructions when she tells me to clean out the basement: "Just throw everything away." Spoiler alert: I still haven't taken her advice.

Moreover, the "how" is equally crucial. How are you going to fund that European "carb-fest" (because that's definitely what it is)? Create actionable steps that help you visualize your journey. Whether it's saving a specific amount monthly, starting a side hustle selling your famous peanut butter cookies (I've 'experimented' with a few recipes—some are just glue with sugar), or canceling that subscription to the "Monthly Sock of the Month Club," which is obviously just your excuse to justify parking your body on the couch, your action plan needs to fit like that favorite pair of sweatpants. And we all know how good those feel after a long day.

Now, let's sprinkle in a bit of reality because we all know life is less of a fairy tale and more of a roller coaster designed by a toddler. You'll encounter barriers like unexpected bills that come out of nowhere like a ninja cat during your nap time, fluctuating incomes, or your Aunt Gladys deciding she needs a new "chandelier" for her bathroom. Be prepared for these unexpected events. Include a "safety net" goal—this is your fund dedicated to helping you recuperate from the financial punches life likes to throw. "Oh, what a thought! A financial cushion, like having an inflatable donut while roller skating!" The trick is not to fall manically in love with setting lofty goals without recognizing the importance of flexibility and adaptability.

Lastly, let's celebrate your progress because you don't have to wait until you've paid off $50,000 in student debt or finally bought that yacht you've been eyeing to indulge yourself in recognizing your achievements. Set mini-milestones and reward yourself for reaching them, like the time you managed to resist buying the latest shiny gadget that you absolutely didn't need. Treat yourself to a fancy coffee, take a solitary trip to Target where you allow yourself to buy one unnecessary item (like a cactus—you know you need a new succulent friend), or perhaps write yourself a fancy financial certificate that says, "I have made progress!" Feel free to frame it and hang it next to the 48 questionable pieces of art crafted by your kids.

In summary, setting your financial goals is less about magically changing your life overnight and more about taking deliberate steps that make sense. Just remember: clarity, actionability, adaptability, and celebration are the key ingredients for your financial cake. And if it flops, don't worry. Just toss some frosting on it (because frosting makes everything better), and get back to the drawing board of your financial wonderland because your journey to financial freedom is just beginning. You got this!

Creating a Personalized Action Plan

Creating a personalized action plan is like trying to assemble a piece of IKEA furniture without instructions, and you're pretty sure you lost one of the important pieces in your dog's toy box. You dive in with enthusiasm, convinced you can just wing it because, hey, how hard could it be? Spoiler alert: things can get messy, so let's arm ourselves with the necessary tools (a.k.a. your curated list of financial goals) and a hefty dose of humor.

First, we need a blueprint—the foundation of your action plan. I like to think of my financial aspirations as a magical recipe where each step is crucial to avoid setting my potential earnings on fire. Take a moment to lay everything out. I'm talking not just about your earnings and expenses; get real with yourself here! List out your goals, such as paying off debt, building an emergency fund, and maybe setting aside a little cash for your dream vacation in a place where piña coladas flow like water. The more detailed your blueprint, the fewer surprises you will encounter—kind of like a well-planned vacation versus a spontaneous road trip with your crazy Uncle Earl who insists on taking the scenic route.

Next, we need to create a timeline—because what good is a plan without a ticking clock breathing down your neck like me at the grocery store when you start tossing ridiculous things into the cart? You'll want to set deadlines for each of these goals. Let's say you aim to pay off that credit card debt; you might decide you want it gone within the next 12 months. That's a realistic timeline, unlike my niece's promise to be a YouTube star after her first video (girl, that's a different level of planning!). Map out when you want to achieve milestones, and make these deadlines visible, maybe even slap them on your fridge or stick them in your bathroom mirror. Trust me, seeing those deadlines every day will be a motivator—not just for you, but for anyone else in your house who has to see your determined face every morning!

Now, as we forge ahead, let's discuss the "how" of your plan. Break down those grand goals into bite-sized, manageable pieces—like those glorious bite-sized candy bars that somehow feel like they don't count as a full bar (just me? Okay!). With your credit card debt goal set, you're going to want to know how much you need to pay every month to reach that deadline. If you need to pay off $1,200 in one year, that's about $100 monthly. Bam! You're brilliant! This step can feel monumental, but treat it like your morning coffee, engaging in spirited debate over how much cream is too much (note: there's never enough).

As you navigate your action plan, don't forget about the power of routine! If your morning ritual includes coffee, avoiding eye contact with responsibilities, and praying that your financial spreadsheet magically updates itself, it's time to switch things up. Make your action plan a regular part of your routine, whether it's a Sunday afternoon session with Netflix playing in the background or your midweek zen moment where you sip green tea and chant affirmations like "I AM A BUDGETING QUEEN!" Pick a time that works for you and stick to it—put it in your calendar, like a very important brunch date, because guess what? It is!

Now, what about accountability? You won't want to take on the wild world of money alone (unless you're auditioning for a financial superhero movie, in which case I need a ticket!). Grab a friend, a family member, or even someone on social media who's obsessed with tracking their daily expenses (they do exist!). Share your journey, and squash the myth that finance should be a lonely road. Celebrate even small victories with them—a little "hey, look at me, I paid down $200 this month!" text can do wonders for motivation. Match the excitement of tracking progress to how you feel when finally ripping good news from a soap opera cliffhanger.

And lastly, let's talk about flexibility. Just like my aunt's well-meaning yet paradoxically terrifying advice on baking, "Don't worry if you run out of flour; it will be fine without it!" Just kidding, Aunt Gladys! Not all of us are born master bakers! The road to financial victory isn't always a straight line. Life will throw curveballs—like unexpected expenses or more enticing sale ads than you can handle. Your action plan should have room for pivots; don't be afraid to adjust it. No car journey has ever gone completely as planned, and neither should your financial adventure! Check in with your plan at least every month—adjust, recalibrate, and keep your vision alive as you realize, "Oh wow, my dog just had an emergency vet bill; I need to recalibrate my goals."

Creating a personalized action plan isn't about fitting a mold but crafting a unique pathway that aligns with your financial goals. Armed with your detailed blueprint, timelines, bite-sized steps, and a generous side of accountability, you're now ready to dive headfirst into your financial revolution. Just remember to keep your sense of humor close and use it freely as you uncover the strange and often absurd adventures of your financial life, because at the end of the day, you're not just creating a plan; you're embarking on a journey that is truly yours! Now, let's tackle the financial world with the gusto and flair of a superhero in their prime—cape optional!

The Importance of Mindset in Financial Success

The importance of mindset in financial success is akin to the magical ingredient in a recipe that isn't listed: it's that pinch of nutmeg that elevates your pumpkin pie from "meh" to "Shut the front door, how did you make this?" You see, when it comes to navigating the labyrinth of finances, your mindset acts as your compass, guiding you away from the banana peels of bad decisions and toward the pot of gold (or, at the very least, a competent budget). A positive and open mindset transforms those cringeworthy financial moments into learning experiences wrapped in a not-so-serious bow, making you the financial hero of your own story, not unlike Batman, but, you know, with a checkbook instead of a cape.

Let's kick off with the principle that every successful financial guru—and I mean the real ones, not the "I just Googled it" crowd—shares: your mindset is the lens through which you see your financial world. Picture this: you've just received your latest bank statement, and it's not pretty. You could spiral into despair (cue the sad trombone), resigning yourself to the belief that you're destined to have a financial reputation akin to monsoons in Georgia (chaotic and frightening), or you could flip the script and view this as an opportunity for growth. "This is not the end; this is merely a plot twist!" you might shout, while your eyes twitch slightly and your dog cowers in the corner. Suddenly, that disaster becomes a launchpad for action. A little reframing can turn any financial fiasco into a character-building story worthy of narrating over family game nights.

But wait, here's the kicker: a positive mindset doesn't mean living in a fantasy world where financial rainbows lead to pots of gold. Oh no! It's about acknowledging words like "budget," "savings," and "debt" without cringing. It's the difference between saying, "Oh, I can't afford that" and "Let's be responsible and save for what I really want." There's power in recognizing that finances are not the enemy; they are merely numbers on a screen waiting for you to take control. That's right! You are the master (or mistress) of your financial fate, armed with the knowledge and tools needed to conquer the battlefields of loans, interest rates, and that pesky urge to devour every sale that pops up on your phone! Embrace the reality instead of hiding behind denial like it's a great pinot noir.

Now, let's get a bit philosophical—grab your zen moment—because making peace with your past financial mistakes is crucial. No one is perfect. Not even those people with perfectly manicured lawns who always seem to have their lives together. Sure, I've made more questionable financial decisions in times of hardship than I'd care to admit. But I learned that each misstep is merely a twist on the winding road to prosperity. Treat failed investments or impulse purchases like a slightly embarrassing ex-boyfriend; rather than letting them haunt your dreams, acknowledge them, learn from the experience, and move on. It's time to pencil your mistakes in the journal of life lessons and, possibly, medium-sized regrets. Just don't take yourself too seriously—money will come and go, but your sense of humor should always be capped with an unlimited supply.

When it comes to cultivating a mindset for financial success, you want to establish a cherished belief system that complements your actions. Start developing a mantra that resonates with you, something that makes you feel empowered! You know, something like "I am an unstoppable budget warrior!" or "Every dollar saved leads me closer to my goals!" (with matching dramatic arm gestures, of course). The more you repeat these affirmations, the more you will internalize the belief that you are in control. Picture yourself as the Joan of Arc of personal finance, holding your sword (the mighty pen) aloft, paving a path toward your dreams of homeownership, financial independence, or even that fun trip to Bali where you can sip out of coconuts.

Finally, it's important to surround yourself with positivity. Just as you wouldn't hang out with a grumpy cat when what you really want is a fluffy golden retriever that will chase its tail and make you giggle, you should curate your financial circle. Seek out friends, mentors, or communities that spark joy and motivate you to reach your financial goals. Look for people who radiate positivity about their journeys. Their contagious enthusiasm will often be the motivating force during your moments of doubt. You could meld your Sunday brunch with financial chats, trading stories about wins and losses, learning from each other, and getting pumped up for the next big budgeting battle. A support network can turn your solo journey into a fun-drenched galaxy of camaraderie.

In conclusion, mindset isn't just a catchphrase; it's the secret sauce in the recipe for financial success. It's all about perspective, resilience, and a bellyful of determination. Embrace every hurdle like a bad hair day—awkward, yes, but completely surmountable with the right mindset and a killer hairstyle fix. With a steadfast belief that you've got this and that you can navigate the twists and turns ahead, victory in financial endeavors is within reach. Now, let's roll up those sleeves and unleash our inner financial superheroes—with a dazzling smile and a seasoned sense of humor—because you, my friend, are destined to fly high over the mundane misadventures of personal finance!

Overcoming Fear and Resistance

Overcoming fear and resistance in the world of finances is akin to facing off against the neighborhood dog that thinks it owns the entire block. You know you should just stroll by without making eye contact, leaving the territorial little beast to bark its insecurities away. But there you are, frozen in place, heart racing, staring at the rippling muscles under its fur as it releases a cacophony of growls that say, "Get off MY lawn!" Much like that dog, our financial fears can be loud and scary, keeping us from moving forward. The good news? Just like that brave neighbor who walks past the beast with confidence and maybe a steak in hand, you too can crush those financial fears and resistance.

First, let's recognize that fear is entirely normal, like finding out that your favorite snack has mysteriously disappeared from the pantry, only to discover it was your partner who snacked it all away. In the realm of money, fear often arises from impending doom scenarios: "What if I go broke?" "What if I can't save?" or "What if I open a financial statement and it explodes in my face like a confetti party gone wrong?" Fear is loud, obnoxious, unpredictable, and often baseless, and all too ready to drag us into the abyss of procrastination. Admitting that fear exists is the first step towards liberation. Just like others might refuse to adhere to the "one-more-bite" rule, kindly tell fear it's welcome to hang around—but it sure as heck isn't going to run the show!

Next on the agenda? It's time to get cozy with your discomfort. The only way to overcome fear and resistance is to face it like a bad episode of reality television: head-on and ready to shout out your "I can't's" with full conviction. So, instead of letting those tiny whispering thoughts paralyze you when it comes to saving or budgeting, snatch those thoughts right out of the air and turn them into conscious challenges. "I can't afford this" quickly becomes "What can I do to afford this?" This simple mental pivot is more powerful than it sounds. It has the capacity to bring about shift after glorious shift in your mindset, transforming obstacles into thrilling adventures, kind of like jumping off the high dive for the first time and realizing you can swim.

But just diving headfirst into the unknown isn't enough. You have to work through the resistance, too, as fear doesn't want to relinquish its grip on you easily, much like that one weird aunt who refuses to leave your family barbecue even after being offered leftover potato salad. So, set clear intentions for your financial goals, and maybe jot them down in your favorite color (bonus points for glitter pens!). Create a visual representation—a poster board of your dreams, adorned with cutouts of your ultimate vacation destination, a picture of that fabulous new kitchen you envision, or even some inspirational quotes that make you leap for joy. Every time you glance at that vision board, you'll feel a spark of motivation replace the fear that previously held you hostage.

Now, let's not forget the magic of breaking it down into smaller, manageable steps. Ever tried to devour a whole pizza in one sitting? Exactly! Brutal! But if you slice that pizza into pieces (and maybe share a slice with your neighbor who happened to provide the "motivation" with his delicious toppings), you'll find it's easier to chomp down without feeling like you need a nap afterward. Similarly, break your financial goals into tiny, digestible bits. Start by tackling one expense to cut, one dollar to save, or one budget category to revamp. The smaller the change, the more triumph you'll experience, and suddenly, the fear that used to chain you down will begin to loosen its grip. With each small win, you'll find yourself inching closer to that robust sense of accomplishment that will inspire even more bravery in your choices.

Speaking of victories, make sure to celebrate every single victory, no matter how tiny. This part is crucial, folks. You face down the fear of making that first investment, and voilà! You earn the right to reward yourself! Whether it's allowing yourself a night out (with responsibly budgeted drinks, of course) or splurging a smidge on those fancy shoes you've been eyeballing, nothing fuels resilience like a good old-fashioned celebration. Do the victory dance in your living room, play music loud enough for your neighbors to question your sanity, and soak in the momentum you've created. Like a cactus blooming in the desert, you're radiating success, even if you're in the midst of prickly challenges!

Lastly, find your tribe. Share your journey. Surrounding yourself with fellow warriors—the friends, the family, or even that eccentric lady down the street who dreams of starting an online business selling artisanal potato chip keychains—creates a safe space to acknowledge fears and process hurdles together. I mean, there's something powerful about airing out your worries while sipping on overpriced lattes, right? Communities can provide encouragement, laughter, and unexpected wisdom. The importance of connecting with like-minded individuals echoes throughout history, from ancient times when warriors relied on their clans to modern-day support networks for personal finance.

In summary, overcoming fear and resistance in finance doesn't have to feel like an insurmountable mountain. It's about digging deep, facing the lion that roars in your mind, and embracing the toddler-like tantrums that enter your brain when confronted with numbers. Acknowledge the fear, take deliberate action, and remember that every small victory counts. So, take a deep breath, summon your inner tenacious beast, and shout, "I'm ready!" Just like that neighbor who finally retrieved their beloved garden gnome from the dog's mouth, you'll reclaim your financial freedom in no time. With a little humor and determination, you're bound to emerge victorious, ready to tackle whatever financial adventures life throws your way. Let's roll forth, gutting the fear out of our financial lives, one quirky step at a time!

Taking Action: Your First Steps Toward Financial Freedom

Taking action toward financial freedom is like pulling off a long-overdue band-aid—painful at first, but exhilarating once you realize it was just a mental block, not an actual limb that had to come off. The truth is, achieving financial independence isn't a mystical journey to a land of unicorns and endless macaroni and cheese coupons; it's about rolling up your sleeves, getting a little sweaty, and making deliberate choices that transform your financial future. So, grab your metaphorical pickaxe, because it's time to mine for your financial goals, and I promise it can be as delightful as pie (especially if that pie is made out of your favorite desserts and entirely calorie-free).

Let's kick things off with the most vital step: *start where you are.* Don't scroll through your social media feed and convince yourself that you need a unicorn-like level of financial acumen right out of the gate. You don't need to scream "I'm financially fabulous!" from the rooftops on your first day—just knowing your starting point is a winning first move. Take a moment to look over your income, expenses, and debts like you're inspecting an odd piece of art at a gallery, tilting your head to see if it makes sense. Develop a sense of awareness! This is where first steps turn into magnificent strides. Ask yourself where your money is going, what your basic living expenses are, and what discretionary cold hard cash you can factor into your financial plan.

Next up, let's talk about setting realistic priorities because, contrary to popular belief, you can't jump straight to the top while wearing roller skates on an escalator. Prioritize the pressing matters first. Do you have debt looming over your head like a cloud of bad decisions? Figure out how you can tackle it. Maybe it's time to contemplate the excitement of the "debt snowball" method, using small wins against your smaller debts to build momentum. Or perhaps it's about looking hard at your impulse spending habits. I mean, do you really need that collection of limited-edition cat-themed action figures, or is it time to bid farewell? Some serious reflection may be required to thrive in the world of financial maturity.

Now, once you've established your priorities, it's time to create a *budget* that brings you joy rather than dread! Sure, the word "budget" can cause some to convulse slightly, envisioning a life devoid of fun and equipped only with loan statements and turkey sandwiches. But let's flip that script! Think of your budget as a financial roadmap rather than a set of inflexible shackles. It's your personalized treasure map, guiding you toward the riches of financial freedom while allowing for occasional detours to good times without going broke. Include all your income sources and allocate funds to essential areas like housing, groceries, debt repayment, and yes, even modest entertainment (a little junk-food splurge never hurt anybody!). You're still allowed to have tacos on a Tuesday without feeling guilty, because who doesn't love taco-filled evenings?

As you embark on the thrilling journey ahead, creating an *emergency fund*—your trusty safety net is important. This is the buffer for life's "surprise, I'm here!" moments—like when the car breaks down or an unexpected vet bill pops up, demanding your attention. Fortunately, cultivating that emergency fund doesn't require becoming a hermit. Start small! Even if you save just $5 a week, you're one step closer to having the magnificent semblance of a financial safety net, just waiting to catch you when reality tries to knock you down if you've ever seen any of those cat videos where the feline hero solves every conundrum with a harmless leap, you, too, can flourish by securing that mat of cash because, just like cats, you deserve the slow-motion bounce back to glory.

After you've established your emergency fund and budget, *commit to taking consistent actions*. Just as people don those ridiculously colorful running shoes to train for races that result in sore legs and impressive bragging rights, your financial progress requires regular dedication! Treat this endeavor like a new exercise routine—show up every month, assess your progress, and re-evaluate your goals. Be prepared for setbacks—like accidentally farewelling your healthy snack habits when the holiday cookies start rolling in—but don't let those deter you. Instead, view them as learning experiences and laugh them off like the joyous journey it is.

Use tools and apps to keep track of your progress. Document your milestones, even the small ones. If you've successfully paid off a credit card, toss confetti like it's New Year's Eve! Record every dollar saved or every menu meal made at home that reminds you of carefree college days—keep it fresh and fun! A little determination and panache will eventually lead you down the yellow-brick road to your very own financial freedom, where you'll discover the magical pot of gold shimmering before you!

In summary, taking action toward financial freedom involves bold choices, heightened awareness, and a commitment to maintaining a light-hearted approach. Understand and prioritize your financial landscape, budget like a planner of epic proportions, establish an emergency fund that screams "I'm prepared for this!", and consistently take action in spite of hurdles. With a sprinkle of determination and the right attitude, you will build the financial future you desire, one fabulous step at a time—and soon you'll be dancing down the road to financial freedom like nobody's watching! Let's make those first steps spectacular and, above all, enjoyable!

www.ingramcontent.com/pod-product-compliance
Lightning Source LLC
Chambersburg PA
CBHW071158070526
44584CB00019B/2844